T0207616

At the Wording Desk

Notes Nimble and Spry about the Origin of Words

BILL CASSELMAN

 www.trafford.com

North America & international

toll-free: 1 888 232 4444 (USA & Canada)

fax: 812 355 4082

Dedication

For my friend David Dick

Sine amicitia vera vita vacua nullaque est.
"Without real friendship, life is bereft and empty."

Contents

List of My Published Books

Author's Note:

This list of my publications is more extensive than usual in the front matter of a new book, but it is my wish that it be presented here. Please note that most of my books are out-of-print. Two are available online as e-books. The others may be purchased used online from various discount sellers.

1.

Casselman's Canadian Words: A Comic Browse through Words & Folk Sayings Invented by Canadians 1995
1st edition 1995 Copp Clark ISBN: 0-7730-5515-0
2nd edition 1997 Little, Brown ISBN: 0-316-13350-7
3rd edition 1999 McArthur & Company, Toronto, Canada
many reprints through 2006
ISBN: 1-55278-034-1

2.

Casselmania: More Wacky Canadian Words & Sayings 1996
Little, Brown Canada Ltd, Toronto, Canada
ISBN: 0-316-13314-0

3.

Canadian Garden Words: The Origin of Flower, Tree, and Plant Names, both wild and domestic, entertainingly derived from their sources in the Ancient Tongues together with Fancy Botanical Names & Why You Shall Never Again Be Afraid To Use Them!
1997 McArthur & Company, Toronto, Canada
ISBN: 0-316-13343-4

4.

A Dictionary of Medical Derivations: The Real Meanings of Medical Words
1998 Parthenon Publishing Group, London and New York
ISBN: 1-85070-771-5

5.

Canadian Food Words: The Juicy Lore & Tasty Origins of Foods That Founded a Nation
1998 McArthur & Company, Toronto, Canada
1999 reprinted with new cover McArthur & Company
ISBN: 1-55278-018-X

6.

Canadian Sayings: 1200 Folk Sayings Used by Canadians, Collected and Annotated by Bill Casselman
1999 McArthur & Company, Toronto, Canada
ISBN: 1-55278-076-7

7.

What's in a Canadian Name? The Origins and Meanings of Canadian Surnames
2000 McArthur & Company, Toronto, Canada
ISBN: 1-55278-141-0

8.

Canadian Sayings 2: 1000 Folk Sayings Used by Canadians Newly Collected and Annotated by Bill Casselman 2002
McArthur & Company, Toronto, Canada
ISBN: 1-55278-272-7

9.

Canadian Sayings 3: 1000 Folk Sayings Used by Canadians Newly Collected and Annotated by Bill Casselman July 2004
McArthur & Company, Toronto, Canada
ISBN: 1-55278-425-8

10.

As The Canoe Tips: Comic Scenes from Canadian Life July 2005
McArthur & Company, Toronto, Canada
This is the first collection of my own original funny pieces, satire and nonsense.
ISBN: 1-55278-493-2

11.

Canadian Words & Sayings July 2006
McArthur & Company, Toronto, Canada
This collection includes new sayings and classic Canadian word stories suitable for the whole family and APPROVED FOR CLASSROOM USE.
ISBN: 1-55278-569-6

12.

Where a Dobdob Meets a Dikdik Mid-October 2010
A Word Lover's Guide to the Weirdest, Wackiest, and Wonkiest Lexical Gems
Publisher: Adams Media
57 Littlefield Street, Avon, Massachusetts 02322 U.S.A.

For the printed paperback -
ISBN 10: 1-4405-0636-1
ISBN 13: 978-1-4405-0636-1
To order the e-book version -
eISBN 10: 1-4405-1004-0
eISBN 13: 978-1-4405-1004-5

Partial Contributions to other books by Bill Casselman (William Gordon Casselman)

1.

Article on "Canadian Folk Sayings" in
The ITP Nelson Canadian Dictionary of the English Language
ITP Nelson, a division of Thomson Canada Limited, 1997,
Scarborough, Ontario, Canada
ISBN: 0-17-606591-1

2.

Essay "See You When the Ice Worms Nest Again" in
Inside Language: A Canadian Language Reader, eds. Jennifer
Maclennan and John Moffat
2000
Prentice Hall Allyn and Bacon Canada, Scarborough, Ontario
ISBN: 0-13-011267-4

3.

Essay "*Barrelhouse Kings*: Something Barry Callaghan Left
out of his Memoir" in
Barry Callaghan: Essays on his Works
ed. Priscila Uppal
Guernica Writers Series # 24,
Guernica Editions, Toronto, Canada, 2007
ISBN-13: 978-1-55071-253-7
ISBN-10: 1-55071-253-5

4.

Chapter 32 "Digitariat" and Chapter 35 "Bafflegab and
Gobbledygook: How Canadians Use English to Rant, to Lie, to
Cheat, to Cover up Truth, and to Peddle Bafflegab" in
Readings for Technical Communication, ed. Jennifer MacLennan,
Oxford University Press Canada, 2008
ISBN: 978-0-19-542322-8

5.
Essay "A Blunt History of the C-Word" in
Vocabula Bound: Our Wresting, Writhing Tongue: Essays on the English Language from The Vocabula Review (online magazine about words)
ed.

Robert Hartwell Fiske
Vocabula Books, Rockport, Massachusetts, USA, 2008
ISBN: 978-0-9774368-6-6

Introduction

We, all of us, deem ourselves worldly-wise yes, but how about wordly-wise? Here's a book to help you in that regard. How does a modest vocable attain wordhood? Two necessary properties comprise wordness. A word must have a meaning. A word must have a history of use. This volume is primarily about etymology, the historical roots and developed meanings of a word as it is spoken and written throughout history. Linguists call the basic, abstract lexical unit of a language a lexeme. Most words are lexemes. A headword entry in dictionaries is a lexeme. Such an entry might be: *stone*. It may have a variety of inflectional endings, such as a plural form like *stones* when the lexeme *stone* is a noun. To stone may also be a verb with a past participle like *stoned*.

How, why and whence did a word gain advent into the bountiful vocabulary of English? That question has hundreds of thousands of vivid, sometimes funny answers, although a reader might not recognize etymological laughter, after reading some of the dour and sour lozenges of despair dispensed from the current medicine box of writers about words. With all due lack of humility, I can state: this book is different! This book has some of the more colorful and more interesting word origins and, if an author may cast off an ill-fitting cloak of modesty, may I say these word stories are told with my lively sense of humor.

This volume is not dry-as-dust word lore. Sometimes I have to attack twits and ignoramuses. Here's a small sample about the false origin of the last name *Cooper*. "The internet smolders with infernos of fallacy, junk-littered repositories of nincompoopery. The errors would cross a wise man's eyes.

Chief among these unsightly sites lurk dank web grots which claim to tell the visitor "the meaning of your baby's name" or "the meaning of your surname." Many of these blunder-stuffed babblings are superintended by persons who can barely spell, let alone navigate the billowy babel of multiple languages. Also nodding by their keyboards at these toddler-dubbing sites are sclerotic knitters with an excess of needles lodged in their skulls, a trait seldom conducive to accurate word lore. At one such boo-boo circus I found a passage boldly stating that the English occupational surname Cooper always meant a coppersmith. Utter drivel. In fact, Cooper as a last name seldom means coppersmith. There are a tiny few Coopers of such an origin, but they are rare." In this book in the relevant chapter, I then explain legitimate meanings of the surname Cooper. I think you'll find it interesting.

Why do I discuss so many rare words in this book? My merry opus wants a reader to learn new words, not the relatively common terms one finds in *Reader's Digest* quizzes – although there is nothing wrong with the acquisition of ordinary words. I hope inquiring readers will pick up new technical terms from modern science, words you may see on medical advice sites and in an article on oceanography on the science pages of good newspapers. These are not the terms you'll pick up doing crossword puzzles – although some of the keenest worders I know are *Kreutzworträtselsüchtigen* (German 'crossword puzzle addicts').

As we delve into the origins of these more complex English words you will learn their Latin and Greek roots, and this knowledge will open up dozens of similar words to your immediate understanding, often without recourse to laborious riffling through large dictionaries.

Explanation of 2 Linguistic Signs Used in this Book

In linguistics, a right chevron (>) points right. A left chevron (<) points left.

Borrowed from mathematics, they are often called inequality signs. In math notation, a right chevron means "more than" so that 5>4 means 'five is more than four.' Therefore 4<5 means 'four is less than five.'

In linguistics, chevrons are used to shorten sentences about derivation, about where words come from. Thus Late Latin *combustio* > Old French *combustion* > modern English *combustion* means that the Late Latin word *combustio* evolved into Old French *combustion* which in turn was borrowed into modern English to give us our current word *combustion*.

The left chevron is used to show the opposite direction of word development. Thus modern English *sword* < Old English *sweord* < Old Frisian, Middle High German *swert*. Compare modern German *Schwert*. This means the modern English word *sword* appeared in Old English as *sweord* and in Old Frisian as *swert* and is completely Germanic when we see that the modern German word for the sword is *das Schwert*.

One Small Note on a Special Asterisk

When in this text you see an asterisk (*) placed in front of a word root, it means there is no printed proof of such a word root. The asterisk means the form is a hypothetical or conjectural construct, not an actual word root. Yes, even etymologists have to guess sometimes. The asterisk makes clear that fact of origin remains distinct from mere theory of origin.

Why Else Should You Bother to Learn Complex Words & Their Roots?

Why learn long, hard words? Because it makes you smarter. I acknowledge that I am preaching to the converted here. But for the etymological neophyte who may have wandered threadless into the cave opening (introduction) of this labyrinth of words, please let me unburden you of initial questions.

Every scientific study of increased vocabulary points to benefits, no matter the age of the new-word learner. Students get better marks the more words they know. Grannies stave off the onset of Alzheimer's by learning new words. Proven in tests! Do you work for a company? Most executives have better communication skills than workers at the bottom of the pay scale. To reach the top in any field, one usually must learn many Englishes. You may retain how you learned to speak at home (called your idiolect or dialect). But, to be of maximum use to your company, you must understand and use easily the private scientific vocabulary used in the sciences that form the basis of your company's manufacturing or business procedures. You must also learn SE, Standard English.

That's three Englishes for most of us. Each one of those Englishes relies on new words, new relevant vocabulary. The more words you know, the higher your potential intelligence. Nincompoops are correctly called dummies, because they can't talk well. Nincompoop probably derives from an old Latin phrase for someone who was insane, who was *non compos mentis* Latin, literally 'not sound of mind.'

No matter what the monosyllabic, illiterate baboons grunt, no matter that some goofy doofus mocks your superior hoard of words, all those who increase their vocabulary increase their salaries, their status, and their position in life. That's all any word-seeker has to know. Start learning more words!

Grass, Sky, Song is a book about prairie birds written by Trevor Herriot. Gliding passages of his book teem with exquisite expository prose, flowing language abounding in specificity and love of subject. At one point in his narrative, Herriot addresses the necessity, for an educated person, of ever bothering to learn the correct ornithological genus and species of his beloved prairie avifauna. He writes, "I began to see that learning the names of things mattered, not so much in the possession it afforded, as in its capacity to call things forth from generality into a particularity that allowed for admiration, familiarity, even wonder." Many a word lover shares that call to a humility that allows us to enjoy even as we marvel at our English language, a trove so full of wonders.

Bill Casselman, April, 2016
website: wordingroom.com
email: wordingmail@wordingroom.com

Chapter 1

Our Word *Travel* comes from *Trepalium*, a Roman Torture Device

Our English word *travel* descends from *travail* in Old French whose first French meaning was *le travail d'enfant* 'the pain of child-birth,' so we're not talking about some trifling inconvenient discomfort.

The first meaning of *travailler* in Old French was to suffer real torture. The first English meaning of travail was painful corporeal toil or oppressive suffering. The word travel in its earliest English semantic outing also meant toil and trouble, even the travails and difficult labours of child-birth.

In Medieval French *travailler* implied odious and literally painful forms of transporting oneself. From these uncomfortable meanings evolved the modern English meanings of travel, which don't begin to appear in Britain until the onset of the fifteenth century. In French and Spanish, the derivatives came to signify hard work: *le travail* and *el trabajo*.

From 1080 CE we have record of *travailler*'s ancestor, a vulgar Latin verb *tripaliare* 'to be tortured with a tripalium or trepalium, a device with 'three stakes' as the Latin name implies: Latin *tres, tris, tri* 'three' + Latin *palus* 'wooden or metal stake.' It probably involved impalement of the human body in some gruesome torture beloved of the Romans. The instrument of torture arose from trepalium's first Latin meaning, a farmyard and blacksmith's contraption with three stakes used to immobilize horses and oxen while putting on or changing horseshoes. If you have ever seen a drama depicting gladiatorial practice, you may have seen a junior gladiator swinging his gladius or short sword at a wooden dummy driven into the sand of the arena. This too was named *palus* by the Romans.

The Pale of Etymology

Latin *palus* gives several English terms. A well-known phrase in Irish history is 'beyond the pale.' A pale is a stick with a pointed end meant to be driven into the ground, a stake, a boundary peg, a fence stake.

Fans of old western movies will remember early forts built by pioneers conquering the American West. Such forts were almost always surrounded by a palisade, a high fence of medium-thick local tree trunks sharpened at one end and driven into prairie ground, the word ultimately from old Spanish *paliçada* 'fence made of pounded stakes,' through a Middle French form like *palissade* from French for 'stake' *palis*, Spanish *pal*.

"What You Say, Nigel, is Really Quite Beyond the Pale, Old Chap."

To repeat a stale joke, "Beyond the pale is not where you go when you have kicked the bucket." Something beyond the pale was anything outside of civil rule, anything beyond the agreed (staked) boundaries of custom and propriety, any opinion or territory in which a traveler might find himself at the mercy of letterless yahoos or thuggish do-badders.

Two historical references contributed to the frequent use of the phrase in English. The earliest has to do with Irish history. By the fourteenth century there was a part of Ireland under English control. This "Pale of Dublin" was fenced, with a once guarded boundary. According to the English interlopers, inside the British-controlled Irish Pale of Dublin, culture and human dignity reigned, but beyond the pale the most uncouth depths of Celtic boorishness and beastliness abounded. Inside the pale or palisade, superintending behaviour by the might of armed soldiers was possible, but, beyond the pale, why — a Dhiaa! — a gentleman might be forced to eat a potato or permit an untoward affront by a leprechaun.

A *locus classicus* of the phrase in English prose occurs in Charles Dickens' The Pickwick Papers (1837 CE) when Mr. Pott says to Mr. Slurk: "I look upon you, sir, as a man who has placed himself beyond the pale of society, by his most audacious, disgraceful, and abominable public conduct."

Pale of Settlement

The next most famous protected area of jurisdiction using the phrase was the Pale of Settlement in Russia in 1791 CE, created by Catherine the Great, who, true to her German origin, positively glowed in the dark with poisonous anti-Semitism. Catherine gave this name to the western border region of Russia, the one area where Jews were allowed to live ghettoized in impoverished *shtetlach* (Yiddish 'little towns').

Catherine the Not-So-Great wanted to restrict trade between Jews and native Russians. It wasn't fair, the empress may have thought, Jews can add and subtract and they're civilized — unlike the barbarous Slavic louts and sword-happy Cossacks sent on horseback pogroms to burn Jewish farms and villages and murder every Jew in sight. But some Jews, useful to Catherine and her court, were allowed to live 'beyond the pale of settlement.' The English term was a direct translation of Russian *cherta osedlosti* 'boundary of settlement.' This prison of specified districts restricted Jewish residence in Russia and Russian-occupied Poland from 1791 CE to 1917.

But now, gentles, I simply must get back to the pet cage, where I am teaching my Rocky Mountain whistling marmot to hiss the opening bars of several Barbra Streisand songs.

Chapter 2

Tournure: Rare but Elegant Noun

Tournure (**turn**-yer) is a word borrowed from French meaning 'graceful deportment,' a noun now obsolescent but one worthy of revival.

Tournure pays semantic attention to beauty of bodily movement, to agile suppleness, to a willow's winsome pliancy, to the nimble ease of choice poise.

Nowadays so scorned a mode is grace that the wedding bride arrives stoop-shouldered and shod in rubber boots. Upon the very table of the nuptial feast yawn too wide bouquets of plastic lilies which accomplish one thing: they obscure from view the people sitting across the table from you. Of course, once one has spoken to those tablemates, the bride's rural cousins clad in what appears to be binder twine and spit, it is possible to be grateful for too wide bouquets. But, oh my, those lily stamens made from pipe cleaners, now that's clever! What a glutinously ornate wedding cake, and with a shelf life of 300 years. Yummy. At head table, directly in front of the microphone, the hunched-up groom blows his nose into a handkerchief and then opens the hanky to inspect discharged mucosities and comment freely upon his own nasal ejecta to revolted fellow symposiasts.

Only in Victorian poetry are we any longer likely — alas! — to encounter upon a magical evening a lissome sylph lithely gliding in fluent tournure down the twilit lawn.

Etymology

The French *tournure* stems from very late Latin *tornatura* 'the way a thing is turned or made, its pleasing roundness,' from the more ancient Latin verb *tornare* 'to round off, to make an object round by turning it on a lathe,' from one of the Roman words for a turner's lathe, *tornus*, borrowed by the Romans from an ancient Greek word for lathe *tornos* 'lathe-chisel or compasses: a carpenter's tool used to draw a circle.' Derivatives in modern languages include Dutch and High German *turnen*, Spanish *tornar* and Italian *tornare*. Note that our weather word *tornado* gets gusty first perhaps as a past participle of the Spanish verb *tornar* 'to turn, to return, to twist back around.' This etymology seeks the name in the shifting, roiling whirl-a-gig winds of the storm.

One who, in golden days of yore, was adept at merry tournure was Hebe (HEE-bee), Olympian goddess of youth and spring and the spritely vernal delight of dance. Now let us skip off sportively to the next chapter, remembering Milton's lyric adroitness in his 1645 CE poem "L'Allegro" (Italian: 'the happy person'):

> "Haste thee, Nymph, and bring with thee
> Jest, and youthful Jollity,
> Quips and cranks and wanton wiles,
> Nods and becks and wreathed smiles
> Such as hang on Hebe's cheek,
> And love to live in dimple sleek;
> Sport that wrinkled Care derides,
> And Laughter holding both his sides.
> Come, and trip it, as you go,
> On the light fantastic toe. . ."

Chapter 3

Epaulettes, Spatulas & Spades

This chapter's glide down the slide of etymology whisks us from the word *epaulette* to a spatula to that homey implement, the spade.

How did early anatomical nomenclature arise? What were the sources of ancient Greek and Roman names for parts of the human body that English borrowed and still uses today? Well, ancient body-part names began as the simplest, homiest of metaphors and comparisons.

Here are a few. For example, the few scraps of ordinary Latin speech recorded in ancient Roman texts reveal that the colloquial word for penis used by the common folk of the Eternal City was *gladius*. Gladius was a name for a short Roman army sword. The root also shows up in English garden vocabulary, where *gladiolus* 'little short sword' was used to describe the slender sword-like leaves of a familiar garden plant. Where does one put a sword? Into a scabbard or leather sheath. What is the Roman soldiers' word for such a sheath? *Vagina*!

The sheath protects the sharp blade of a sword when not in military use. Just as the long muscular vaginal tube lined with mucosa evolved during mammalian development to receive the penis and its spermy deposit during copulation, so the leather sheath received the Roman sword or gladius.

Consider the Latin word *uterus* meaning 'womb' and compare a similar Latin word *uter, utris* 'big wineskin' or 'water sack made of leather.'

Scapula, our medical word for shoulder blade, in my Casselman etymology, is a diminutive form of Latin *scapus* 'the stem of a plant, the upright of a door frame, the beam of a steelyard.' A human shoulder blade could easily be supposed to help support the skeletal anatomy of a human. The noun *scapus* is available with many of its meanings in polysemous Latin having to do with uprights that support things. We also know that the father of anatomical naming, Hippocrates, used the Greek word *spathe* to name the shoulder blade. In ancient Greek *spathe* had meanings like 'flat wooden blade of an oar' and 'wide scooping, digging stick.'

Épaulette

This military shoulder patch often dangling with fancy golden braid, in spite of its effeminate array of flaunting flutteriness, is often the strutting pride of macho generals.

The flamboyant shoulder ornament takes its name from a diminutive of the French word for shoulder, *épaule*. Earlier forms include Middle French *espaule* from Old French *espalle* from Late Latin *spathula* 'little broad sword' from *spatha* 'short broad-bladed Roman army sword.' The word was borrowed directly from ancient Greek *spathe* 'flat sword.'

Cognate are the English word *spade*, the German word *Spaten* and the Latin *spatula,* all descendants of Proto-Indo-European **sph-d* 'long, flat piece of wood' whence also Hittite ishpatar, 'spear.' In botany the root gives two names of modestly sword-like flower parts: *spathe and spadix.* The black figure on playing cards, spade, is from a related Italian word for garden tool blackened by immersion in soil: Italian *spade*, plural of *spada* 'sword.'

Épaulement 'shouldering' is a stance in ballet where the head is turned to look over a forward shoulder when the other shoulder is drawn back. In the obsolescent vocabulary of fortification, an epaulement is a heap or mound, a shoulder of earth, thrown up to protect soldiers from enemy fire. But let us move forward, for, in the next chapter, strange winds await.

Chapter 4

Wind Words like Simoom & Williwaw

An Ancient Greek Wind God

Among Grecian and Roman deities of yore, Aeolus was blustery regent of the winds, superintendent of tempests, justly weather-vain, Caesar of the sirocco, the rex in the storm, monarch of the mistral, whistling conductor of whirlwinds, in short: the pomposity of ventosity (*ventus* Latin 'wind'). Think of that spritz of urinary sagacity embodied in the Latin proverb: *vir prudens non contra ventum mingit* 'a wise man does not piss into the wind.'

The Greek Aiolos (or Aeolus in his Roman form) was a mortal king, ruler of the island of Aeolia, a real isle, and, so Homer tells us, one visited by Odysseus and the setting of an episode of the *Odyssey* (see below). No divine, deifying ichor flowed purple in his human veins and yet Aiolos controlled the winds. His name may be Greek, from their adjective *aiolos* 'changeable, quick-moving, rapid.' But Aiolos could have been borrowed earlier than classical Greek from a Semitic language like Phoenician, where *aol* means 'whirlwind.'

Ulysses (Odysseus) Gets Bagged

In the *Odyssey* Homer tells my favorite story about Aeolos. On his return voyage, Odysseus (Ulysses to the Romans) lolled pleasantly on the Aeolian isle for weeks, bloviating amiably with the wind god. "Hey, Aeolus, flip me a mermaid on the half-shell!" So charmed by his visitor was Aeolus that he gave Odysseus a going-away present: a plump, capacious bag of mighty winds to help blow his ships home to Ithaca. But, once outbound for home, the scurvy crew of sailors and unsavory layabouts on deck accompanying the Greek hero were full of discontent and bloated with nautical bitchiness built up after years at sea, and these ocean scum grew more and more curious to see what perhaps golden or silver treasure lurked in that vast swollen leather bag they had loaded aboard when embarking from Aeolia.

Of course, the crew ripped open the bag; all the stored winds rushed out and blew with force. Odysseus' ships were blown back to the isle of Aeolia by those escaping winds. But, as the sailors clambered bedraggled and besalted up the beach to his palace, the king of the winds showed the revenant miscreants no sympathy. Thus came the gift of Aeolus to naught. Curiosity, like other human traits, must be kept in check.

Simoom

These wind words and names are ones whose ventose sonority appeals to me. Simoom is as slippery a toxic wind as ever sanded a camel's hump. The engulfing simoom withers and desiccates all it passes, hauling sandy dust over most of the Middle East, blowing across the Sahara, gliding over Israel and Palestine, grit-whipping Jordan and Syria and the Allah-loving, woman-hating deserts of Araby. Over dune-strewn wastes both African and Asian, simooms waft and squall in lethal wheeze. Simooms can boil at 54°C (129°F) or parch a throat at 10% humidity. In his 1968 book *Climatology*, G. R. Rumney wrote: "The sirocco is known as the *khamsin* in Egypt, *leveche* in southeastern Spain, where it is usually quite dry, *garbi* in the Aegean, *samoon* in Algeria, *sahat* in Morocco, and *ghibli* in Libya. There are many foreign versions of the word: *samoom, samum, semoom, simúm, samoon, samun, semoun, simoon, and simoun,* among others.

Etymology of Simoom

Simoom — the very word summons up Death in a billowy burnoose of ebon velvet, opening skeletal arms to enfold, embosom and suffocate you in its smothering shroud of gasps. Simoom is the poison wind. In Arabic samūm 'the poisoner' from the verbal root *s-m-m* 'to poison.'

Wuthering

One of the best weather adjectives pops up in northern British regional English, namely *wuthering.* In the best Emily Brontë novel, it inhabits the title: *Wuthering Heights.* Her definition in Chapter One is tasty too:

"Wuthering Heights is the name of Mr. Heathcliff's dwelling. 'Wuthering' being a significant provincial adjective, descriptive of the atmospheric tumult to which its station is exposed in stormy weather. Pure, bracing ventilation they must have up there at all times, indeed: one may guess the power of the north wind blowing over the edge, by the excessive slant of a few stunted firs at the end of the house; and by a range of gaunt thorns all stretching their limbs one way, as if craving alms of the sun."

Was inclemency ever better limned? The etymology can be explained as a mere vowel gradation of *weathering.* *Withering* exists. But the word is thonged with Viking leather too. In Old Norse, proto-Scandinavian language of the Vikings raiders of northern Britain, are stout terms like *hvitha* 'high wind, squall' to which may be compared a modern Norwegian verb *kvidra* 'to dart back and forth, to stop and start,' perhaps cognate with Old English words for 'glowing light' or 'aura,' *hwitha* and *hwithu.*

Katabatic & Anabatic

Two little technical terms from meteorology are fun to know. Katabatic is said of winds, like Canada's Chinook, that blow down a declivity or hill or Alp, cold air flowing downward by gravity. Cold air of course weighs more than hot air, to which any trip to London, Washington or Ottawa bears witness. Greek *katabatos* = *kata* 'down' + *batos* 'able to go.'

Anabatic wind flows upward like all warmed air. Greek *anabatikos* = Greek *ana* 'up' + *batos* 'able to go.

Mistral

This cold, dry northerly of France gusts down through the Rhone valley, across the south of France, always affecting the weather in Provence, finally to dissipate far out over Mediterranean midwaters. The word is ancient, from Old Occitan, a southern dialect of French where it had forms like *maestral* and *maistral*, clearly showing its classical Latin etymon, *magistralis* 'masterly.' For it is the master wind, in the sense that the mistral influences all weather on the Levantine littoral whenever on a winter's day it gales stiff breezes to the south.

More than one writer has borrowed the wind's name, most prominent being Chilean poet Lucila Alcayaga whose nom de plume was Gabriela Mistral. The pioneering writer of the first comprehensive Occitan dictionary was Frédéric Mistral. A famous French train that ran between Paris and Nice was the Mistral. Between 1993 and 2006 Nissan made a Mistral automobile.

Even ancient Greeks recognized that this dangerous warm wind, the mistral, could make humans do strange things. Greeks called the mistral *kakoscholai pnoai* "bad-leisure winds."

Williwaw

What a roistering, sea-salt-soaked word! At first a williwaw was a blustering squall at sea, like those common in the Straits of Magellan, a phenomenon of northern latitudes, a whaler's nightmare wind-roar, and a cold wind blowing offshore and descending onto waves and men in ships from coastal mountains. No one knows the word's root, although it sounds as if it might stem from a northern aboriginal language of North America. There is a Scottish dialect word, *whilly-wha* which means lip-flap, idle speech, deceptive blather etc. But the semantics of the two words seem distant and rapprochement unpromising.

Well, blow me down, wind-mates, the captain's coffer for this wee chapter yawns void. She be empty as a harlot's promise, me hearties. And yet, the ship nears port; the gangplank sways; the dock creaks. Sure now, we'll return to wind words someday eftsoons, ye scurvy sea-dogs. And we'll do so before a pelican can dance a jig on a dead man's collarbone.

Chapter 5

You Bastard! Coward! Dullard!
Lubbard! Sluggard!

being a brief jaunt during which I examine the origin of English words which end in the pejorative suffix –ard.

Bastard!

The late French linguist Albert Dauzat came up with the most picturesque origin of the word *bastard*. Dauzat's notion was that the insult derived from an Old French word *bast* meaning 'packsaddle for a mule' or 'saddlebag slung over a mule's back' + the negative French suffix *-ard*. Thus a bastard was probably the love child of a man who herded mules and one night enjoyed a carnal connection with some highway hussy using his saddlebag as a pillow during their sex. No kidding! Was this a particularly weird way to name an illegitimate offspring in medieval European languages? Too bizarre to have ever accounted for the word's accurate origin? No, not at all.

Compare some other European words for a wretch begotten out of wedlock.

Old French had a word *coitrart* 'quilt-child.'

German has *Bankling* 'bench-child,' suggesting a quick copulatory alliance on a tavern table. Low German had *Mantelkind* 'cloak-child,' summoning up the picture of a torrid coupling under a greatcoat in a ditch at the side of a medieval highway.

Even the Vikings had a word for bastardy. In Old Norse *hrissungr* means 'brushwood-child.' Ragnar got lucky in the shrubbery.

Victorian English sniffed haughtily at such corporeal wallowings and gross affinities and, sneering through its tortoise-shell lorgnette, termed the loathsome product a 'love child.' In British legal terminology, the word *bastard* referred specifically to an illegitimate but acknowledged-by-the-father son of noble gentry or royalty. Some etymologists state that this *fils de bast* 'child of a packsaddle' is dubious both chronologically and geographically.

Differing proposals for the root of 'bastard' abound. The notion is posited that a Germanic root **bast* 'marriage' is the origin, with the pejorative suffix *–ard* added to mean that it was the child of a 'bad' marriage with a wench of low estate or that a bastard was the peasant offspring of a Christian and a pagan, a conjointure not sanctioned by holy ritual. But that guess reads to me as a conceit no sillier than the packsaddle one.

Others offer a 'lost' Proto-Germanic word for barn, namely **bansti*, that may be akin to Gothic *bansts* 'barn son.' So that a bastard is a 'son of the barn,' whose straw-bedded conception featured a clodhopper diddling a milkmaid in a haystack.

Where Did –Ard, the Suffix, Come From?

The Old French operative, negative suffix *–art* or *–ard* was copied from the Germanic adjective *–hart* or *–hard*, an extremely frequent component of two-part Teutonic warrior names like Richard. Remember that the two roots in each Germanic binomial name did not have to make clear sense; they merely had to be taken from an agreed-upon list of "name" roots. Richard = *Reich* Germanic 'kingdom' + *-hardt* Germanic 'enduring, tough, hardy.' Gerard is similarly *Gar* 'sword' + *-hard*. Everard or Everett is *Ebur* Germanic 'wild boar' + *-hardt*. Leonard means 'brave as a lion' from German *Leonhard* = *leo, leonis* Latin 'lion' + *-hard*.

In Old French this usually negative suffix *–ard* was extremely productive, for example in French words like *bastard, couard, canard, mallard, mouchard*, and *vieillard*. After the Norman Conquest these words poured into Britain and, by the time of Middle English, we had borrowed *wizard, placard, standard*. Then, in forming new English words, the ending *–ard* came to mean 'one who performs acts to excess or to his discredit' in words like *buzzard, drunkard, laggard*, and *sluggard*.

Most provocative of all is that many of the English nationality names may have begun as insults, as depreciatory snubs like *Spaniard, Lombard, Savoyard*. The semantic weight of 'something hard' survives in other words with this suffix, e.g. *billiards, petard, poniard* and *tankard*.

Coward

This word for a craven, white-livered weakling goes all the way back to the Latin word for tail, *cauda*, perhaps because a coward turns tail and runs away with his tail between his legs. The line of derivation may look like this: Old French *coart/cohart/cuard/cowairt/couard* > Provençal *coart* > Italian *codardo* = *coda* + *-ardo* pejorative suffix> Italian *coda* > Latin *cauda*.

Some Familiar *–ard* Words in English:
Drunkard
Dullard
Laggard
Lubbard – a big, clumsy oaf
Sluggard

Wizard — sage or magician, but wizard began as an insult equivalent to 'smart ass' or 'big brain', from the adjective *wise* + *-ard*.

Lizard — sometimes assimilation of the –ard suffix occurred, as in the form of lizard from Old French *lesard* (modern French *lézard, lézarde*) and Italian *lacerta*, both from Latin *lacertus* and *lacerta*. The usual ending in Old French would have seen a form like *lesert, but people thought it was the *–ard* ending and pronounced it that way.

Mallard = Middle English < Middle French *mallart* < Anglo-Norman *malle* male + French suffix *-ard,* hence a meaning like 'excessively masculine in behaviour.' Our ending is usually quite pejorative and in the word *mallard* may be also. In this species of common wild duck, Anas platyrhynchos (Latin and Greek 'flat-billed duck') the "very" male mallard is deeply interested in duck sex but makes the female brood the eggs, raise the ducklings and feed them, while he swims lazily about the pond preening his feathers. Mallards were the source breeding stock of most domestic duck hybrids in the West.

Mustard

Mustard got its name because the original condiment was ground mustard grains mixed with most or must, unfermented grape juice, hence *most* + *-ard*. It entered our language after 1066 CE as Anglo- Norman French *mustarde, mustard, mostart, moustard*. The postclassical Latin *mustardum* was a medieval form borrowed from French and relatinized. The word did not exist in ancient Rome, where the Romans borrowed the Greek word for mustard. Mustard in classical Latin was *sinapi*.

Hence the spurious etymology seen so often on the internet is a deeply ignorant guess, namely: *must* 'grape juice'+ *ardens* Latin 'fiery.' So mustard is fiery grape juice, is it? This utter claptrap is found in bad dictionaries and on word websites that are not reliable, such as the infamous "*podictionary*" whose writer, with no discernible scholarship in word study, is taken in by every folk etymology that comes down the pike and who appears to do NO investigative research into etymology but instead riffles through pop word books, copying whatever origin is colorful, no matter how ignorant. All one need do to know that *sinapi* is the Latin word for mustard, not *mustardum,* is to look it up in a cheap seven-dollar English-Latin paperback dictionary. The pod person who compiles "the podictionary" could not even be bothered to do that. What a *schlub*! What contempt he displays for his readers. *Mustardum* as a form did not exist until the 12th or 13th century.

A Few Uncommon English *–ard* Words:

Ballard- obsolete word for a bald-headed person from *bald* + *-ard*

Bullard – keeps a bull, shortened from bullward; nothing to do with –ard suffix

Bombard – old word for bumblebee

Canard – is the French word for 'duck' as well as its other meanings like 'hoax' or 'false story.' Its roots are Old French verb *caner* 'to quack' + *-ard* as operative suffix, hence *le canard* is 'the quacker.'

Clochard – French word for 'beggar' used by Hemingway from *clocher* French 'to limp.'

Bugiard – a liar

Croisard or **crusard** – neat but obsolete insult for a Crusader

Dizzard – a dizzy dolt, a fool, a simpleton ---- obsolete but worth reviving

Doddard – a pollarded tree

Babillard – chatterer, a bird name

Blinkard – an obsolete word for a doddering old, blinking fart. A word well worth reviving, due to the paucity of insult words in English.

Boggard – a bogey, a goblin

Boinard – obsolete word for a fool
Buffard — a rare word for a silly fellow

Here's one from French: *le Père Fouettard* 'Father Flogger,' is a continental French bogeyman, an evil man dressed in black who stuffs bad children into a big bag and wallops them with a stick or a whip. He is a nightmare version of the punitive father.

I wish to end this piece by coining a cheap new word. I hereby propose the hybrid word **schleppard** for a goof-off who drops the ball, a loser who never puts the puck in the net. Perhaps some religious saviour having an off day could have been called The Good Schleppard? Or perhaps not? Guards! Seize the coiner of that neologism, innocent little me!

Chapter 6

That Namby-Pamby Narcissus
— and Garden Advice Too!

Here I traipse through the origin of the flower name *narcissus*, but I wander a few word paths that diverge from that floral route, chiefly to examine odd byways of vocabulary and Greek myth.

Every September, North American gardeners plunge fat bulbs deep into autumnal loam and await a narcissine awakening. Whether dubbed daffodils, jonquils, paper whites or trumpet-flowered narcissi, these heralds blow chrome-yellow fanfares that sound each spring the melting retreat of winter.

The genus *Narcissus* was named by Linnaeus from a figure in Greek mythology, Narkissos, a beautiful boy in the old myths. The genus *Narcissus* comprises about forty, mostly European species. The horticultural forms have been crossed and recrossed for hundreds of years, and now number in the thousands of varieties and cultivars.

"Beauty Too Rich for Use, For Earth too Dear"

Although Shakespeare puts the words above into the mouth of Romeo when first he beholds young Juliet's virgin glow (Act V, Scene 1, *Romeo and Juliet*), the sentence applies to the myth of Narkissos too. The passage boasts four of William Shakespeare's best lines, in which the word music of his English flames like honeyed fire. Such mastery bears repeating.

"O, she doth teach the torches to burn bright!
It seems she hangs upon the cheek of night
As a rich jewel in an Ethiope's ear —
Beauty too rich for use, for earth too dear!"

One Strand of the Narcissus Myth

Oh yes! That Shakespearean line could have been the motto of Narcissus. Narkissos was a Greek lad so handsome that he spurned the love of women and men. But, one sunny Hellenic afternoon, kneeling beside a lonely forest pool, the lad found at last his own true love—himself. Pertly prone on a downy moss pad and gazing at his reflected image in the sparse ripples of the pond, Narkissos murmured to himself, "What a cute little stud muffin I am! By Zeus! I'm way too beautiful to be defiled by concupiscent deities and randy godlets, manhandled by coarse charioteers or lustful ladies who want merely to use me and then toss me back, depleted and bereft, on the barren moss. Nobody's ever going to flip up my chiton for a quickie at noon. I'm just too, too precious." Nowadays, Narkissos would have made a perfect simpering shill in one of the more lurid advertisements for male cologne.

Chiton versus Tunic

The short chiton, by the way, when worn by male children and slaves, was the ancient Greek equivalent of the brief tunic of casual Roman dress. The chiton or tunic was a very short, sometimes sleeveless shirt of wool or, during high Athenian or Roman summer, the chiton might have been made from a lighter, gauzy, translucent cotton material. Clowns in Greek and Roman comedies often wore chitons or tunics so short that their genitals were exposed for the audience to laugh at.

Outrecuidance — Obscure Synonym for Narcissism

One wants to avoid otiose sentences in which superfluous doublings like Narcissus' narcissism must be referenced. Outrecuidance might help. Its pronunciation usually attempts to follow the French: ootruh-kwee-DANSE. This interesting verbal rarity was borrowed into English in the fifteenth century or before from a word attested in Old French by the 12th century, where *outré* meant 'excessively beyond normal' + the verb *cuider* meant 'to display self-satisfaction or conceit.' In 1819, Sir Walter Scott used it in his novel Ivanhoe: "It is full time… that the outrecuidance of these peasants should be restrained."

Narkissos Again

Moss-cushioned and recumbent on a forest pool's ferny brim, Narkissos kept reaching to grasp his own reflection in the water, but each time he touched the surface, his image disappeared. The boy could not bring himself to leave the bank of the pool and so he stayed there, forgetting to eat, entranced by his own handsomeness — O fatal lingering!

When eventually the vain boy expired, the Greek gods took Narkissos up into the supernal ethers of Olympus and metamorphosed him into a golden flower, in order that they might each spring enjoy his beauty.

Note that I have omitted the Echo strand of the Narcissus myth. It was an addition to the earliest Narcissus stories and may be found on any site devoted to retelling Greek myths.

Etymology of Narcissus

The ancients thought that Narkissos' name was related to a Greek word for stupor or stunnedness, *narke*, a noun that is the source of English words like narcolepsy, narcotic, and Nark Squad. The prime meaning of the noun's antecedent, the Attic Greek verb form *narkoun*, was 'to make numb, to deaden feeling in.' By this reading of his name, Narkissos was "stunned" by his own gorgeousness. I think we have all observed a few Olympic swimmers who seem burdened with a similar malady, especially after springing forth, all fresh and lovely, from their anabolic steroid showers. My preferred motto for the Olympics has always been: "Let the injections begin!" I object to the title "Olympics." Far apter would be: World Youth Drug Trials.

But Greek personal and place names suffixed by -*issos* were borrowed from other languages, as -*issos* is not of Hellenic origin. So it seems likely this mythical figure first arose in the ancient Near East, and the Greeks borrowed the name and the story, and by folk etymology made it look as if it were related to *narke*. Orientalists have not so far found the foreign source of the word *Narkissos*.

Narcissism

Havelock-Ellis and Sigmund Freud used narcissism to label an early stage of sexual development wherein our own bodies arouse erotic feelings in us. According to Freud, most of us outgrow this fixated period of intense self-love. Freud, of course, never sat beside the runway at a fashion show. But ancient peoples knew well the high price of physical hubris, the sin of pride in bodily appearance. It is a common insight of Greek tragedy. And no wonder twelve chapters of the biblical *Book of Ecclesiastes* are devoted to warnings about "vanity of vanities; all is vanity."

The Plant Family of Narcissi

Narcissus belongs to Amaryllidaceae, the amaryllis family. In Greek myth, Amaryllis was a beautiful shepherdess in the pastoral poems of the third-century BCE Greek author Theocritus. Her story was borrowed into Latin poetry by Ovid and Virgil. Her name derives from a Greek verb *amaryssein* which means 'to have sparkling eyes.'

Species

Many, beautiful narcissus hybrids are widely available, but do look out for some of the smaller Narcissus species offered for sale from time to time. Among my favourites is *Narcissus poeticus* or Pheasant's Eye Narcissus with very fragrant, wavy-edged, white petals thinly margined in deep red. *Narcissus minimus* (Latin, very small) is among the smallest bulbed plants in the world, native to Asturia in the Spanish Pyrenees. One cultivar "Jack Snipe" is available early in the fall at garden centres. Try a dozen of these tiny beauties tucked into a nook beside your front door.

Etymology of Daffodil

Asphodel, the name of a narcissus frequently mentioned in ancient poetry, derived from *asphodelos* Greek 'a lily.' But during the rough and tumble of word borrowing from one language to another through history, plant names get tossed and jumbled.

Thus asphodel first entered English texts as *affodill*. Then, somehow, it acquired an initial /d/. The Oxford English Dictionary (2nd ed. 1989) opines imperiously that "the initial d has not been satisfactorily accounted for." Harrumph! Well, some of us who study words disagree. "The asphodel" in Middle Dutch was *de affodil*, borrowed into English a second time, where the Dutch definite article sounded to English ears as if it was part of the word and not the Dutch word the. That confusion and ignorance of Dutch produced the English form *daffodil*. It has taken many playful English forms through the years, such as *daffodilly* and *daffydowndilly*. At first daffodil referred to the asphodel but then became a name for English narcissi species and has remained the name for those species to this day.

Jonquil

Jonquil entered English from early French *jonquille*, *Narcissus jonquilla*. French borrowed the word from *junquilla* Spanish 'little reed,' named because of the rush-like leaves of many narcissi species. The Spanish word goes back to *iuncus* Latin 'rush, reed.'

Unmanned Lads of Greek Myth

Narkissos belongs to a small group of vaguely sexless flower-boys of Greek mythology: Hyacinthus, Adonis, Attis, Hermaphroditus and several more obscure prancing ephebes. These mythic namby-pambies were either denied normal male sexual function in their folk tales, through interference of goddesses or, more horribly, through self-castration.

Those who study the historical and psychological underpinnings of Greek mythology suggest that these asexual boys hark back to a time of brutal matriarchy in early Greece, when queens ruled tribes, and men were mere ambulatory sperm-bags and hunters.

The folk memory of this era, when females ruled all of Hellas, lingered toxically in the Greek male mind. Hellenic men who came after this dread epoch of gynarchy made certain that women never again ruled Greece. So say some scholars. Women became not only feared but vilified as not-very-interesting baby-machines, preferably mute ones. Other classicists adduce these early matriarchies as one of the reasons for ancient Greek pederasty.

We shall terminate this flamboyant narcissine extravaganza with William Wordsworth's poem "The Daffodils." But, remember, I don't want anyone climbing up on the kitchen table and tossing rose petals at the plumber.

Such indulgence is not fitting, and it might lead to wanton
tunic-lifting.

The Daffodils (1804)

I wander'd lonely as a cloud
That floats on high o'er vales and hills,
When all at once I saw a crowd,
A host, of golden daffodils;
Beside the lake, beneath the trees,
Fluttering and dancing in the breeze.
Continuous as the stars that shine
And twinkle on the Milky Way,
They stretch'd in never-ending line
Along the margin of a bay:
Ten thousand saw I at a glance,
Tossing their heads in sprightly dance.

The waves beside them danced; but they
Out-did the sparkling waves in glee:
A poet could not but be gay,
In such a jocund company:
I gazed -- and gazed -- but little thought
What wealth the show to me had brought:

For oft, when on my couch I lie
In vacant or in pensive mood,
They flash upon that inward eye
Which is the bliss of solitude;
And then my heart with pleasure fills,
And dances with the daffodils.

William Wordsworth, 1770-1850

Chapter 7

The Fiery Sheen & Lustrous Tincture of Copper

Ductile, hammerable copper, bringer of bronze weapons overthrowing the Stone Age, quack's cure for arthritic stricture, valid trace element in human nutriment, malleable for maidenly bracelets, the metal's distinct color compounded of red and brown chromas, of golden undertone, of russet luminance, of cupric hue, of auburn glint, all copper properties which have been millennial pleasures to the eye and hand of humankind.

Our English word *copper* stems from an early Germanic borrowing of the Latin *cuprum* 'copper.' Where did the word begin? On the stark and lovely Mediterranean isle of Cyprus, we think, where, at least one thousand years before Christ, copper mines abounded. In a syllabic script called Mycenaean Greek Linear B, there appears a demonym, the name for an island dweller, recorded as *ku-pi-ri-jo* 'person of Cyprus, a Cypriot.'

What bedevils linguists still is the ancient chicken-and-egg query. Did copper take its Greek name from the island, or did the ancient Greek name of the island *Kupros* come first and have a meaning now lost to history, while later giving the local metal its name? The Greek *Kupros* may be cognate with more ancient Sumerian words like *zubar* 'copper' and *kubar* 'bronze.' Other theories of the word's origin are twaddle, spurious folk etymology untested by any sound linguistic parameters.

In early Latin the first name of copper was *aes Cyprium* 'metal of Cyprus;' only in Late Latin did it dwindle to bald, lowly *cuprum*. By the way, *aes, aeris* is exactly cognate with our English word *ore*.

Other Meanings, Other Origins

Copper was once British thieves' cant then general North American slang for policeman, arising from the slangy British verb *to cop* 'to nab, to hold, to sneak' because the coppers were the ones who might catch do-badders. Probably *to cop* is a very early import of the Norman French verb *caper* 'to seize, to lay hold of.'

A copper penny was so-called because many early low-denomination coins were minted from copper. My country, Canada, recently abandoned copper pennies because the metallic copper needed to make a penny was worth more than one red cent. A red cent was another synonym referencing copper's colour.

Cop is an obsolete English word for a spider, but it survives in the compound *cobweb*.

A False Etymology of the Surname *Cooper*

The internet smolders with infernos of fallacy, junk-littered repositories of nincompoopery. The resident errors would cross a wise man's eyes. Chief among these unsightly sites lurk dank web grots which claim to tell the visitor "the meaning of your baby's name" or "the meaning of your surname." Many of these blunder-stuffed babblings are superintended by persons who can barely spell, let alone navigate the billowy babel of multiple languages. Also nodding by their keyboards at these toddler-dubbing sites are sclerotic grannies with an excess of knitting needles lodged in their skulls, a trait seldom conducive to accurate etymology. At one such boo-boo circus I found a passage boldly stating that the English occupational surname Cooper always meant a coppersmith. Utter drivel. In fact, Cooper as a last name seldom means coppersmith. There are a tiny few Coopers of such an origin, but they are rare.

A cooper is a barrel-maker, a deft fitter of staves bound fast by copper hoops, the cooperage full of casks, tubs, churns, hogsheads, tierces, rundlets, tuns, butts, puncheons and firkins. Of course there hasn't been a big order for firkins for some centuries. But, hey, a barrel-maker can dream too.

After the dawn of surnames in Europe and England it was not long before the occupation became a surname, at first George the Cooper, then George Cooper. This Cooper/Copper comes from Middle Dutch *kūpe* "basket, wood, tub." Possibly an ultimate or penultimate etymon may be Latin *cupa* 'vat.' Cooper surnamed early in English history. From 1181 CE survives a document naming Selide le Copere of Norfolk. In the Friary Rolls of York for the year 1424 CE reposes John Copper. By 1562 CE there was Richard Cooper of Ecclesfield in Yorkshire.

Cooperage as an occupation was widespread in medieval Europe and produced barrels of surnames. Consider last names like French *Tonnelier*, German *Fassbinder* (literally cask-binder), *Böttcher* (tub maker), *Fässler* and *Keiper*, Hungarian *Kádár*, Polish *Bednarz, Bednarski,* Ukrainian *Bondarenko* and Russian *Bondarev.*

From the Latin *cuprum*, English obtains scientific words about copper like cupric and cuprous, medical terms like cupremia 'copper in the blood,' and cupriuria 'excessive copper excretion in the urine, seen in copper poisoning.'

Earth's Classiest *Station de Métro*?

The most beautiful subway stop in the world is the *Arts et Métiers* subway station in Paris, entirely clad in the fiery sheen of lustrous copper sheeting. The station is so named because it is the nearest subway stop to the *Musée des Arts et Métiers*, a Parisian museum displaying French scientific instruments and inventions. The station was designed to resemble a giant imaginary machine, replete with colossal cogwheels, plus a cornucopia of implemental paraphernalia including doohickeys, thingamajigs, gizmos, widgets and whatchamacallits. Do visit it, especially if you dwell in cities with shabby subways unfit for rats.

But now, my fellow metallurgists, we gotta slam a topper on this copper hopper.

Chapter 8

It is, M'Lud, in Point of Fact, a Tort!

The legal term I hear most bungled in everyday speech is *tort*. *Tortum* is the source, a medieval Latin word simply meaning 'injury' or 'wrong done.' M'lud is a common contraction of "My Lord," a servile designation by which every British lawyer during court must address a presiding judge.

At English law, in preciser definition, a tort is a wrongful act, excluding breach of contract, for which the victim of the tort or wronged party may seek damages in a lawsuit. In a tort, a duty of reasonable, careful knowledge was owed. But the duty owed was breached and harm occurred. Actual or proximate cause arose from the tortious act. Proximate cause, a phrase beloved of lawyers acting for the plaintiff, means a reasonable person ought to have "foreseen the harm." Prove that at law and you'll be sailing through the Caribbean on your bought yacht for years.

Examples of Legal Torts

Other torts may arise from a doctor removing the wrong kidney or a slum landlord permitting a tenant to keep a Rottweiler and then said canine bites some fingers off a visitor, little crippled Bobby. Look out, landlord! In a grocery store, Mrs. Lipidsky slips on wet cabbage that has fallen to the floor and not been cleaned up. Tort City!

Of course, the tort may not be a crime. It may comprise negligence. The injury may be emotional, reputational (that is, comprise defamations like slander and libel) or economic. Copyright infringement is a tort, so too is false imprisonment. If I can prove your breakfast cereal seriously harmed but did not kill my children, you may be a tortfeasor (committer of a tort). If you subject me to untoward invasions of my privacy, that may be a tort. Almost all auto accidents are tortious acts.

A lawyer adds this. Normally the plaintiff has to prove some act of negligence on the part of the defendant and this can be problematic as sometimes accidents just happen, i.e. driver had a heart attack, or famously a bee stung a female driver on her breast. However, some tortious conduct is automatic. A famous British case involved the plaintiff's neighbour manufacturing dynamite, and, being inherently dangerous, the act was found to be tortious *per se* without proof of any negligence on the part of the tortfeasor when the sucker blew the hides off some of the neighbour's prize cows."

The definition of tort in the *Oxford English Dictionary* emphasizes the cast put on a tort in British law: "The breach of a duty imposed by law, whereby some person acquires a right of action for damages."

In American tort law, intentional torts are frequently recognized, where a person or, say, a food company, has intentionally acted in a way that harms another. U.S. product "strict liability" permits the remedy of recovery without the legal need to demonstrate negligence.

In tort law, the plaintiff has a lower burden of proof than in criminal cases. Preponderance of evidence is often sufficient as opposed to the more complex burden of proof beyond a reasonable doubt, for example, in a case of murder. O.J. Simpson, e.g., was acquitted in criminal court and later found liable for the tort of wrongful death.

Etymology

Tort entered English from Norman French sometime in the thirteenth century. The medieval Latin root word *tortum* 'injustice' gave rise to Spanish *tuerto* and Italian *torto*. *Tortum* 'wrung, twisted' is the past participial adjective from the Latin verb *torquere* 'to twist, to wring, to torment.' Do not confuse a tortuous path with one abounding in torture. A tortuous path is a twisty one. Consider the old French joke about the river that was so winding and twisting, that its fish had to have hinges.

The Torture of Cognate Words

English abounds with other words ultimately derived from *torquere*, the most familiar is perhaps *torture*. It entered English from twelfth-century French as *torture* from Latin *tortura* 'twisting a body to cause human pain, wreathing, torment, torture.'

Extort

To twist a confession out of a reluctant victim is to extort a confession. One might extort ransom from a nervous parent. The Latin source is another verb *extorquere* = Latin prefix *ex* 'out of' + *torquere* 'to twist,' to wrest or wring (something) from a person or to extract by torture.

Extortion is often the illegal 'twisting out' of money from otherwise reluctant donors.

Contort

To contort is to twist together, to draw something away from its normal course or meaning, from the compound Latin verb *contorquere* = Latin prefix *con-* (from *cum* literally 'together' but often a simple intensifier of the root meaning, here for example where contort means to really, really twist things up) + *torquere* 'to twist.' A contortionist does such ultra-twisting with his or her own body. Then the audience sees a distorted image of a human body.

The Root Hidden in a Flower Name

Nasturtium = 'nose-twister' in Latin, so named because its flowers have a pungent aroma, from classical Latin *nasus* 'nose' + *tortum* 'twisted.'

Burn, Baby, Burn!

Middle English gave us *torch*, from Old French *torche*, from late street Latin *torca from Latin *torquere*. The idea is that dried plant material dipped in oily pitch or tar and 'twisted' around a pole gave humankind its earliest torches.

Torque

The rotary force or 'twist power' of an engine is its torque.

To examine a true English cognate of Latin *torquere*, look up the word history of *thwart*. It derives from the same Indo-European root as Latin *torque-*.

But now, we needs must call a stop to these sinuous circuits of anfractuosity, these torques, these torches, these torts.

Chapter 9

Lawn: a Word Headed for Oblivion?
& Grass: a Word That Will Survive?

100 years from now, will *grassy lawn* be an obsolete phrase? In the midst of parching drought, the state of California has outlawed (2015) the watering of lawns. In a future, climate-changed world, the very word *lawn* may fall upon the listening ear as exotic, as preposterous, as fable-borne as *elf* or *sprite* or *fairy on tiptoe at the bottom of the garden.*

Lawn Ago & Far Away

Like an arpeggio strummed on a harp, played as merry elves scamper down a twilit lawn in a movie, the very sound of the word *lawn* may someday thrill or startle or be a criminal utterance. How unfortunate, even calamitous that shall be, for lawn enunciated, its central vowel spun out to a pleasing amplitude, prompts happy memories. For me, lawn summons boyhood play during long, school-free summer afternoons. Boys just knew those days "under the apple boughs" would never end. Mom sat watching us on the back porch and the lawn was wreathed in the fieldy aroma of new-mown grass. And this summer Dad might let us boys cut the lawn a first time!

Origin of the Word *Lawn*

Whence then did this labial delight enter our English word-hoard? The word *lawn* is the same root and is but a variant of the word *land* through an intermediate form *laund* from Old French *launde* or *lande* 'ground with trees' from an unrecorded Old Celtic **landa* source of cognates in the later Brythonic languages Welsh *llan,* Irish *lann* and Breton *lann.* In most languages of the world, words begin in semantic generality and narrow in meaning to evolve into complex specificity. A perfect example is *land* becoming *lawn.*

Think of Welsh place names with the familiar prefix *Llan-* which at first designated a cleared and enclosed area of land. Eventually the *Llan-* prefix began to name holy land in Wales occupied by friaries or Christian communities of monks or nuns. Then evolved Welsh place names like Llanbadrig (Saint Patrick) so that Llanbadrig implies a convent or priory sacred to Saint Patrick. Other saintly sites are Llandeilo (Saint Teilo), Llandudno (Saint Tudno) and Llandrindod, named to honour the Holy Trinity, in Welsh *y Drindod.*

The Idea of Lawn

Lawn as a concept first sprouted in medieval hamlets of France and England where common grazing sites were set aside, where amiable winters and warm-dewed humid summers favoured the burgeoning of grass. Thus were born the village commons, the common, the green, all small tracts of grassland to be shared by domestic animals. In smaller settlements, the commons were often in the centre of a tiny community so that all neighbours with grazing animals could share the greensward and mild kine could chomp and munch their graminaceous fodder contentedly. Were I more of a Pecksniffian word snob I might have written "poaceous fodder," for *Poaceae* is the giant plant family to which all grasses belong.

The thousand-year span of grassy commons is more than ample proof of that biblical verity from the book of Isaiah (40:06) "All flesh is grass."

The Word *Grass*

From its source, grass is indeed Teutonic turf. The word began in Old English *græs* and harks back to the supposed Old Germanic root **grasom.*

Even farther back is an Old Aryan stem **ghrā-* to grow, whence Latin *gramen* 'grass,' source of yet another botanical name for the grass family, namely *Gramineæ.*

To stray from agriculture and momentarily pay court to the Muse, here's a complete poem by Emily Dickinson.

PRESENTIMENT IS THAT LONG SHADOW ON THE LAWN

> "Presentiment is that long shadow on the lawn
> Indicative that suns go down;
> The notice to the startled grass
> That darkness is about to pass."

Unlike that fatal carpet, the water-wasting, endangered lawn, I predict that the word *grass*, especially with newer semantic luggage such as its synonymy with marijuana, yes, grass will outlast its lush and wastrel massing in lawns. Potheads will be smoking grass and ingesting it in brownies and spliffs long after the sad, browned, penultimate smudge of lawn has blown away, drought-blistered to oblivion.

Chapter 10

Heavens! Obscure Words for Heaven like *Welkin* and *Firmament*

To begin, I lodge a mild dissent concerning descriptive adjectives used by most dictionaries when referring to words rare, obscure or obsolete. Our two synonyms for 'heaven' under discussion today, *firmament* and *welkin*, both suffer from slipshod, uncareful and deficient labelling.

The Firmament Fuss

The Oxford English Dictionary in particular seems loath to even mention satirical or playful or lightly jesting uses of a rare or obsolete word. Take *firmament* as example. If you know the Book of Genesis in the KJV, the King James Version of *The Bible,* you will exult in the orotund majesty of *firmament*, a synonym for heaven reverberant when spoken aloud like the blast of an angel's trumpet. A place of locative authority and environing certitude, the firmament is, by the very sound of the word, confident of its existence and certain of its divinity. *Genesis 1:6* tells the reader "And God said, Let there be a firmament in the midst of the waters, and let it divide the waters from the waters."

Oxford says modern use of firmament is "only" poetic or rhetorical. So wrongly incomplete! I've read the word *firmament* used whimsically, playfully, magnified for comic exaggeration or employed viciously in an anti-religious newspaper column by a militant atheist. Such uses of the word in print have shown up throughout my life. Yet in its many quotations demonstrating various uses of *firmament*, Oxford shows not one quotation that is sportive or frisky.

Further in the OED's long entry, the great dictionary states a definition of firmament: "Heaven, as the place where God dwells" Then, with dark, excluding authority, Oxford rolls sonorously onward to assert that the word is "obsolete except in Biblical and liturgical phrases." Poppycock! Illogical Hooey! How about a recent (August 2015) American newspaper columnist describing Donald Trump as "arriving freshly jetted from the firmament." Satire! The journalist is making fun of Trump's pseudo-godlike shenanigans, with a reminder to his Bible-knowing readers of God's dwelling place, namely the firmament. The word's use is NOT obsolete. Firmament is alive in comic mode. Therefore it behooves the OED, in its monumental, century-long revision, to begin to include such jolly usage in lists of exemplary quotations.

There endeth my rant. Now commenceth my etymology of firmament.

Firmament's long word history fascinates. Its immediate etymon is classical Latin *firmamentum* "something that or an object which lends solid support to, holds up, strengthens" from the Latin verb *firmare* from the old Roman adjective *firmus* 'solid.'

Myles Coverdale, early translator of the Bible into English, found it in the fourth-century Latin translation of the Bible by Saint Jerome commonly called *The Vulgate*, not because it was vulgar but because Saint Jerome's translation became widely popular and sometime in the 13th century, nine hundred years after Jerome translated, his work was dubbed the *versio vulgata* Latin 'the commonly-used edition.' Saint Jerome also wanted the Bible to be readable by ordinary, literate-in-Latin people (Latin *vulgum* 'the people').

Myles Coverdale made the word *firmament* popular in his 1535 version of the Bible. But Coverdale had found the word *firmament* in an earlier William Tyndale Bible, where Tyndale

had perhaps Englished the word from its Vulgate Latin form
firmamentum. Unlike Coverdale, Tyndale knew the Hebrew
of *The Old Testament* and the Koine or Hellenistic Greek of
The New Testament, so his translations were freshly made
from Hebrew and Greek texts. He knew that Saint Jerome
had selected Latin *firmamentum* as a translation of a biblical
Hebrew word *raqiaʿ* which meant the overarching vault of the
sky, that is, heaven.

The trilitteral verbal root in Hebrew, *raqaʿ* has a neat
significance. It was a Jewish blacksmith's verb and meant 'to
pound out metal into a thin sheet.' Thus we have one idea
of how very early Hebrew writers thought of heaven. They
imagined it was a sheet of metal separating the watery abode
of rain and hail above from the rivers and streams and seas
below. Now let us return to that line from Genesis quoted
above. One may see that, from an ancient Hebrew point of
view, the mysterious double mention of water begins to make
sense. "And God said, Let there be a firmament in the midst of
the waters, and let it divide the waters (above) from the waters
(below)."

I now tiptoe tentatively out on a precarious semantic limb,
to make an educated guess about why those ancient Hebrew
bible-writers might think of the sky as a sheet of thin metal.
I remember being backstage at a commercial theater during a
production of Shakespeare's *King Lear*. When Lear raves in
the storm, the sound of theatrical thunder was provided by a
large sheet of thin tin or very thin iron suspended backstage
on thick wires from the rafters. A stagehand merely shook the
thin sheet of metal violently and the most realistic rumbling
thunder roared forth and filled the theater. I believe some
ancient scribe had watched and listened to a blacksmith pound
to flat resonance a sheet of metal in some sooty Judean smithy,
then the scribe heard the sheet shaken and recalled the vibrant
hollow rumble of booming thunder.

New Testament Greek used *stereoma* 'solid thing, firm structure' to translate the Hebrew raqia'. It sprang from the Greek verb *stereoun* 'to firm up, to be solid' and was of course a translation for the Latin *firmamentum*.

Heavens Above and Below

Through centuries of use in standard and dialectical forms, English spellings of the word *heaven* were diffuse and manifold. There are dozens of orthographical variants, but consider only the opening line of the Lord's Prayer in Old English (from perhaps 950 CE).

"Our father who art in heaven"
Fæder ure thu the eart on heofonum;
Literally: Father our, thou that art in heaven.

When heaven is plural (the heavens,) it is often an English translation of the Biblical Hebrew noun *shamayim*. To translators not deeply versed in Hebrew cases, *shamayim* looks like a simple plural form; in fact it's a dual. The dual was used in many ancient languages as a special plural for objects that customarily appeared in pairs, in twos. Thus words like eyes, human legs, hands, human arms would appear in the dual case. There are some scholars of Biblical Hebrew who say *shamayim* is in the dual case because "the waters" in the Hebrew scriptures came in twos, water, abode of rain above the firmament, then the metallic sheet of "heaven" intervening, separating the earth-bound water of streams, rivers, oases and seas below. Hebrew *mayim* means "water or waters." Hebrew scholars today argue still whether *shamayim* is cognate with *mayim*.

Do you think all this has little to do with the everyday English you speak and write? Think again! The two little tips of our letter /M/ represent wave tips. The letter **M** is derived from the Phoenician *mem*, via the Greek *mu*. Semitic *mem* probably originally pictured water. It is thought that Semitic people working in Egypt c. 2000 BC borrowed a hieroglyph for water that was first used for an alveolar nasal /n/, because of the Egyptian word for water, *n-t*. This same symbol became used for /m/ in Semitic, because the word for water began with that sound.

Returning to heaven, Saint Jerome's Vulgate Latin was *firmamentum* and also used was the plural of the Romans' word for sky, *caelum*, plural *caeli*. Modern English contains derivatives like *celestial.*

The Koine Greek of *The New Testament* used ouranos 'sky' to also mean Christian 'heaven.' English like Latin abounds in derivatives of that Greek word. Consider the planet Uranus, ancient Greek Ouranos, the name of the husband of Gaia (Earth) and father of Chronos (Time). Chronos in turn was the father of Zeus. As many of the other planets were named after gods and divine messengers of ancient mythology (e.g. Mars, Jupiter, Mercury, Saturn) so too was Uranus dubbed. I now blush to include a cheap, unsavoury joke from the realm of a famous sci-fi television adventure show. It is not a clean jest and will surely corrupt the lily chastity of youth. Too bad. So sad.

Question: Why is the U.S.S. Enterprise like toilet paper?
Answer: Because both circle Uranus looking for Klingons.

Another derivative of Greek ouranos 'heaven' is uranium, named by its discoverer German chemist Martin Klaproth (1743-1817) who dubbed the element in the late 1780s in honor of the planet Uranus which had been discovered only a few years earlier in 1781. In Latin, Urania was the 'heavenly' muse of astronomy.

Welkin: Most Obsolete Heaven Word?

Welkin's prime meaning in Old English was 'cloud.' A totally Germanic root it is; compare the modern German *die Wolke* 'the cloud.'

In Old English plural citations, "the welkin" usually means not "the clouds" but "the heavens." E.g. Old English *under wolcnum* 'beneath the sky' or 'under heaven.'

By the time of Middle English, after 1100 CE, welkin named the dome of heaven, the overarching vault of sky, the biblical firmament.

The word has been obsolete since the sixteenth century, says the all-knowing *Oxford English Dictionary*. Really? Why then is there a reference in Shakespeare's *Twelfth Night* that appears to mean welkin is still a current, apt term in 1623 CE? In Act 3, Scene 1, line 57 we read "Who you are, and what you would are out of my welkin, I might say Element, but the word is ouer-worne."

Minced Oath?

Possibly from the fifteenth century, for several hundred years, welkin was used in exclamations and asseverations, usually, I believe, as what we call in word study, a minced oath. To mince your words means 'to choose words so as not to offend anyone.' This particular expression began as a substitute for an outcry of angry condemnation, namely, "by Heaven!" or "by Heavens!" But the speaker decided that using heaven's name in this way was blasphemous and therefore substituted something milder, less religiously offensive for the word *heaven*. Thus "By heaven!" or "By the heavens!" became "by the Welkin." Consider this Elizabethan passage from 1602 CE by Ben Jonson "This villainous poetry will undo you, by the welkin." And two hundred years later, 1823 CE, in Sir Walter Scott's *Peveril* "Which, by the welkin and its stars, you would not be slow in avenging." The reader must keep in mind

Scott's archaizing tendency, his habit of using obsolete words to lend his prose a bygone prospect and a sound of yore.

Another example of a minced oath is *Jumping Jesus!* turned into *Jumpin' Jehoshaphat!* An Elizabethan phrase of shock, horror or surprise was "God's wounds!" This was a clearly blasphemous reference to the crucifixion. To diminish the impiety, Elizabethans, including Shakespeare, shortened and condensed the phrase to "Zounds!"

Like firmament, welkin may still find use in waggish prose, rhetorical exaggeration and even below in my pseudo-poetical, valedictory claptrap.

Go therefore and let the starry welkin ring with rigorous approvements of an ampler parlance. Cast up celestial nets to snare a firmament of frolic. Let stern obsolescence yield to blithe merriment, to learned whimsy of usage and stoop down betimes to chuck the chin of our nursling, the still young English language.

Chapter 11

Alarm! A Militant Order

ALARUM!

When alarum, later alarm, first resounded to English ears, it was a shout exhorting civilians to go to war — an Italian phrase to begin with: *all'arme!* "To arms!" In other words: Men, take up your weapons whatsoever they may be.

Fisher, seize that trident (three-pronged fish spear).

Farmer, grasp that pitchfork.

Woodsman, heft that broad-axe.

Reaper, hone a sickle's blade until it slices soldier-neck wide-open.

The Italian battle-cry arose from the simple Latin plural noun *arma* which even to the Romans signified the implements of war: swords, spears, shields, daggers and all the armaments of combat.

Stage Direction: Exit Thespian, Following Lesson in How to Speak Shakespearean Verse — or— Why Iambic Pentameters Need Not Induce an Actor to Swallow his Pretty Tonguelet!

Then, in English, alarum came to mean the sound itself, perhaps a trumpet's blast or a drum's roll. Soon after, alarm named the feeling stirred in human hearts by bugle's blare, and, erelong, the hurried actions of men caused by hearing such alarms, leading to one of Shakespeare's choice stage directions: *alarums and excursions*. This instruction called for soldiers or crowds to dither and flither to and fro across the stage indicating preparation for battle departure, done amidst drum trill and trumpet screech. The hullabaloo and brouhaha of hubbubbed rumpus has brought many an otherwise hushed scene of Shakespeare to a finale more spirited than the actors' wan performances may have merited.

Anything that caused shocked attentiveness was an alarm, and so, through weary daily use, through the iterance of utterance, the word's force dwindled down to our drab modernity where it resides in the humble name — alarm clock. Alarum! A once martial word that broke blood's levee as onrush through the veins of warriors now serves to summon round-shouldered minions crawling by glum busload to their ordained work cells. But such is the sandpaper of time which abrades the semantic sheen of even the noblest word.

Etymology

Latin *armum* is a reflex of the PIE morpheme (Proto-Indo-European word root) *areh whose prime meaning was 'fit on, equip for battle.' It is cognate with Greek words like *arariskein* 'to fasten to, to fit to, to make suitable for' and has a Sanskrit reflex in *arpayati* 'he gets ready for.'

Interesting extensions of the PIE or Aryan morpheme *areh are Latin *armus* 'shoulder,' English *arm* 'upper limb of the human body,' Old High German *aram* 'arm,' Greek *harmos* 'joint,' Sanskrit i*rmas.*

Blare The Tucket! Blast The Sennet!

As ornithologists covet rare birds, *rarae aves*, so we wee word lovers sometimes append a verbal oddity to our work. Today, for your especial logophilic delectation, I offer two terse musical terms, also from Elizabethan drama: *sennet* and *tucket.*

A sennet was a cornet or trumpet flourish, a stage sound meant to accompany the entrance or exit of some actors. It differed musically from an alarum but, alas, we know not how. The word's provenance is likewise obscure. Is sennet a dialect variant of sonata, diminished by apocope and vowel gradation? Most scholars think that a daft conjecture. So mopes the sad wordlet, forsaken, solitudinous, bereft of ancestry and embalmed in the embosoming amber of obsolescence.

A tucket is a trumpet fanfare or sequence of notes signalling soldiers to start marching. Cavalry troops were traditionally called to follow a leader by the sound of a tucket. *Toccata* in Italian and *touchet* in Old French are similar and mean 'trumpet flourish.' Tucket may be a diminutive form of tuck 'trumpet blast' from Italian *tocco* 'clock or bell strike or stroke' < Italian *toccare* 'to hit, to strike, to poke.' Both tuck and tucket could also signify a short drum exclamation.

In Shakespeare's 'Henry V' we read: "Then let the Trumpets sound The Tucket Sonuance, and the Note to mount."

I conclude with this richly sonorous passage, one of the high water marks of dextrous English, the sarcastic honey spooned out during the opening speech of Shakespeare's hunchbacked king-to-be *Richard the Third*.

"Enter GLOUCESTER, *solus*
GLOUCESTER
Now is the winter of our discontent
Made glorious summer by this sun of York;
And all the clouds that lour'd upon our house
In the deep bosom of the ocean buried.
Now are our brows bound with victorious wreaths;
Our bruised arms hung up for monuments;
Our stern alarums changed to merry meetings,
Our dreadful marches to delightful measures.

Grim-visaged war hath smooth'd his wrinkled front;
And now, instead of mounting barded steeds
To fright the souls of fearful adversaries,
He capers nimbly in a lady's chamber
To the lascivious pleasing of a lute."

Chapter 12

Cruising for a Bruising

Ever sailed on a big luxury cruise, me hearties? Now we humbly serve you the origin of the word *cruise*.

Etymology

Here is my elaboration of the usually unclear dictionary entry about 'to cruise.' The metaphor appears to have originated in Holland during naval record-keeping, in sailing journals and mapmaking. In 16th-century Dutch nautical cartography, *kruisen* was a verb meaning to make an "x" mark or a series of "x" marks, that is, serial crosshatching, to show on a nautical chart that a ship had "crossed" a certain expanse of water. Straight and dotted lines indicated the possible but uncompleted sea path of a voyage. A cross-hatched line sometimes indicated the part of the voyage completed.

All other meanings of 'to cruise' in Dutch, in England, in French, seem to descend from this initial practical use by Dutch navigators. By 1678 CE, the verb has skipped from making marks on a naval chart to making actual voyages, for Dutch sentences like this appear: *kruyssen op de Zee* 'to traverse and cross the seas' and French in 1688 has *croiser la mer* 'to cruise up and down the sea.' Middle Dutch had *cruce* 'cross' from Latin *crux, crucis* 'cross.' Consider other appearances of that Latin noun in English borrowings like crucifixion and crucial and in the wonderfully silly, pseudo-learned term for one who solves cross-word puzzles, namely, cruciverbalist.

Is it unusual for English to have borrowed Dutch nautical terms? Not in the least. There are dozens of watery Dutch loans. Consider Dutch originals like *yacht* and that nautical interjection beloved of old pirate movies *Avast*! That is Dutch *houd vast* 'hold fast or hold steady.' Middle Dutch gives English *buoy*, a noun that names a water marker chained to the bottom as a *boeie* or *boei*, from agricultural Latin *boia* 'a fetter, a halter.'

There you are. Yes, it was a short cruise!

Chapter 13

Hammada, Erg & Médano:
Lost in the Desert?

The percipient logophile – you, dear reader – will not stroke out to learn that several technical terms in English geography naming kinds of deserts and desert features were borrowed chiefly from Arabic, words like *erg*, *hammada*, *nabkha* and *médano*. Today, here in my word-tent, these obscure, legitimate and delightsome wee vocables shall doff their crimson-felted fezzes, fling away hooded djellabas and reveal themselves unto you word-naked and aglow in the pristine dawn of their creation.

Hammada

Hammada is the stony desert, common in parts of the Sahara, a boulder-strewn flatness from whose surface wind has blown away much sand and left rocks large and small.

From Arabic *hammada* is the desert word closest to my heart, because it once exploded a front tire on a little Peugeot I was driving through what I may call the "foot-sands" of the Sahara south of Marrakech. I suffered a mild sunstroke and swerved the little French rental car off the road. It bumped and screamed as it jolted over the roadside hammada pebbles and stones. Two sharp little rocks then pierced one tire. It hissed and deflated — most tiresomely. The Peugeot and I came to a kidney-in-mouth halt.

Dazed by heat and sun, I flung open the driver's door and collapsed, gasping like a docked carp, on the hot leather car seat. By quite undeserved luck, a Berber truck driver was passing by. He stopped and offered to affix the spare tire. The Peugeot had no jack. The trucker pointed at a rock and told me to fetch it. I remember the Berber word for rock is *azrou.* Somehow he pried that rock under the front axle and was able to put the new tire on. I offered him the equivalent in Moroccan dirhams of thirty dollars. He would not take one Moroccan *santim* (from French *centime* 'penny'). The Berber truck driver said I might pass him fifty kilometers up the road beside his broken-down truck and he would expect me to stop and help him. I said in halting Arabic that I would indeed help him, *inch' Allah* (God willing). At the mention of Allah, the Berber truck driver spat derisively. Berbers are animists. God is omnipresent, in everything, everywhere. It was a superintendent godlet of rocks who had helped that truck driver find the proper-size rock to put under my axle. Allah, the truck driver implied, had nothing to do with it.

Stony-desert, low-sand wasteland is hammada in North Africa, *gobi* in Mongolia, and *gibber-plains* in Australia. *Giba* is a word for stone, boulder or rock in Dharug, an extinct Australian Aboriginal language.

Erg

Erg is the desert mode most familiar to us, large sand dunes carved by earth's deft sculptor, the wind, with its keenest chisel, the air. These are the susurrant sands of purificatory solitude in films like "Lawrence of Arabia," where the dune mirage is not anything as vulgar as rippling water or date palms doing the hula. Instead, alone in the void, you see to the bottom of your heart. The tepid shallows of your squandered soul are rendered clear and oyster-lustrous, reflected back at you fiercely, so that you may purge the dross of a shabby self and come back to the oasis of life rinsed, scrubbed free of the washable demons and renewed to an

Edenic vigour. The erg's enticement of errant mortals is often a mere visual bribe: a soothing plethora of crescent dunes contoured by a mischievous Eros into languorous swirls of sand-flesh, curved dune-thighs whose sandy lips gape wide, luring men to a pert but empty wakefulness or to soporous peril.

The Arabic and the best English plural of erg is areg. Don't use ergs. It brands you as a doofus, an infidel who probably lost your pants when they were eaten by a camel. The word is of North-African provenance, *arq* 'dune field,' borrowed into Arabic from a non-Arabic language like Berber. Remember too, from the bothersome annals of disambiguation, that the form erg also names a calibrated unit of work. But the plural form areg does not.

As the sci-fi author Frank Herbert reminded us in his "Dune" novels (first one published in 1965), ergs are found on other planets and on bits of interstellar bric-a-brac. Venus and Mars have ergs and so does Titan, one of the moons of Saturn.

The world's largest erg or sand desert fills the lower Arabian Peninsula. It bears the brooding Arabic label, Rub' al Hali 'the empty zone' and spreads its desiccant vacuum across 650,000 square kilometres.

Desert

As any mystic knows, the desert is not empty. It is full of God. For no other reason did Jesus decamp into the wilderness. The New Testament's Koine Greek uses the word *eremos* 'forsaken, desolate place.' Of Jesus' trial in the wilderness, the Latin Vulgate, thus eventually giving us our English word desert, uses *desertum: tunc Iesus ductus est in desertum ab Spiritu ut temptaretur a diabolo* 'Then Jesus was led into the barrenlands by the Holy Spirit in order that He might be tempted by the devil.'

Desertus, deserta, desertum is a Latin adjective, here in its three gender presentation forms. As an adjective it is a perfect passive participle of the verb *deserere* 'to abandon, to forsake,' literally *de* a negative prefix+ *serere* 'to join together,' hence 'not joined together with anything, hence abandoned.'

Here's a note of intrigue from Wikipedia. I don't agree with it, but still it lingers hauntingly: "The transliteration of the Ancient Egyptian term for the Red land (i.e. the deserts on either side of the fertile Black land irrigated by the Nile) is dšrt (conventionally pronounced deshret); it has been stated that 'it is not impossible that the very word *deserta* entered the Latin language by way of Egyptian'." This is ingenious but highly unlikely, given the clear Latin ancestry of *deserta*.

By the way, the word *dune* is a mere variant of the noun *down*, possibly influenced in its English spelling by French *dune*.

Nabkha / Nebkha

This is the old Arabic word for a type of sand dune that forms around a vegetative obstacle in a desert. Clumps of shrubs and grass begin to gather windblown sand and a small bit of vegetation takes root on a broad, flat sand sheet. When the sand accumulates, the little plant clump grows thicker and perhaps taller, permitting more sand to gather around it. I prefer one of the English synonyms for nabkha. Some of the desert-loving explorers who first encountered these little bush-mounds called them "hummocky dunes." There are nabkhas in Kuwait, China, New Mexico and Mexico.

Médano

In South American Spanish geographic vocabulary and in English descriptions too, the word *médano* refers to a continental dune and *duna* refers to sand drifts on the coast. Médanos may have sparse vegetation or none at all. This lovely, voluted word slipped into early Spanish under Moorish influence in Andalusia. Arabic *máydan* meant 'sandbank or hill of sand' from Arabic *maydan* 'field, arena, open tract'.

Harena

Above is the original Latin spelling of the word English spells as arena. It's the Latin word for 'sand,' and, in the days of gladiators and finely diced Christians, arena gave its name to the building in which gladiatorial combat took place. Sand was put upon the floor of an amphitheatre to absorb the blood of the slaughtered animals and people.

No more pleasing egress to our dune meditation is there than a passage from the American writer who wrote best about deserts.

"Water, water, water.... There is no shortage of water in the desert but exactly the right amount, a perfect ratio of water to rock, water to sand, insuring that wide free open, generous spacing among plants and animals, homes and towns and cities, which makes the arid West so different from any other part of the nation [USA]. There is no lack of water here unless you try to establish a city where no city should be."

— Edward Abbey, *Desert Solitaire: A Season in the Wilderness*

Chapter 14

Canopy First Meant 'Mosquito Net'

The English meaning of ornamental cloth suspended over a bed or altar came directly from Medieval Latin *canopeum* > classical Latin *conopeum, -eum, -ium* 'net of fine gauze about the bed, mosquito net, tent.'

The Latin was borrowed from Attic Greek *konopeion* 'an Egyptian bed or couch with mosquito netting' < *kanops* 'gnat, mosquito.' Its Greek form and spelling were perhaps influenced by the name of the ancient Egyptian city of Canopus. Compare canopic jars containing the embalmed innards and bundled disemboweled entrails of mummified Egyptians. But the word itself, *kanops*, according to J. B. Hofmann's *Etymological Dictionary of Ancient Greek* and Eric Partridge's *Origins*, is a direct loan from Hieroglyphic Egyptian *khenus, khnemes* 'gnat, mosquito, housefly' with the addition of a familiar Greek noun suffix – *ops, opis*.

Our English poets have clasped the word to their talkative bosoms, especially to denote the heavens above, the starry welkin, and the overhanging sky. Notable among users was the Bard of Avon, exampled in the profligate beauty of Shakespeare's Elizabethan word music which as prose adorns this passage from Act 2 of *Hamlet* (1604 CE) where the gloomy Dane attempts to delineate his sad humour:

HAMLET
"I have of late, but wherefore
I know not, lost all my mirth, forgone all custom of exercise;
and indeed, it goes so heavily with my disposition;

that this goodly frame the Earth, seems to me a sterile
Promontory; this most excellent Canopy the Air,
look you, this brave o'er-hanging, this Majestical Roof,
fretted with golden fire: why, it appears no other thing
to me, then a foul and pestilent congregation of vapours."

Forest Canopy

The most modern meaning of canopy in English is the
dense crown of leaves and branches formed when tropical
trees "crowd into a shade," to quote the lyrics from one of
Handel's pretty tunes "Where're You Walk."

Other Meanings of Canopy

The part of a grapevine that grows above ground has the
technical name in viticulture of canopy.

The cloth and suspensory apparatus of a parachute are its
canopy.

The canopy at a Jewish wedding under which the happy
couple stands is in Hebrew a *chuppah*, in English a canopy.

A pope may award to a particularly supine basilica,
one whose prelates toady to all papal nincompoopery an
ornamental *umbraculum* (Latin 'little shade'), often called in
press releases a quilted canopy or *ombrellino* (Italian 'little
shade').

Canopy in French

Latin *canopeum* also billowed gently over fifteenth-
century French in forms like *conopée* or *canopie* 'tent' and
canapé 'sofa, couch.' Around the end of the seventeenth
century, French chefs filched the word to name choice dainties
and saliva-inducing savouries served atop crisp bread squares,
so-called little "canopies" to cover the bread cube.

Thus a new meaning of *canapé* appeared, this sense still alive in pompous culinary English: The Countess of Reflux swished into the banquet hall and whispered to her maid, Pyrosis, "I don't think that larks' tongues served on a bed of lattice is too arcane a canapé. The lattice-lettuce pun will surely register agreeably with all my guests and literate diners, *n'est-ce pas, ma petite Pyrose?*"

Chapter 15

Apothecary & Derivatives like Boutique

Somewhere in the glum gloom of the old part of a European city I enter a medieval apothecary's shop, recreated for tourists to a detailed and eerie perfection. Labels on vials of quicksilver fetched from strange strands glimmer in mercuric liquidity on shelves. Crystals of potassium bitartarate lurk stoppered under brown glass, beside herbed potions and pots of glutinous unguent which promise surcease of pain or at least an afternoon's intermission from agony. At the front of the shop on an oak counter, ceramic mortar and stone pestle sit, now still as death, smelling faintly of unknown crushed spices, of balms too rare for lay persons to know even their names. In a corner sits is an alembic, an apparatus no longer abubble, no longer distilling down its long neck some condensed elixir of recovery.

An alembic was a simple pot still or retort: one pot contained the liquid to be distilled by boiling, attached by a tube to another cooler pot into which the vaporous effluvia are led and in which the distillate is condensed. The word came into English, French and Italian through Greek from an Arabic word for a still *al-anbiq*. Elizabethan English boasted several spellings of the word *alembic*. In Sonnet CXIX, Shakespeare's obsessed lover laments:

> "What potions have I drunk of Siren tears,
> Distilled from limbecks foul as hell within. . ."

On a side table await beaker, bowl and bucket, eager to receive the powdered and stirrable grounds of *materia medica*. For apothecaries were the physicians of their age as well as its pharmacists and chemists. The entire experience in the little shop made me ponder the sweetly sayable word *apothecary* and its odd, direct derivatives like *boutique* and *bodega*.

The Outset of Our Apothecary Quest

Let's begin with a simple Greek verb *tithenai* 'to put, to place' which eventually produces hundreds of English derivative words, many of the technical kind that give readers trouble. Yet, by simply memorizing a few Greek root words such as *tithenai* and some of its forms, one may understand much polysyllabic jargon with ease.

One of the common nouns derived from the verb *tithenai* 'to place' is *theke* 'a receptacle, a box, a cover, a case, a sac, a cell, a hollow space, into which one places something.' Think of the French word for library, a building-size receptacle into which one places books. The Greek word for book is *biblion* and one Greek word for storage-place is *theke*, so the French library is *la bibliotheque*, from Latin *bibliotheca* 'library' from Greek *bibliotheke* 'book-case, library.'

First Name of the Bible in Old English

One of the synonyms for the Bible in Old English was *bibliotheca* 'book-like receptable that holds all the parts of the Bible.' In fact, the first word used to name the Bible among the early Anglo-Saxons was Old English *bibliothece*.

"O true apothecary! Thy drugs are quick."

Within a vault of doom in fair Verona, Romeo utters his antepenultimate praise in Shakespeare's star-crossed tragedy. Apothecary began as an ancient Greek word for storehouse *apotheke*, from *apo* 'away, nearby, beside etc.' + *theke* 'storage bin.' The verb was *apotithenai* 'to store out of sight, to hide away, to put by for later, to put beside one for easy access.' In Late Latin an *apothecarius* was a specific sort of store-keeper who kept in his shop products that would last awhile like preserved fruit as jams, candies, spices and "simples" that is, commonly known drugs. The word came into English from French. By early in the seventeenth century the London trade guilds were noticing the new use of the word, for in 1617 The Worshipful Company of Grocers permitted a group of merchants to break off from them and to call their guild (an early trade union) The Apothecaries' Company of London.

Worldwide Spread

Such a term filled a verbal blank, as witnessed by its speedy acceptance all over the world where a common word for drugstore, pharmacy or chemist's shop was needed:

Pharmacy in Dutch
apotheek
Pharmacy in German
Apotheke, Pharmazie
Pharmacy in Swedish
Apotek
Pharmacy in Luxembourgish
Apdikt (pl. Apdikten)
Pharmacy in Indonesian
Apotik
Afrikaans Language
Apteek
Danish Language
Apotek
Estonian Language
Apteek

Finnish Language
Apteekki
Icelandic Language
Apotek

Shopping Around for Shop Words

While *la boutique* is merely the common French word for small shop, boutique has acquired, during its sojourn in English, a fashionable elite sense, for example, a boutique where designer clothes are sold. In Swinging-Sixties English, boutique became an adjective so that one could read of "exclusive boutique wines for sale." Surprisingly boutique began in ancient Greek as *apotheke* too. Its path of transformations looks like this: Greek *apotheke* 'depot, storage place' > Latin *apotheca* 'storeroom' > Italian *bottega* 'shop'> Old Provençal *botica* 'little shop' > medieval French *boutique.*

Bodega

This current Spanish word for wine-shop also is a descendant of Greek *apotheke* and it too invaded England, as the name of cellar shops selling only wine. Compare Italian *bottega.* Spanish *bodega* had intermediate forms like *apodeka,'podeka, bodeka,* and finally *bodega.*

Now, though, we exit the apothecary's shop. We break in two the glass ampoule holding the wizard's magic liquid, the enchanted potion that brings silence. As the ampoule's shards smithereen upon the cobblestones of the Old City, yes, one can almost hear the silence and the advancing of the next chapter.

Chapter 16

The Hubbub over Haboob

We'll continue for one more chapter with winds because here I present my suggestion for a new origin of the English word *hubbub*.

The prime semantic force of the word *hubbub*, from its earliest appearances in English, has been loud noise; the roar of a crowd is a hubbub; so too is a raw war cry from a thousand throats spritzing hatred.

The Oxford English Dictionary presents one of its most vertiginous etymologies for hubbub, stating that hubbub derives from a Scottish Gaelic interjection of shouted contempt "*ub! ub! ubub!*" or from *abu!* "war cry of the ancient Irish." Darn, and I thought the Irish war cry was "Give us another pint of Guinness then."

In fact, the historical evidence for a Celtic origin is skimpy, not to say invisible. A far more likely ancestor exists and it is the thousand-year-old Arabic name for 'howling sandstorm,' haboob.

A haboob is a powerful sandstorm, from Arabic *habub* 'blowing violently, blowing as a high wind.' The Arabic verbal stem *habb* means 'to blow.' As one American traveler wired home, after being caught in a Sudanese haboob, "It's one hell of a lollapalooza. Lasts three hours but that's way long enough and it can drive sand grit straight into your skin."

In 1972, I was in a Moroccan haboob, on a sandy *piste* of a road leading southward from Marrakesh to a then forsaken hamlet in the foot-sands of the Saharan desert named Zagora. I remember the name of the little Berber town meant in Tuareg "twin peaks" named as it was after a nearby small but bifid mountain. The chief feature of the town back in that day? Zagora boasted an outpost of *la Légion étrangère*, the French Foreign Legion. But I encountered neither Buster Crabbe nor Burt Lancaster. When I was about fourteen years old, Burt made a foreign-legion movie called "Ten Tall Men." For one year afterward, I dreamed of chasing desert brigands on camelback across undulant swells of wind-furrowed dunes, all whilst clad in khaki and gripping a 9mm pistol, maybe the FL's preferred MAB Parabellum made by Luger.

Zagora today

Like a sad, collapsed tire, the semi-ruins of a giant French hotel cheaply built in the 1940s squatted in the centre of Zagora, its mud walls of *pisé* or tapia ever so slowly dissolving in the infrequent rain. The night I resided in that two-hundred room shambles there were exactly two guests, my sandpapered self and a Moroccan tax collector. As the haboob whooshed through town, so loud outside that we all had to shout at each other to be heard over the screaming sand blast, the manager of the hotel and his servants appeared in the lobby and brought a huge laundry tub of bed blankets and large towels soaked in water to the front steps of the hotel. Our cars were parked in the open, because there was no garage. I was helped by the hotel workers to cover, to plaster my tinny Peugeot with wet blankets and towels, so that the hard-driven sand of the haboob would not remove the body paint from the car. The sand stung my skin and the noise of the haboob was like water pouring over Niagara Falls (I was born 40 miles away from the Falls) but water pouring as if the medium was not water, but gritty sand.

Do British word-sifters mean to tell us that no English traveler, returning home from Middle Eastern desert storms of dust and sand EVER brought the word *haboob* back to Merrie Olde England? I don't believe that for a second. Hubbub is so obviously formed on *haboob*, with the utterly familiar and common gradation of its internal vowels, vowel-shifting that occurs inside thousands of words borrowed back and forth between languages. Just say aloud some of the spelling and pronunciatory variations of hubbub that have occurred in English orthography over the past several centuries: hooboube, hooboobe, howbub, how-bub, huboob, hub hub, huboob and, as quoted in the Oxford English Dictionary, even hubbub!!! No relationship to haboob? Surely British word mavens jest?

Sudan's capital city of Khartoum has dozens of haboobs every year. Kuwait, Iraq and the arid baking sheet of the Arabian Peninsula all regularly suffer haboobs. Lest Americans consider them foreign winds, Texas and Arizona experience haboobs. Phoenix and Yuma have three or four a year. Of course, Americans object to their winds having an Arabic name. The Depression-era dustbowls of the "Dirty Thirties" that carried away so many tons of prairie top soil and so many farmers' dreams were often haboobs. These oppressive blows can propel not only cheek-stinging sand grains but also tiny razor-edged pieces of rock that sculpt an uncovered forehead with hieroglyphics of blood and abraded skin.

The *haboob* phenomenon is essentially the massive downdraft of air from a collapsed thunderstorm supercell. As the gusting, descending air barrels into the ground it picks up volatile debris like sand grains and motes of dust. It can then propel them by the ton in a dense wall or column 3,000 feet high attaining breadths 60 miles wide. That's no mean storm. The wise among the haboob-engulfed seek whatever shelter is propinquitous and procurable.

So we too should imbibe the wisdom found in the last verse of "The Day is Done" by Henry Wadsworth Longfellow (1807-1882):

"And the night shall be filled with music,
And the cares, that infest the day,
Shall fold their tents, like the Arabs,
And as silently steal away."

Chapter 17

A Vault of Ninnies

You Moping Fonkin!
You Peevish Numpty!
You Poop-noddy!
being a modest trove of synonyms for the word fool,
*a diverting hodgepodge of odd, archaic, obsolescent
and new equivalent terms for fool, such as pillock,
joculatrix (Latin, literally 'female joker'), muggins
(gained wide use in the 18th and 19th centuries as a
term for a simpleton), schmeckl (Yiddish, diminutive of
shmuck 'penis' literally 'little penis') and dickwit.*

A Synonymy of Fools

A fool and his synonyms are soon parted. The reason is simple. English has a sparse stock of insult words. Consequently those few abusive terms our language does possess are used and re-used and become stale clichés quickly. Shouting 'Ass!' at the committer of some moronic act gets lame quickly. Insult does not bear repetition. The wimpy-gripped stumblebum who dropped the rare Limoges dinner plate and smithereened it on the tile floor of your kitchen will hardly even hear your calling him a fool. But if you machine-gun at him "You fumble-fingered fonkin!" he will at least pause to scratch his furfuraceous noggin, wondering what precisely you meant. Half the superior joy of insulting those who err is their not understanding the very insult.

Thus stands English ever in need of fresh invective. By inventing new insults and exhuming buried verbal treasure of yore, it is my humble hope in this brief endeavour to rescue tongue-lashing from letterless clods and return it to purveyors of high word art.

Fool Itself

"I had rather have a fool to make me merry than experience to make me sad," says Rosalind during her pleasantly stichomythical meeting with Jaques in the forest of Arden, at the top of Act IV in Shakespeare's *As You Like It.*

So, first, a brief peek at fool's interesting lore. It began as *follis*, Latin for a sack of flour, a bellows or an inflated ball that Roman gentlemen used as part of their exercise at the baths. Already by the time of late Latin, it was used as an insult for a windbag or blatmouth. Entering Old French, *follis* became *fol* and in modern French *fou* 'mad, insane' but note that *fou* the adjective is still *fol* before a vowel and its feminine is *folle.*

Fol entered English with the Norman Conquest of 1066 CE. By the start of the 13th century, in Middle English, *fol* meant 'stupid person.' Fool's overuse in subsequent English centuries has caused the word to be uttered more vehemently and made it carry a heavier semantic weight of contempt than earlier it bore. *Fool* is a stronger putdown than its weaker adjective *foolish.*

Fonkin

A word we must rescue from the dusty shelf of near oblivion is fonkin. A fonkin is a ploppy, blobby type of fool, his brain a puddle of cerebral porridge, his plumpish flesh unlived-in and virginal although always scrubbed clean of dirt. Fonkins bathe obsessively. The fonkin boing-boings down a street, bobbing obscenely like Tweedledum or Tweedledee. Your average fonkin is soft, pliant, unmanly in his folly, fatuous, inept, hesitant.

Fonkin is synonymous with that solid British slang word for fool, *prat*. In London I heard a Cockney who had watched an assistant at a vegetable market drop a large watermelon and smash it, "Prat! Ee's daft as a fried smelt." At rest the fonkin can often be seen to protrude his tongue-tip between his teeth and sit immobile and idle for hours, torpid as a sunned skink.

Above all, fonkins believe what you tell them, whether it's a racing form or Holy Writ. They are the credulous ninnies of orthodoxy. Flying saviours, multiplying loaves of bread, out-of-control fish replication, no religious preposterosity is too outré for the wide-eyed idiot smile of the hapless fonkin.

Do not bestir yourself, gentle reader, to look up preposterosity in a dictionary. I made the word up, a legitimate descendant of preposterous whose clustered, gobbling, pompous polysyllabism suits perfectly its meaning.

Bumpkin is Kin

True, fonkin is obsolete and obscure. It was last used in printed prose in CE 1591. But so what? It is a compound of *fon* 'a fool' but from an earlier verb *to fon* 'to lose flavor, to become insipid' then 'to be foolish' + the common Germanic diminutive suffix *–kin(s)*, in meaning either dismissive or affectionate. Peterkins is a mother's pet name for her son Peter. Bumpkin is a short, stupid fellow, the word quite probably from a Dutch diminutive like *boomken* 'stumpy tree' or *bommekijn* 'little barrel.'

Recent additions to the synonymous tribe of fools have entered English from New York City Yiddish, from Hollywood and from showbiz in general, and from various Jewish-American writers. Thus a few of the Yiddish insults now seen in English include:

Nebbish - 'a nobody, a nothing, an insignificant non-entity,' from Yiddish interjection *nebekh* 'poor thing!' from Czech *nebohý*

Schlemiel - 'a fuck-up, a bungler, from a Hebrew adjective meaning 'ineffective'

Schmendrick – a chump, a screw-up,' from Yiddish *Shmendrik*, from the name of a character in an operetta by Avrom Goldfaden (1840-1908), father of Yiddish theater.

Shlimazel 'unlucky jerk,' from German *schlimm* 'poor, lacking' + Hebrew *mazzal* 'luck'

Schlub - a clumsy, stupid, or unattractive person, from Polish Yiddish *zhlob* 'hick,' from Polish *zlob*.

Cretin

Cretin began as a term of compassion. *Crétin* was a southern French dialect word that meant 'Christian person' (from Latin *Christianus*). Cretin was first applied to deformed and mentally retarded persons found in certain alpine valleys that lacked iodine. *Crétin* was used in the sense of 'that poor unfortunate may be deformed and retarded but he or she is still a fellow Christian and demands our compassion as a fellow human being, in distress true, but still a congenial wayfarer on the same stony path of life we all needs must travel.' Then, gradually in French then English, cretin became an insult tossed at people slow on the uptake or remarkably stupid.

Ignoramus

Today it means a person devoid of knowledge or uninformed of matters commonly known to a community or people. But it is fourteenth-century British legal Latin. In classical Latin it means 'we do not know.' In its British legal use, ignoramus meant 'we take no legal notice of [the prosecution's indictment]. It was, as the *Oxford English Dictionary* states "the judgment made by a Grand Jury upon a bill presented to them, when they considered the evidence for the prosecution insufficient to warrant the case going to a petty jury."

The meaning was then generalized to a stupid person, because of the similarity of the verb to the much more widely known adjective *ignorant*.

Pillock

This putdown of an idiot or fool is still in wide British usage, derived from a very early English word meaning 'penis,' thus equivalent of modern American slang like *dickhead* or the Yiddish insult *putz*.

Constult: My Favorite Obscure Fool's Verb in English

When reasonably intelligent people assemble to be thoughtful, they consult. When fools assemble, they constult, from the Latin adjective *stultus* 'foolish.' *Stultus* may also be a noun, 'fool.' Think of our verb *stultify*. The verb was coined and used briefly in the middle of the seventeenth century. Constultation takes place daily in many corporations and households.

Neologies

Do investigate on your own the vast *omnistultium* of foolish synonyms in English. *Omnistultium* is my coinages. I fashioned it on the model of pandemonium. Instead of naming a swarm of demons as pandemonium does in Milton's *Paradise Lost*, omnistultium signifies an array of clods, a vast stumblebum swamp of soon-to-drown nincompoops.

Chapter 18

Dross Words: Scoria, Dregs, Recrement, Scobs, Slag, Draff, Lees, Offscourings. Do You Know Them All?

Lamentable Lacunae of Lame English

Today I take my scorn, unleashed, for a walk. Compared to other prominent languages of the world, English has a tiny supply of insult words. On the other hand, Yiddish sparkles with inventive invective. Chinese has 400 phrases insulting to denizens of the white West. "Round-Eyes" and "Dead Mushroom Face" are the merest start to the racist Chinese concatenation of odium against foreign westerners. The French bathe daily in a word-tub of disdain for everyone on earth who is not of pure French provenance. But diffident, hesitant English purses its proper lips and squeaks in Uriah Heepish mode, "If you can't say anything good, then don't say anything at all." Such goody-two-shoes propriety sucks and sucks big time! I say: Label and dismiss all crap, both inanimate and human!

This English shyness about making negative words legitimate must be overcome, flung down and throttled. So today I offer a thorn-bush of words that prick, stab and draw the blood of disapproval: dross, slag, lees, scoria, recrement, draff, offscourings, dregs, scobs.

Why We Need Impertinent Words

Some of these putdowns you will know; others will be new words, fresh, razor-sharp and ready to wound the commercial thieves and crooked business swine who have so burdened us. We need a militant vocabulary of thing-abuse that bristles, because our modern world presents us daily with objects that fail their purpose: a shampoo making one's hair dirtier, a stool softener that produces a Gargantuan fecal bolus requiring either reparative anal surgery or "the jaws of life" applied to one's arse, car "safety" bags that explode and kill drivers, all manner of industrial product failure and subsequent customer injury and defilement.

We need spoken and written ploys of language that name, confront and dismiss these affronts to out timely progress through the day. It therefore behooves the careful English speaker to be armed with a stout quiver of keen-fletched arrows to pierce shoddiness, zinging words to make everything slipshod fall wounded to the linoleum floor where, with a vengeful smirk of satisfaction, we may observe it exsanguinate.

Dregs

I begin with dregs, useful for rundown goods and inferior people. The most frequent use is the dregs of wine, the lees of wine, the sedimental residue that makes it necessary to decant port. But the lowest order of the *profundum vulgus*, the great unwashed, are the dregs of society. Dregs can also signify the last little bits, remnants almost unworthy of notice.

Dregs is a bestowal to English from the Vikings. In their language, Old Norse, *dregg* was the lees of wine. Dregs is cognate with Swedish *dragg* 'dregs,' Latin *fraces* 'dregs of oil' and Greek *tarattein* 'to stir, to disturb' and with Albanian *dia* 'dregs of oil' and even with Old English *deorc* 'dark' as a colour.

Let us not forget the apt but seldom used adjective *dreggy.* Wonderful word! Let me use it in an exemplary passage from my failed science-fiction novel: "A couple reported they had been abducted by aliens, a dreggy little duo from West Virginia, Ethel and Ben Klort. Of course, on the rocket ship driven by giant bumblebees from the planet Nargon, there was the always-reported cold aluminum probe introduced by the alien doctor into Ethel's body, or, as Ethel said so becomingly, "They stuck it in 'down there.' That's right, Ethel, logic assures us that aliens voyaged through thousands of light years, across the vasty blank of the universe, expending numberless units of intergalactic fuel, just to look up under your dress. Something Ben hasn't done for decades."

Dross

This sleek monosyllable is veneered with scorn. The evil, susurrant sibilance of the terminal esses make the word easy to spit forth with salivary contempt. Dross began as the scummy matter that floats to the top during the smelting and refining of metals. Dross was worthless impurity, trivial matter best consigned to the garbage heap. "He was wide-awake and his mind worked clearly, purged of all dross" wrote Vladimir Nabokov. A film reviewer reported that "bad as the film is, Thomas Haden Church ('Sideways,' 'Smart People') somehow manages to rise above the dross as a self-absorbed reporter."

Dross' early appearance in Old English as *drosna* or *drosne* found the word with meanings like "sticky dirt, ear wax, lees, yeast gone bad." Dross harks all the way back to a Proto-Indo-European etymon *dhrak- or *dhrag- ʃ 'mucky sediment, yeast.'

Because the singular form of the noun *dross* has come to have a collective meaning, the plural form is not used enough. Yet drosses, with its double-sibilance of dismissal, can render most aptly what is loathsome and inutile. If I may be permitted yet another brief fictional outing, consider this offering. "Frequently Ted was overwhelmed by bitter memories of an abused childhood. Why, he had been deprived of licorice at the age of seven! Ted's boat of memory was inundated by the swamping drosses of a resentment which at times engulfed him and made him incoherent."

"The owner was upset because the new, fancy, up-scale restaurant across the street had skimmed off his best customers and left him with the dross, the putative *beau monde* of downtown Toronto, eaters who dined out but didn't mind picking their nose before tucking into the chateaubriand."

Another rarer significance appears in the obsolescent phrase *opium dross*, the scrapings of a smoked opium pipe reboiled and manufactured anew as a kind of second-class prepared opium.

Draff

Draff is a Germanic husk of a word that first meant "grains of malt, barley and cereals left over after brewing, the swill and refuse fed to pigs. In 1623 Shakespeare waxes proverbial about it. Act 4, Scene 2 of *The Merry Wives of Windsor* opines "Still Swine eats all the draff." Draffsack is a now sadly obsolete insult for a low gluttonous lout with a beer belly or wobbling paunch.

Residuum

A word that merits wider use is one of the classical Latin words for residue, something remnant, that which remains after a good or useful process has occurred, namely *residuum*, used in English since at least the sixteenth century and still in current scientific use to name a smudgy deposit left after a process like evaporation or combustion, a lowly sediment.

Residuum's twin *u*'s, the first short, the second long, lend a lingering to the word's pronunciation that may be employed to append depisement or affix opprobrium to an utterance. For example, "His political support has dwindled to a pathetic residuum of toadies, lickspittles and lifelong brown-nosers."

Offscourings

This excellent word, usually a plural form treated as a collective singular, is in the earliest English bibles including King James and Tyndale, e.g. Lamentations (KJV) iii. 45: "Thou hast made us as the offscouring and refuse in the midst of the people." Offscourings are the rubbish scraped off completed objects to be thrown away as useless. The word is applied to persons as often as it is to things. Edgar Rice Burroughs in his seminal *Tarzan of the Apes* (1914) wrote of "a vessel of the type often seen in coastwise trade in the far southern Atlantic, their crews composed of the offscourings of the sea — unhanged murderers and cutthroats of every race."

Charles Frazier wrote one of the best Odyssey-like journey novels about a civil war soldier who deserts the slaughter and walks overland back to his waiting lover in the deep South. The book's title is *Cold Mountain* (2000 CE) "He commenced pulling the trigger out of sheer frustration with the willfulness of these sorry offscourings."

Recrement

A cousin of excrement (feces), recrement is refuse, useless scum, rubbish, dregs. Both excrement and recrement derive from classical Latin nouns. To the ancient Romans, *recrementum* meant 'dross, waste material.' The verbal source is Latin *cernere* 'to separate, to decide.' Thus, etymologically, excrement is 'that which is separated from the body. Recrement uses the Latin prefix *re-* not in its literal meaning of 'backwards, back, again, repeated' but rather as *re-* is used in many Latin words that made their way into English as a general intensive prefix, a developed sense beyond its prime repetitive meaning. Thus recrement is matter that *really, mightily, truly* deserves to be separated from what is useful, that is, dregs, refuse, etc.

It may be of interest to note that one of our Germanic English words for excrement applies the same semantic ploy. Common English *shit* is ultimately a past participial form of a verbal root that appears also in our verb *to shed* and in modern German *scheiden*, past tense *schied*, past participle *geschieden* 'to divide, to separate, to put aside.' Thus shit like German *Scheisse* is what must be put away from us, be separated from us by defecation.

Unlike most of the other drossy words in this column, *recrement* is seldom used figuratively. What is figurative language? It is use of a word with a sense different from its literal meaning. Some of the figures of speech are metaphor, simile, symbol, metonymy, synecdoche, hyperbole, litotes, personification and apostrophe. There are plenty of other figures of speech (and of written language). Seek them out if you don't know them all. They will help your understanding of and your flair for English prose composition.

A rare figurative use of recrement is found in a 2006 article in the Richmond (Virginia) Times Dispatch: "Richmond's best feature: The remnants of its courtly charm. Richmond's worst feature: The recrement of bigotry that hides behind the above."

Scobs

Scobs is rare but when found used only in the plural. It too refers to the dross floating to the surface of smelted metal ore. It may also mean ground-up metal filings, powdered ivory, shavings, etc. An ancient Roman word, it was *scobs, scobis* in Latin meaning 'sawdust, filings, scrapings,' a noun from the verb *scabere* 'to scrape,' whence other English words like *scabies*, an itchy skin disease, but not related to English *scab*. The English verb *to shave* is however very probably cognate with Latin *scabere*. An interesting Roman menu item was *scobs citreus* 'grated lemon-peel,' reminding gourmets that the French did not invent everything in the kitchen!

Scoria

Largely used only in its technical meaning in metallurgy and volcanology, scoria came to us through Latin from ancient Greece where Greek *scoria* meant 'dross from refining metals,' its exact meaning still in modern English. It is related to a Greek word for dung *skor, skatos,* from which English gets scatology meaning 'dirty' writing, anything obscene. To those who study volcanoes, scoria is often used in its Latin plural form *scoriae* to signify bubble-like masses of molten lava cooled on the surface, its bubbles made by gases escaping from the lava during the cooling process.

Slag

Slag has many meanings developed from its prime sense of smelting refuse in metal refining. The word source of slag is the dread o.o.o. 'of obscure origin.' Applied to persons, slag is insulting. It may mean a coward, a bully, a low lout worthy of contempt, a petty criminal, a whore.

Spodium

Here we tiptoe down echoic corridors of seldom-visited word mausolea. Spodium and spode are rare words once used in English to signify fine white powder made from calcined material. Latin *spodium* was borrowed directly from ancient Greek where it was a diminutive form *spodion* of *spodos* 'ashes, dross, dust.' One of the forms of magic divination, where the seer foretells the future by poking through warm ashes, is spodomancy.

Lees

To conclude, one of the most familiar of the dross words, the lees of wine, that is, the insoluble settlings during fermentation and aging. Wine lees are chiefly deposits of residual or dead yeast that collect at the bottom of a vat or, as in port, at the bottom of a bottle.

The word has a singular but infrequent form *lee* from Middle French *lie* < Medieval Latin *lia*, not a Latin word but probably borrowed from a Celtic language by Roman soldiers in northern Gall and so akin to Old Irish *lige* 'bed, grave, something you lie in' and to a Welsh word *llaid* for mud. Lie is cognate too with Latin *lectus* 'bed,' Greek *lechos* 'bed' and Old Slavic *lezati* 'to lie down.'

One proverbial phrase is common. "I shall drink life to the lees." I shall consume all to the very bottom of the bottle of vital delight, but not before I banish from my presence the human recrement clustered 'round the portals of my abode, the teeming, wailing dross, the dreggy choir chanting hymns of whining entitlement, retunded slags who would fritter away one's precious time begging for contributions to, say, the National Home for Unwanted Perspiration Stains or polluting television by selling us bad cars. Be gone, you lumpen-scobs!

Chapter 19

Dolphin Words

Dolphin, the Swimming Womb

In sassy arcs, high over the brine bath of the sea, vaulting above the bounding swell, the dolphin has spanked across the wide bay of human imagination from our first tentative sightings, voyaging on tree-branch or hollowed trunk. Darting through shallow seas above continental shelves, dolphins are found in all temperate waters. Dining daintily on little squids and slippery fishlets, they join humans in being happy piscivores. A carnivore eats meat; a piscivore eats fish. All the ancient peoples who encountered these playful marine mammals fell in love with dolphins. Friendly intelligence — how rare on earth is that? — and their curved mouth, the famous delphinine smile, insured humanity's affection.

Etymology

The word *dolphin* sailed into English from Old French daulphin < Medieval Latin *dolfinus* < classical Latin *delphinus* < Hellenistic Greek *delphinos* < classical Greek *delphis*. The term is related to the Greek word for uterus or womb *delphys*. The ancient Greeks saw the sea mammal bearing live young, hence womb-fish? And did the glistening shimmer of the dolphin look like a womb to those randy Hellenic fishermen? Perhaps. The Greek womb word *delphys* may be a reflex of the Proto-Indo-European morpheme *dhel- 'to be hollow, to be split' suggesting a male naming of the vagina. Perhaps even more apt as a source is an extension of that PIE morpheme, namely *dhelbh- 'dig, excavate, insert, delve.'

Iconic Pioneer

One of the earliest icons of joy in the annals of European art is 'boy on a dolphin.' Both joyous and erotic the image was, for most depictions display a slender nude youth firmly astride the moist flanks, muscled thighs clamped to the comely womb-fish. I'd say that perks up the erotometer into at least slight overdrive?

Greek myth told that any sailor drowned and lost at sea would have a dolphin bear his soul to shore. Dolphins were said to have rescued men who fell into the sea.

The primary myth is the story of Arion. The Greek historian Herodotus tells the tall tale. Arion, a singer, was returning to Greece from several lucrative gigs in Sicily and Magna Graeca. He boarded a Corinthian merchant ship for his return to Greece. Now it was Arion's custom of a morning to sit upon the gunwales of the ship and sing for an hour. The second day, bound out from Tarentum on the Apulian coast of southern Italy, the crew of Corinthian cut-throats suddenly mutinied and turned piratical, threatening all passengers with death. Arion began to sing. The pirates stared at him. Then Arion jumped into the sea. The pirates guffawed loudly. But all around the ship, dolphins splashed and waited, for they had heard Arion singing across the waves and, charmed by his voice, had encircled the ship to listen. Once in the water, Arion climbed onto the back of one, and the dolphin swam him back to Corinth, where Arion went to the king, reported the pirates and saw them all hanged. It turned out that, in collecting Greek folk tunes, Arion happened to remember a salty wee ditty a fisherman had taught him years before, a tune specific to the task of luring dolphins ashore. The moral of the story? It never profits a *chanteur* to neglect his songbook!

A possibly mangled version of that same story tells of the god Dionysus once trapped by pirates. For some divine reason known only to Dionysus, the god dumped the brigands into the sea to drown, but then Dionysus had second thoughts, and turned them all into dolphins, who swam away to safety.

Related Words

1. **Delphinium** was named because the flower's nectary is vaguely dolphin-shaped.

2. **Dauphin** was an honorary official title of the eldest son of every King of France from 1349 to 1830. Among manifold earlier forms of the word were *daulphyn* and doffin. A French dictionary suggests that the title arose from an actual surname Delphinus whose held lands were the French province of *le Dauphiné*. When the last lord of *le Dauphiné* had to give up his province to a more powerful nearby princeling, he insisted that the title should become hereditary and be borne by every eldest son of every succeeding French king. The historical proof of this is scanty. A more cogent guess is the supposition that Dauphin began as a nickname for some early important person, who was perhaps overly fond of swimming, so his boyhood companions named him after one of ocean's happiest swimmers, e.g. "*Voici Pierre le dauphin.*"

3. **My Brother, the Womb-Sharer.** The ancient Greek word for brother is *adelphos*. A brother is one who shares a womb (Greek *delphys*) with his siblings. The initial /a/ is not the usual alpha privative or negatizing particle; it is rather a copulative prefix, joining root

meanings together. Consider too the Greek word for 'brotherly love' *philadelphia.*

4. **What about the Oracle of Delphi?** If the blushing author may be permitted here to insert a modest note of disambiguation, please take notice that the famous oracle of Delphi (ancient Greek *Delphoi*) did NOT take its place name from dolphins. The name derives from *delphys* 'womb.' The site was also called in antiquity the *omphalos* (umbilicus) of the world, the navel center of earth, the planetary bellybutton, the Hellenic focal point. There may have been uterine caves in the vicinity suggesting a vaginoid entrance to the underworld. Therefore the first god worshipped at Delphi may not have been Apollo, but rather the goddess Gaia, ancient Greek Earth Mother.

One Hideous Nickname!

An obsolete Germanic-based name for the supple sea-gliding dolphin was in English the word *mereswine* 'sea pig.' Really! How could one stand at the helm of a tea-clipper, nostrils besprent with salty spume, suddenly spot the sportive sea-leap of a merry dolphin and think *mereswine*? Well, apparently one could, if one were an early German or Dutch merchant sailor or naval functionary who abominated all earthly creatures who were not human and were therefore perhaps edible. This sleazy term has cognates in most of Germanic and Scandinavian languages. Compare Dutch *meerzwijn* and German *Meerschwein*, Icelandic *marsvín*, Swedish *marsvin*, Danish *marsvin*. Both parts of the compound are Germanic, *Meer* 'sea' + *Schwein* 'pig.'

I think we all know who the mere swine of the oceans really were, the unsavoury slew of imperialistic aquatic piggies and nautical marauders, like Viking raiders and history's sailing oppressors like the British navy and the Dutch merchant marine.

Another Porcine Name

Dolphin would not be the only comely swimmer of the seas to be tagged with a piggy name. Look at the etymology of that other smaller delphinoid whale of the family Phocoenidae, the noble porpoise. The word came over to Britain with the Norman conquest of 1066 and shows up in thirteenth-century Anglo-Norman in forms like *pourpas*, *porpeis* and *porpes* from a Late Latin compound *porcopiscus* 'pig-fish.'

Creepiest Related Word: Dolphinarium

It's a circus-like aquarium where dolphins are kept in a watery prison pool for public entertainment. As a British newspaper *The Daily Telegraph* reported in 1984, "a large number of dolphins and killer whales imported. . . to perform tricks in dolphinaria die after only a short time in captivity." Want to help dolphins not become extinct? Do not patronize dolphinaria. Don't attend cutesy-poo aquarium shows where captured, enslaved dolphins, in an obscene aquatic vaudeville, are trained, in self-degradation, to perform pelagic clown acts in front of brain-dead hardware-store owners from Mutantville, Wisconsin who squat *en famille* on pink plastic bleachers, slushie-slobber drooling down the chinless skull of Little Bobby, their sullen spawn, a child with the IQ of a mollusc. Beside Little Bobby, maternal buttocks explode in a steatopygous paroxysm, a climax of fat-assedness, a consequence of unwisely purchased spandex tights. If, one sunny afternoon at Boredom of the Sea World, Mommy thinks Little Bobby needs to see a mammal with a fish, kindly suggest to Mommy that she toss Little Bobby into the shark tank.

Chapter 20

Pukka, Sahib! Top-Drawer!

(An email question) "Dear Bill Casselman:

I, Dorothy, received a sterling silver milk mug for my first birthday years ago from a British relative. It is engraved in script; the saying is "Pucca Dotty." Stamped on the bottom of the little mug are the words: London, England. The daughter of the British relative said she only knew my infant self as Pucca. The only reference I have of that name was on that mug. I have tried to find out about Pucca but no luck. Anything you can come up with will make me smile and probably cry a little. Now I'm questioning the spelling. Maybe Pukka?"

My answer:
Dorothy -

The word is *pukka.* "Pukka Dotty" in British slang between, say, 1890 and 1940, would be an affectionate nickname that meant approximately "the best Dorothy that ever could be."

Pukka is one of those Punjabi or Hindi words that wandering Brits brought back to Old Blighty, that is, back home to England from any of various military duties in India. It's a handy little adjective of many meanings, both in its original languages and adopted into English.

In ancient Sanskrit it was *pakva* 'cooked, ripe, ready." In Punjabi (Indian) or Panjabi (Pakistani) and Hindi, developed senses occur like 'mature, of good substance, permanent, of high quality.' All these meanings entered English too.

The British liked the word as a synonym for 'real' or 'genuine' or 'first-class' or 'top drawer.' E. M. Forster uses it in his famous novel *Passage to India* writing of two English characters described by a native Indian: "Mr. Fielding wasn't pukka, and had better marry Miss Quested, for she wasn't pukka." They were not of the best class of person, it seems. It is still in use that way: "In very proper, upper-class, sniffish Oxford tones, she responded in a pukka English not heard since her grandfather returned from his tour of duty during The Raj."

In modern London slang, young people still use the word. "Dude, those tats are pukka!" (translation: I like your tattoos!) "We lived in a small hut at first; then we build a pukka house." A real, genuine residence.

The only common compound is a double-decker noun, *pukka sahib* 'a person of sound credentials and probably of a rich family.' The term is often gently satiric nowadays and suggests British stuffed shirts oozing haughty disdain for lesser mortals. "He owned a Bentley and so he thought himself a very pukka sahib type; the fact that the family had accrued its wealth from a line of popular toilet cleaners did not in the least faze the uncouth baboon." Sahib is an Urdu word, borrowed from Arabic where *çahib* meant 'friend.' Formerly in India, sahib was the polite equivalent of adding "Sir" to a statement, when an Indian was addressing a European. The man's wife would be addressed as *memsahib* (English ma'm for madam + *sahib*). The normal Urdu feminine, *sahiba*, never caught on in English.

I'm quite cheered that we could elucidate so niftily this pukka puzzle. Now, let us withdraw to the refectory, nibble on a warm scone slathered with Marmite and sip mayhap a soothing cup, ere long, of Oolong.

Chapter 21

Solstice or "Sun! Stand Thou Still!"

The nano-moment of winter solstice falls due on the day of the planet's extremest axial tilt. States lordly Wikipedia with unhumble certitude, "The winter solstice occurs exactly when the axial tilt of a planet's polar hemisphere is farthest away from the star that it orbits."

Solstice is one of two times in the year when the sun is farthest from the equator and *appears* to stand still. The farthest northern point on the solar ecliptic is winter solstice; the farthest southern point is summer solstice. The word *solstice* derives from the deeply mistaken ancient belief that the sun could stand still. It cannot, without quite severe consequences, enumerated later in this chapter.

Etymology of solstice

Solstice was borrowed early into English from French *solstice* < Medieval Latin *solsticium* < classical Latin *solstitium* < Latin *sol* 'sun' + -*stitium* suffixal form 'a standing still' > participial stem of the Latin verb *sistere* 'to stand still,' citational forms of the verb: *sisto, sistere, steti, statum,* a verb at the root base of hundreds of English words such as assist, consistent, desist, exist, insistence, persist, substance, transistor, and— my fave— to stand up against someone or something again and again: to resist.

Miraculous Solstices

In various compendia of religious thaumaturgical phenomena (translation: tall tales from the ancient Near East), the sun stands still. Notable in Christian fabledom is Joshua's solar dictum in the Old Testament, Joshua, Chapter 10: (KJV) "Then spake Joshua to the Lord in the day when the Lord delivered up the Amorites before the children of Israel, and he said, in the sight of Israel, 'Sun, stand thou still upon Gibeon; and thou, Moon, in the valley of Ajalon.'" There follows the usual biblical account of some major-league smiting and divine clobbering in which God obliterates all the enemies of the Jews.

Naturellement, no biblical mention is made of the catastrophic interplanetary consequences of our sun standing still, such as these never-happened-in-history disasters: The principle of the conservation of angular momentum of rotating bodies would apply. Therefore the entire Rocky Mountain cordillera would topple like a squishy Popsicle into the Pacific Ocean, creating thousands of mighty tidal waves per hour, which would sweep over earth's continents drowning all of humanity, even Rabbis and Donald Trump. Oy! Winds of five or six hundred miles per hour would howl and blow and scrape the earth raw of all buildings and structures. With everyone on Earth dead, some Sunday school classes would have to be cut way back.

Chapter 22

What is a Wind-Rose? What is Advection?

A wind-rose is nautical chart of wind directions, its centre a circular compass surrounded by various wind heads blowing into the central compass rose.

Etymology of Wind-Rose

The word *wind-rose* was formed on the analogy of "compass rose," which was a card showing the 32 points of the compass for mariners, likened to a rose in its form.

In modern usage, a wind-rose is a graphic used in meteorology to show the amount of time the wind blows in each compass direction at a specific geographic location. Wind-roses also indicate wind speed, temperature, frequency, and force.

From the technical vocabulary of meteorology and oceanography comes **advection**, a noun denoting the transfer of heat or energy by air movement, with its accompanying verb, to advect. The noun was borrowed directly into late Victorian English from a German oceanographic term, *die Advektion* 'heat transfer by oceanic water.' The German is from a classical Latin word, *advectio, advectionis* 'carriage of goods' from the verb *advehere = ad* 'to' + *vehere* 'to carry.'

English Words from Latin Veh- Root

This Latin *veh-* verbal root, cognate with the English noun *way*, supplies dozens of English derivatives with some sense of transference or carrying, words like **vehicle,** literal Latin meaning of *vehiculum* 'little cart.'

In medicine, an agent that carries the bacteria or germs of a disease is a **vector,** Latin 'carrier.'

A **vehement** argument carries great force.

Invective is powerful verbal or written abuse carried against some person or their beliefs.

A **vein** that carries blood is in Latin *vena* 'carrier.'

To inveigh against someone is to attack them with violent words from Latin *invehi* 'to bear in against, to attack.'

To convey something is to carry it. It may be an act of convection.

A convex lens has a curvature that bulges outward; a concave lens goes inward. Latin *convexus* meant 'arched or rounded,' from a past participle of *convehere,* namely *convectus* 'carried or brought together.' When an arch is formed, the outer parts of the surface may be said to have been 'brought together.'

Well, matey, that's the whole parchment on wind-rose. All readers, bound out for the Word Isles, should now be onboard, before anchor is weighed and sails are set. This book of essays — she be a yare vessel — and my previous writings, if consulted, will guide you over the treacherous sea-swell of baloney so often encountered on etymological voyages.

Chapter 23

Spissament: A Cooking Term Chefs May not Know

Some words spurt from the lips with such labial defiance and susurrant delight that they must be put to use no matter how sporadic their frequency, no matter how tenuous their continuance. Such an obsolete rarity is the noun *spissament*.

A spissament is a thickener, any substance that increases density or viscosity. In cooking, a specimen of spissament is roux, flour added to a little fat and cooked until brown, used to thicken French sauces and world soups. One of the Latin adjectives applied to thick liquids was *spissus* 'thick.' From it sprang the later Latin noun *spissamentum* 'thickening agent.'

The Fascinating Origin of a French Accent Mark

In the Romance languages derived from Latin, *spissus* provided a general word for 'thick.' Consider Italian *spesso*, Portuguese *espesso*, and Spanish *espeso*. Modern French for 'thick' is *épais* but it began in older French as *espes, espies* and *espais,* a direct borrowing from Latin *spissus*. *Épais* has an acute accent on its initial *e*. Remember the origin of the acute accent mark in Old French written documents. Monks and other learned men who knew Latin realized that *spissus* was the word for 'thick' but as the early French language developed out of simple street Latin, these men heard people dropping both the normal Latin endings of words and, in this instance, the initial *s* of *spissus*. They thought dropping it wrong. So they added a little mark over the first sound to show that, once upon a not too distant time, the word had begun with an *s*. Thus Latin *spiss(us)* evolved into French *espais* and then *épais*. In sum, the acute accent began as a small letter *s* superscribed above the letter that had once followed the now disappeared *s*, so that *espais* became *épais*.

Sometimes a French circumflex accent mark showed where a disappeared /s/ had been, for example in the name of that small, thin pancake: *crêpe*, as in *crêpes Suzette*, ultimately through sixteenth-century French *crespe* from classical Latin *crispus* 'curled.'

Inspissated is not an Insipid Term

Infrequent but much more common is a related word *inspissated* 'thickened,' found in the technical vocabularies of several sciences. In medicine there is a laboratory machine called an inspissator used to thicken fluids such as blood plasma. Inspissated bile syndrome is a rare disease in infants where thick bile blocks and plugs the bile ducts possibly leading to enlarged liver, persistent jaundice and hemolytic anemia. *Inspissare* is a Late Latin verb meaning 'to thicken noticeably, to congeal.' Inspissation is the plugging of an anatomical tube such as a bile duct, vein, artery or intestine, in which thickened, dried material having lost some of its fluid content, blocks the lumen of the vessel.

Lumen

Lumen (plural lumina) is an anatomical word worth knowing, naming the inside space or hollow cavity of any tubular structure in the body. In medicine one may refer to the lumen of a catheter. The bore of a hollow needle is its lumen. *Lumen* is the Latin noun for 'light' or 'air well' or 'opening.' It shows up in many other words in English ultimately from Latin, words like bioluminescent, illuminate, luminosity and luminary. In the measurement of light in physics and electrical science, a lumen is the unit of luminous flux, calibrating the amount of light given out by a certain source even if fluctuant.

Other Inspissated Forms

Maple syrup gurgled in the cauldron as its slow, sugary inspissation advanced.

A neat little adjective – now, alas, obsolete – was *spiss*. It meant compact, dense, close. But we could revive it. In spiss globules dripped ice-cold water from the cleft in the dike. He was a spiss-headed yokel with the I.Q. of a sow bug.

Boiling the watery broth served a nicely spissative purpose, for it was slowly transformed into a glutinous but hearty soup.

The spissitude of the fool's perception only increased with age.

Our English word broth no longer thickens with spissaments. So such useful terms must be poured into the *olla podrida,* waiting through the night to become tomorrow's soup.

Olla podrida (Spanish 'stinking or rotten pot,' French *pot pourri*) was originally a terra cotta vat or stoneware tub in the kitchen into which leftover stews and soups were poured, to be reheated and consumed on the morrow. *Olla podrida* eventually came to name a specific Spanish stew of pork and beans and sausages and chickpeas and other kitchen veggies and meat scraps tossed into the vast pot, heated for several hours, then served. Like potpourri, the Spanish phrase can be used in English to name a hodgepodge, a diverse mixture, a miscellany.

The best English plural of potpourri is the French form: *pots-pourris* while *olla podrida* is best pluralized in grammatical Spanish as *ollas podridas.*

The current *Oxford English Dictionary* clasps its dainty, manicured hands together and whimpers fretfully "It is not known why *olla podrida* was so called in Spanish; perhaps from the resemblance of the bubbling and swelling appearance of the slow-cooking stew to festering putrefaction. . ."

Nonsense! Piffle! Twaddle! Have any of the etiolated virgins of the OED — I see them clad in Laura Ashley gingham frocks, skipping merrily to library shelves sniffing clove-studded pomanders — have any of these pristine ever entered a working kitchen? Or did servants convey to their upper-class table the daily comestibles? The storage *olla* in a simple Spanish kitchen was termed *podrida* 'stinking-rotten' clearly because unused food tossed into a large clay pot for a day or two stinks, but is not so malodorous that poor people will not try to eat it, however fetid a snippet may be, however abject their poverty, however tepid its *réchauffage*. Honestly, British naïveté is sometimes so cloying it's enough to make a fellow forget to don his spats during inclemency.

Chapter 24

Hysteria: The Just Death of a Loaded Word

Norwegian painter and printmaker Edvard Munch in his famous "The Scream" (1893) may have depicted what psychiatrists would call "an indeterminate figure" in modern art's most wretched cry of obliterating angst. But Ancient Greeks and more modern men too had the sexist notion that nervous afflictions were peculiar to women and were symptoms of various uterine maladies. Plato imagined that the uterus (Greek *hustera* or *hystera* or more usually in the Greek plural *hai husterai*) was a separate spirit and animal part of a woman that only wanted to become pregnant. If it did not, this imaginary uterus-spirit wandered in a fit of mopish pique through the female body causing trouble. When it arrived at the brain, this *hystera* (womb animal) went totally postal and induced feminine hysterics. Consider this quotation from Aretaeus the Cappadocian, a Hippocratic medical writer of the second century CE.

> "In the middle of the flanks of women lies the womb, a female viscus, closely resembling an animal; for it is moved of itself hither and thither in the flanks, also upwards in a direct line to below the cartilage of the thorax and also obliquely to the right or to the left, either to the liver or spleen; and it likewise is subject to falling downwards, and, in a word, it is altogether erratic. It delights, also, in fragrant smells, and advances towards them; and it

has an aversion to fetid smells, and flees from them; and on the whole the womb is like an animal within an animal."

An Attack of "The Vapours"

In case you have dismissed the above fumblings of ancient medical writers as the quaint folly of a bygone day, remember the Victorian British of only a century ago who, before Freud, termed hysteria "an attack of the vapours." According to Victorian and Edwardian physicians, just what were the vapours? Uterine emanations seeping up from the vagina into milady's brain where they overwhelmed the female body! So corporal knowledge had not come too far in centuries, had it? Compare the early 19th century "delicate" German word *Mutterweh* 'mother's affliction.' This was not a euphemism for menstruation but for hysterics.

Hippocrates: Not the Father of Hysteria

Contrary to what is printed in many histories of medicine, the word *hysteria* was not coined by the so-called Father of Medicine, Hippocrates, who was far more of a physician and clinician than Plato—no matter what Plato imagined. The word *hysteria* does not appear in ancient Greek and Hippocrates dates (ca. 460 BCE – ca. 370 BCE) are thus too early.

Hippocrates taught that the cause of what came to be called hysteria was irregular movement of blood from the uterus to the brain. Although such an etiology is incorrect, there is a shred of Hippocratic clinical observation there that far surpasses Plato's insupportable myth-making. Hippocrates had perhaps observed a person in the throes of a potent conversion reaction and noted the elevation in temperature and engorging of the facial skin. Plato, on the other hand, probably has his slaves drive away with long sticks any unfortunate Greek who was having "a fit."

Etymology of the Word *Hysteria*

Husterai or *hysteria* was an Ionian word mostly used in the plural, so that even in ancient Greek *hysterai* was a euphemism whose literal meaning is "the inferior parts" or "the lower parts" — very much like the modern evasion used by western parents to describe young girls' genitalia "down there" or other sexist evasions to name a woman's "privy parts" like the Latin *pudendum* or *pudenda*, in form a gerundive of obligation meaning literally 'that of which one ought to be ashamed.' Compare one of several creepy periphrases in German, *die Weiche* 'the soft parts.' Creepy but slightly more accurate than some other languages' circumlocutionary genteelism.

The form *hysteria* may be Modern Scientific Latin (late 18th-century?) < *hustera* Greek 'uterus' + *-ia* medical suffix 'diseased condition of' <*hustera* Greek, 'uterus' < *husteros* Greek adjective 'the latter, the weaker, the inferior.'

Etymologist Eric Partridge suggested *hustera* might have been an elliptical version of *hustera metra* 'the lower womb.' Having examined the uses of *husterai* in passages of ancient Greek, I think euphemism is a more cogent explanation of the Greek word's origin.

The Latin word *uterus*, adopted into English, may stem from the same euphemistic Indo-European root, *udteros 'higher,' as does the Sanskrit comparative adjective *uttaras* 'latter, higher, upper, northern.' Compare the Hindi name of that flood-prone state in northern India, Uttar Pradesh. *Uttar* means 'northern' and *pradesh* means 'region' or 'state.'

The Roman Catholic Church Finds Good Uses for Hysteria.

Hysterical Witches — Those Bitches!

As a disease, hysteria has had a good, lucrative 2,000-year run of popularity. Hysteria worked nicely for the Roman Catholic Church during the pleasantly corrective era of inquisitions. Hundreds of thousands of European women, tortured and burnt at the stake as witches, showed signs of hysteria. So did cheering mobs of Catholic peasants who gathered eagerly around the burning women who screamed in agony as their hair ignited and their fiery clothes seared their already cooking flesh. It was warmly instructive to attend a good people-fire, to watch human legs and arms crisp up nicely as God's work was conducted by His anointed male fire-brigade of priests and their torch-happy henchmen. All this happened under the benign and divine auspices of what a recent pope, a paleoconservative old horror named Ratzinger, has termed "the only religious body of believers worthy to bear the name 'church.'" *Ja-wohl, Irhe Hoheit!*

Let us not imagine that all hysterical witches were burned upright standing at the stake. Pious Roman Catholic onlookers, quite like holy moderns at a decent fireworks display, demanded variety in presentation. So turning a nude woman on a spit was also ordained by those priests in closest touch with their Lord. That way one could watch the human beings' skin roast and split like pork cracklings. It is recorded that the assembled firewatchers sang hymns to drown out the young girls' screams of pain. Some ancient version, I imagine, of "Jesus wants me for a sunbeam."

I have already received emails of outrage that I should even bring up notes from The Inquisition. One little lily of piety suggested that we ought to forget such slight past errors. Maybe she's correct? Maybe we should forget the Inquisition and The Holocaust?

My inquisitory interval shall conclude with one more historical note. When they were not busy burning young women and buggering altar boys, some of these Roman Catholic inquisitors displayed a zeal for scientific notation that would have made Darwin himself proud.

Here is a Spanish priest's notation exactly quoted as he watched a woman being burnt to death and calmly jotted down a few notes: "I have observed that the breasts of lactating women tend to explode when the fire is high."

In all the horror of human history, I have never read a more obscene, evil sentence. That it was written by a Roman Catholic priest is all I EVER have to know about our very unholy mother, the Church of Rome.

Doubters? Peruse some of the historical record preserved in the following volumes.

Books about the Inquisition

Henry Kamen, *The Spanish Inquisition:A Historical Revision.* (Yale U. Press, 1999).

J.A. Llorente, *Historia Critica de la Inquisicion de Espana.*

R. Sabbatini, *Torquemada and the Spanish Inquisition* (1913).

History of the Inquisition from its origin under Pope Innocent III till the present time. Also the private practices of the Inquisitiors, the form of trial and modes of torture, (1814).

J. Marchant, *A Review of the Bloody Tribunal* (1770).

E.N Adler, *Autos de fe and the Jew* (1908).

Gonzalez de Montes, *Discovery and Playne Declaration of Sundry Subtile Practices of the Holy Inquisition of Spayne*

Ludovico a Paramo, *De Origine et Progressu Sanctae Inquisitionis* (1598).

J.M. Marin, *Procedimientos de la Inquisicion* (2 volumes), (1886).

Simon Whitechapel, *Flesh Inferno: Atrocities of Torquemada and the Spanish Inquisition* (Creation Books, 2003).

Hysteria Comes of Age

During the Age of Reason there was a decline in attention to hysteria, but this was corrected by a big revival of hysterics at the birth of psychoanalysis. Indeed the first psychoanalytic document is often thought to be: "FREUD, Sigmund and Joseph BREUER. *Studien über Hysterie.* Leipzig and Vienna: Franz Deuticke, 1895." This is Freud's and Breuer's account of their discovery of the profound benefits of "free association," in part a result of their clinical experience with hysterics. It is the founding paper of psychoanalysis.

What is Hysteria Called Now?

Today hysteria is usually labeled conversion disorder. Be aware that this is an extremely difficult diagnosis to authenticate.

Note that, even in modern psychiatric literature, women are still the chief hysterics. The diagnosis of hysteria, which was the most common psychiatric label applied to women up until the 1930s, continues to oink its way through shrinks' offices. Thank goodness, horrible surgical procedures like clitoridectomy are no longer suggested as methods of treatment!

For such reasons, and because its diagnosis had much to do with misogynist feelings on the part of male psychiatrists, nowadays hysteria is not generally accepted as a legitimate term for a mental disorder. The use of hysteria as a diagnostic label has declined in western countries almost to zero grade. Hysteria, for example, is no longer listed as a disease in the *DSM IV*; This is the *Diagnostic and Statistical Manual of Mental Disorders*, fourth edition, published under the auspices of the American Psychiatric Association. In the seventeenth edition of the Merck Manual, hysteria no longer has a separate entry.

But hysteria and its adjective hysterical are still current and widespread in ordinary speech, and both noun and adjective are met in historical medical literature. The word is on the way out of legitimate medical vocabulary and that is a just victory for those want to purge medical terminology and practice of male chauvinist notions. Today most psychiatrists consider hysteria to be, in the current charming euphemism of the shrink trade, a legacy diagnosis. Translation: Hysteria has become through ignorant overuse an almost clinically meaningless, catch-all term, much like schizophrenia. Good!

Two useful books:

A. Roy, ed., *Hysteria* (1982)

E. Showalter, *Hystories: Hysterical Epidemics and Modern Culture* (1997)

Chapter 25

A Plenitude of Amplitude

My current antipathies, about one of which I here wax peevish, include public address systems whose announcements are indecipherable due to defective or tatty loudspeakers and insufficiently potent amplifiers. Imagine you are at Nude Fang's, the discount Chinese clothing store, shopping for a modest t-shirt made of reconstituted Shanghai eco-lint guaranteed not to unravel until a first washing. Suddenly throughout the store a warning gong sounds over the P. A. and Adela Adenoid, the nasal voice of the store, warns sternly, "Attention, shoppers."

Here the loudspeakers throughout the department store suddenly go dead and buzzing amp noise ricochets up and down every aisle. After an interval of electronic humming, Adela's speech resumes: "A male dwarf with a loaded Glock is now in Lingerie trying on junior bras. This advisement in no way seeks to demean achondroplastic cross-dressers. However, one clerk has had her kneecaps nibbled in a lewd and wanton manner. Be sure to take Escape Aisle number . . . [loudspeakers here cut out and issue noises like grax-shporp-crackle-rackle-zizit]. All other escape routes lead to certain death. Thank you for shopping at Nude Fang's."

Whew, you think, *at least we're safe*. Then the first Glock bullet smithereens the face on your twenty-dollar Rolex.

Audio design engineers are paid to confect P. A. systems built to convey announcements clearly. Yet never do public address systems convey clarity of word.

Ample

A pleasing rotundness of amplitude swells the sound of our root word *ample*, essentially borrowed holus-bolus from Latin *amplus* 'of large bulk, of abundant extent,' said to be a reflex of the Proto-Indo-European etymon **am* 'graspable' appearing in words like Sanskrit *amatra* 'drinking vessel or hand-bowl' and Latin *ampla* 'handle of a jug,' literally 'grasp-thing.' Ample always suggests a quantity more than needed. George has an ample supply of wood cut for the winter fireplace. Ample gains poetic heft when used in a phrase with internal rhyme, for example, "sampling ample lamplight" shines brightly.

Shakespeare liked the full sound of the adjective. When King Lear seeks to buy his daughters' love, among other pricey choices he dandles in the lap of their filial greed "this ample third of our fair kingdom."

American poetess Emily Dickinson, a sweet judge of words, brought before the court of usage and employed the adjective brilliantly in a short poem she wrote in 1872.

> "Immortal is an ample word
> When what we need is by
> But when it leaves us for a time
> 'Tis a necessity.
>
> Of Heaven above the firmest proof
> We fundamental know
> Except for its marauding Hand
> It had been Heaven below."

Two near synonyms are among adjectives I prize highly: capacious and commodious.

Ampliate

Rare words we promise in each essay and here is the verb *to ampliate* 'to increase in size or amount. Each day, seek to ampliate your vocabulary.

Amplivagant

This word is not merely rare. I admit *amplivagant* is *le mot recherché*, uncommon to the point of pretentiousness. But, *mes enfants*, why else am I here, if not to foist upon innocent readers the most obscure word-mosses scraped from oblivion's grotto.

Amplivagent = *amplus* Latin 'wide, full' + *vagare* Latin 'to roam,' hence our English word *vagrant*. The word means 'roaming widely.'

One day Fred took off on his 750cc Harley, commencing his amplivagant tour of America, promised to himself and pined for since childhood.

The accent falls upon the second syllable, am-**PLIV**-igant.

Thinking about that exemplary sentence and the motorcycle's hot wheels and salvation "on the road", I wonder: Does the American fallacy that fleeing will heal ennui and entropy still prevail? Can an American, stuck in the glutinous mire of home-tedium, still save herself or himself by "lighting out" for parts unvisited. What happened to Ned? *One day he just up and lit out!*

Chapter 26

Chthonic

How dank and deep is the adjective *chthonic*, how expressive of its meaning: of secrets moist and subterranean, of the hidden night-mind of undergods, of infernal arcana. The American pronunciation of chthonic is *thonic*, to rhyme with tonic. What Yankee drabness! The words are *kthonic* and *kthonian*. One ought to vocalize that initial Greek *ch*-sound, as a hard *k*. Educated British speakers do. The British oral mode is better, more steeped in netherness, more mimicking the muculent ooze of hell. Orpheus, lyre in hand, descended into the underworld to sing back to earth from chthonian realms his lost Eurydice. Pluto, despot of Hades, frowned, brooding on his chthonic throne.

The late Mary McCarthy is a writer I enjoy and respect. She was a witty apostle of The Higher Bitchiness, right up there with Truman Capote and Gore Vidal. Mary McCarthy's splendid 1963 college reunion novel, *The Group* reviews a hellish roommate's living quarters: "The chthonic imagery of Norine's apartment, which was black as a coalhole and heated by the furnace of the hostess' unslaked desires."

Autochthonous & Heterochthonous

Compound adjectives include this munchy jawful from mineralogy and geology: heterochthonous (hete-ROCK-thonous), said of stones and rocks not formed where they are modernly found or of fossils re-embedded. Heterochthonous may also be a rare synonym for *foreign*. Autochthonous then may refer to lithic masses originating in situ. An autochthon 'original inhabitant' is found in modern anthropology and biology textbooks. The ancient Greeks used it the way we might use "native" or "aboriginal" from Greek *autochthon* 'from the same earth' < *autos* 'self, same' + *chthon* 'earth.'

Etymology

Chthonic derives from Greek chthon, chthonos 'earth, surface of the earth.' This is a very old Proto-Indo-European root, cognate with Sanskrit *ksami* 'on the ground < *ksam* Sanskrit 'earth, soil'; compare *chamai* Greek 'on the ground' and Latin *humus* 'dirt' 'earth,' Hittite *tegan* 'ground,' and Tocharian *tkan-* 'place.' The most surprising English relative of *chthon* is our adjective *humble* from Middle English *umble* from Old French *humble* from Latin *humilis* 'slight, low-cast, of the mere earth < *humus* Latin 'soil, dirt, earth.' Incidentally our word *human* has the same root.

We Are Only Human

In the *Old Testament* of the Christian Bible, a creation myth lies buried inside the very name of the first man, Adam. Adam was made from nothing, that is, from dust. That's what his name means. One striking feature of the Adam and Eve creation myth in Genesis is the pottery metaphor: a god formed humans from clay or dust. This is a worldwide element in creation stories. Compare the Hebrew and Christian version in Genesis 2:6, 7 as translated in the King James version of 1611: "There went up a mist from the earth, and watered the whole face of the ground. And the Lord God formed man of the dust of the ground. . ." So, even today, in brickyards of the Middle East, does the brick-maker sprinkle water on the clay before he kneads it into shape. The Bible's name for the first man reflects this too. Adam means 'human being, person.' With only a slightly different Hebrew voicing, *adom* means 'red.' Both may be related to Hebrew *adamah* 'clay' or 'red earth of Israel.' In Old Testament Hebrew, it is usually *ha adam* and the definite article *ha* makes some biblical scholars suspect that the name, like some others in Hebrew, was very early borrowed from neighbouring Assyrians. If so, it might stem from Assyrian *adamu* 'to make or produce.' Thus Adam would mean 'the made one, the created one.'

Earthy Ones

In English the term *human*, borrowed from Latin, shares this myth, meaning the ancient Romans believed this story too, reflecting the made-of-dust and/or the pottery myth in creation stories. The prime meaning of Latin *humanus* is 'clayey' or made of *humus* 'earth, soil, clay.' The Roman word for human being or man, *homo*, as in our species *Homo sapiens*, also stems from the same root. In Old Latin it was *hemo* 'the earthen one' or 'the person of clay.' The idea must have occurred early in human history, when primitive humans first dug up an interred body to discover bones and dust. Dust thou art; to dust shalt thou return.

Historical Name: Melanchthon

Philipp Schwartzerdt was a German scholar and religious reformer who lived from 1497 to 1560 CE. Like many medieval intellectuals, he translated his dowdy German name which meant 'black earth' into Greek to make it sound more imposing. He took German *schwarz* 'black' and translated it into Greek *melas, melanos* 'black. Then he did the same with *Erde* German 'earth' and he used *chthon* Greek 'earth' and came forth as the infinitely more sage-sounding and more impressive scholar Melanchthon! Many did it. The founder of binomial botanical nomenclature was a Swede named Carl von Linné. He changed his name to the Latinate Linnaeus. Much more clout and intellectual gravitas abides in the changed surname.

Perhaps I ought to market my little books, not as humble Bill Casselman but as the noble, the stark Basilikander, Prince of Words? After all, a basilica was originally a king's castle or palace and *aner, andros* is a Greek word for man.

Chapter 27

Carpe diem does NOT mean 'Seize the Day.'
Correcting a Clumsy, Vulgar Mistranslation of Horace

Carpe diem is often translated in brutal mode as "seize the day." That command is the title of a Saul Bellow novel. But that translation is primitive, aggressive and reeks of error. The phrase appears in a Latin poem, Odes i. xi, by ancient Rome's best lyric poet, Quintus Horatius Flaccus, known to English posterity as Horace. Here is the Horatian context:

> *dum loquimur, fugerit invida*
> *aetas: carpe diem, quam minimum credula*
> *postero.*

(My somewhat free translation) "Even as we speak here, time zips by, jealous that we humans have enjoyed even these few moments: so delicately pluck the flower of *this* day. As for tomorrow, forget it!"

The entire Latin poem is filled with metaphors drawn from peaceful agriculture, not war. What Horace meant here was an analytic action upon one's present time much more sensitive than seizing, a delicacy of temporal choice apparently unknown to Saul Bellow.

In form, *carpe* is a command, the imperative present singular of *carpere*, a Latin verb with prime meanings like 'to pluck (a flower), to pick (a plant), to cull, to harvest.' Far rarer are the verb's military meanings like 'to seize and carry off.'

The Latin verb *carpere* signifies 'to pick a flower, to harvest.' "Pluck the flower of the day" is the subtle Horatian nuance here. Horace, a great poet, unlike Mr. Bellow, advises a delicate picking of the present time's possibly hidden benefits. *Carpe diem* is an invitation to enjoy the day, not crush it in a vulgar Bellowian grasping clutch.

The metaphor, like the verb *carpere* itself, suggests a gentle harvest of the fruit of the day when it is ripe, not, as Mr. Bellow hints, stomping the day into a mundane mush. The flesh of a fresh apple is always to be preferred to apple sauce. But one cannot explain that to vulgarians who have passed too lengthy a sojourn in hog-butchering Chicago. Yes, you may take it that, in spite of his Nobel Prize, I am no fan of Mr. Bellow's pushy, twentieth-century survival manuals disguised as novels.

Horace followed Epicurean self-sufficiency and moderation in action and feeling, both of which might lead to a contented life. To demonstrate again how distant from Horace is that violent, crass, profane American take on *carpe diem*, it is worth remembering that the ancient Greek philosopher Epicurus wished to strive for a tranquil life of peace, freedom from fear and absence of pain. Since death is the end of both body and soul, Epicurus believed, death should not be feared. No gods reward or punish humans. The universe is infinite and eternal. Not too shabby a philosophy for a guy who lived 2,300 years ago!

Fairness bids us add that, from the paltry biographical scraps extant, Horace was a social climber who did all he could, as the provincial son of an ex-slave, to weasel his artistic advancement into the privilege-granting, marble-floored courts of the emperor Augustus, with the connivance of his *amicus*, fellow poet Virgil.

The Epicurean is a less fretful view of dotage, of the artery-clogging onslaught of old age, than many modern modes couched as they are in denial and euphemism. The golden years indeed!

Etymology of *Carpere*

The Latin verb is a reflex of the Proto-Indo-European root*kerp-*, *skerp-* 'to pluck, to harvest' and has cognates like *harvest* in English and *Herbst* 'autumn, harvest-time' in modern German. The most interesting Greek cognate is *karpos*, the ancient Greek word for fruit but literally 'that which is picked, plucked, harvested off the fruit tree.' English botany is filled with derivatives that describe parts of fruits, terms like endocarp and pericarp and mesocarp. The English fish word carp is not related.

The first carpet was probably woven of pluckings, cuttings of thin rope.

Carpals are part of *carpus*, the bones of the wrist, the part of the arm used to pluck things, to pick fruit, the "twisters" that make things bend in conjunction with the hand's fingers. Latin *carpus* is a direct borrowing of Greek *karpos* 'wrist.' The English word *wrist* itself describes an action similar to the Greek word, where Old English *writh-* is a gradient stem of the verb *wríthan* 'to writhe, to twist.'

Carpire's Russian cognate appears in very plain vestment as the unadorned reflex *syerp*. It is the Russian agricultural word for 'sickle.' What else is a sickle but a reaping-hook, a way to *pick* for harvest a swatch of grain, of cereal, of wheat? Note that many Proto-Indo-European roots which appear in Latin with an initial hard *c* show up in Slavic languages with the *c* softened to as es-sound.

Harpy

Other Greek reflexes of the PIE root lose the hard *c* and give us those razor-talonned witches, the Harpies, from ancient Greek *harpyiae* literally 'snatchers,' from the Greek verb *harpazein* 'to snatch, to seize.' In the *Iliad* and the *Odyssey*, Homer used the plural to refer to whirlwinds and hurricanes that seized things on land and sea and snatched them faraway into the sky. Roman mythology saw the Harpies as creepy birdlike monsters who were ministers of divine vengeance. If Jupiter and Juno arose on the wrong side of the Olympian bed, the simply divine couple might send Harpies to perform hideously bloody revenges of the gods.

Would that modest *moi*, little me, could send the Harpies to claw away the pens of all scribes who translate *carpe diem* as "seize the day."

Chapter 28

Lost Mud Words like Lutulent

Mud is a glutinous German monosyllable, probably borrowed into English from Middle Dutch *modde*, cognate with modern German *Moder* 'mustiness, decay' as in this common German assessment of an old, uninhabited house "*Es riecht hier nach Moder*," 'This place smells musty.'

Poor, bereft *mud* appears to have no fellow cognates in non-Germanic Indo-European languages. However my purpose in this chapter is less an etymology of the word *mud* than increasing the paltry supply of insult and invective in Mother English. Other world languages rejoice and abound in a word-hoard of rude snub, of vile taunt, of low obloquy. English, on the other hand, prissy, hesitant, thinking well of all others at all times, the Little-Mary-Sunshine of world tongues, needs help with nasty and snide putdowns. One neglected source of vituperation is stealing words from the private vocabulary of science. And that, my wee fiends, is what we are up to today!

I want you, hereafter, to refer to dirty politics as a sepulchre of lutulence, that is: a slimy, mucopurulent grave-hole of iniquitous filth. One of the scientific terms for muddy is lutulent, with pounding stress on that first, bald *u*: **LUT**-ulent. Do not palatize that initial *u*. Then lutulent may be spit forth with an enunciatory contempt one can taste.

That Dirty Roman *Lutum*

The source is Latin *lutum* 'dirt, clay, mud, mire, sludge, ooze, silt.' It is not a common root in other English words but the etymon does hide in our word *pollution*, from the Latin verb *polluere* whose original form was as *por-luere with its sense 'to make a liquid thoroughly muddy,' sometimes with the intent of performing a ritual decleansing. *Polluere* = the Latin prefix *por-* (a rarer version of Latin *pro* 'thorough, forth, forward') + *luere* 'to make muddy, to make dirty' and then its various developed metaphorical meanings 'to make morally dirty' hence 'to corrupt, to befoul, to stain, to sully, to soil, to render unclean before a ritual' and its most modern semantic 'to contaminate air and land and water with toxic noxae.'

Related etyma include an old medical word for syphilis from Latin, *lues* 'filth, disease, plague.' *Lues venerea* 'syphilis' is obsolete medical Latin rare in English, but one may still encounter in medical literature *luetic* as an occasional synonym for *syphilitic*.

Even Rarer Dirty Words

Let us consider several recherché gems derived from a word for mud or potter's clay in the koine Greek of The New Testament. And that word is *pelos* 'mud.' It is most familiar in the still extant name Peloponnese, a large peninsula and region in southern Greece, forming the part of the country south of the Gulf of Corinth. *Peloponnesos* means 'the island of Pelops,' a hero in early Greek mythology reputed to have first conquered the peninsula. Pelops was a given name based on appearance, much like Rufus (Latin 'red-head') was first applied to a man with red hair. Pelops is made up of *pelios* 'dark' and *ops* 'face.' His dark face, perhaps swarthier than an olive-skinned Greek, gave him the probably not at that time insulting nickname 'Dark Face.'

Pelophobia is a morbid fear of getting dirty. You've met these obsessive-compulsives. Keeping one's hands clean, for example, washing your hands after you have greeted a politician, is normal, sane procedure. But lathering up your pinkies twenty times a day in a fretful foam-fist of aseptic hygienics is perhaps, crazy.

A pelophile is a plant that thrives in a muddy or clayey environment. So is a pelophyte, whose terminal root is ancient Greek *phuton* or *phyton* 'plant.'

More Dreck

In the verbal annals of scuzz and mire, a more intense ancient Greek word is *rhypos* 'dregs, sordidness, filth, feces, foul matter.' Both Homer and Aristotle used the word.

Rhyparia is an obsolete word that names excreta, defilement of the body, sin, scummy coatings on the teeth and tongue during some illnesses. Yuck! A rhypax is a dirty person. Rhypophagy is eating putrid food. A rhyptic is a medicine that cleanses, clarifies or acts as a cathartic.

You see my point. It is time to start yelling at political rallies "Drop dead, you rhypophagic sepulchre of lutulence!"

Chapter 29

Cuddle, Chowder, Chauffeur, Caldera, Coddle an Egg: All Related Words!

Caudle < Coddle < Cuddle

To administer a warm, soup-like drink to a fellow being who is sick, invalid or, as my Scottish grandmother used to say, "Doing poorly," is a caring, restorative gesture possibly as old as humanity. In any case, in this column you will observe the derivational relationship among words like *cuddle, coddle* an egg, *chowder, cauldron, caldera* and less used nouns like *caudle.*

In a sixteenth-century English manual for midwives we read: "It is a commune vsage to geue often to women in there chylde bed cawdels of ote~meele." 'It is a common usage to give often to women in their child-bed caudles of oatmeal.'

Early in the thirteenth century, *caudle* came into English from Norman French *caudel* < Medieval Latin *caldellus* 'a modest drink of a hot liquid' < classical Latin *caldum* 'hot drink' < Latin *calidus, caldus* 'warm, hot.' We may even have borrowed the general recipe from the Romans for whom *caldum* was a drink for invalids composed of warmed wine mixed with bread, eggs, honey and spices.

Two common verbal derivatives of caudle are *to cuddle* and *to coddle.* First, early in the sixteenth century, arose *to coddle* with its initial meaning of 'to boil gently,' as in the kitchen device, egg-coddler. Developed from that primary meaning are 'to nurse a sick person with warm, nourishing food and drink' and later expansive significances as when *to coddle apples* meant 'to make apple sauce.'

To cuddle 'to hug affectionately, to hold in a warm embrace, to comfort, to fondle' has many, bizarre, suggested sources. The only cogent one I have found, in a long lifetime of riffling through foxed word tomes, is *cuddle* as a vowel gradient of *coddle*. The first use of cuddle in print is 1522 CE.

Back to Latin *Caldus*, *Calidus* 'Warm, Hot'

Ancient Romans had no showers. Common people went out each day to public baths where, for low fees, they exercised, ate, gossiped, visited neighbours and bathed. Before bathing one might have a friend or a slave anoint your body with olive oil and then gently scrap off the oil and any adhesive sweat and dirt of the day with a strigil, a broad, curved, not-very-sharp metal blade with a handle. Next came bath time, in three basic pools: first a plunge into the scrotum-tightening *frigidarium* or cold bath, then a lukewarm bath or *tepidarium* (hence our English liquid adjective *tepid*) and finally, to open the now cleansed pores, a hot bath or *caldarium*. Afterward one lay down to sweat awhile and converse amiably with friends or lovers, perhaps while sipping warm honeyed wine to encourage sudor and to loll and dawdle in perspirant abundance. As immersive ablutions such procedures were quite civilized. They are thus almost utterly unknown to us moderns.

Caldarium > Cauldron

A cauldron is a large kettle or boiler with a clear-cut etymological path from Latin *caldarium,* Roman word for a hot-bath through French and Spanish forms like Spanish *calderon* and Anglo-Norman *caudron* and doublet derivations like standard French *chaudière* 'kettle.'

Shakespeare's witches' spell from Act 4, Scene 1 of *Macbeth* has mnemonic resonance from alchemical days, so let us offer some of the bard's word-conjuring magic:

"Round about the cauldron go;
In the poison'd entrails throw.
Toad, that under cold stone
Days and nights hast thirty one
Swelter'd venom sleeping got,
Boil thou first i' the charmed pot.
    Double, double toil and trouble;
    Fire burn and cauldron bubble.
Fillet of a fenny snake,
In the cauldron boil and bake;
Eye of newt, and toe of frog,
Wool of bat, and tongue of dog,
Adder's fork, and blind-worm's sting,
Lizard's leg, and howlet's wing,
For a charm of powerful trouble,
Like a hell-broth boil and bubble."

Derivatives of Latin *Caldus*

The most familiar to us is perhaps the common French adjective meaning 'hot or warm,' namely *chaud*, directly from Latin *caldus*. A French kettle used to heat liquids is a *chaudière*. Breton fishermen used such a boiling pot to make a fish stew. When they sailed to the New World these denizens of Brittany took their food choices with them and developed tasty *chaudières* of North America, but they became known as Newfoundland and New England *chowders*, a word mangled directly from the northern French of Breton fishers.

The Latin root in *caldus* 'hot' is *cal- and gives other English words like *calor* 'heat', the rarer *calid* 'lukewarm' and the very common *calorie*, an arbitrary French coinage from *calor* used as a metric measurement in food sciences to name an amount of heat needed to raise the temperature of one litre of water one degree centigrade.

An interesting, partially hidden derivative is the English verb *to scald* 'to burn, to make red hot, to heat on high,' from Old French *eschalder* from late Latin *excaldare* where the Latin prefix *ex-* signals 'excessively' and *caldare* means 'to wash in very hot water.' The English spelling may have been influenced by the Italian derivative *scaldare* 'to warm up, to heat.'

In Spanish and in English geology, we have a deep hollow at the top of some extinct volcanoes, shaped like a big iron boiling pot, called a *caldera*, the Spanish word for cauldron or large kettle, from caldaria, the plural of *caldarium* 'hot pool' in Latin or 'big kettle.'

Chauffeur

The most surprising derivative is *chauffeur*, French 'one who or that which heats up.' Now why is one who drives a car for a passenger named a "heater" in French? Easy. A chauffeur was a person who "warms up" or stokes fire in a steam-driven automobile, as the first "cars" were indeed steam-driver. Remember the Stanley Steamer? *Chauffeur* is the agent noun of the French verb *chauffer* 'to heat' from low Latin *calefare* 'to make hot' which itself was Latin street talk for classical Latin *calefacere* 'to warm up.' Notice the Latin root we spoke of earlier, **cal-* 'heat, warmth.'

Sops & Infusion

These two words for hot drinks do not belong here if we are following strict etymology, but we are not, are we? No. For we are free spirits who do but fly wheresoever the wings of probatory trajection may bear us.

Sops

Sops, perhaps a vowel gradient of Old English *sopp* influenced by Anglo-French *soupe* and *soup.* To my Scottish grandmother, sops was a piece of bread dipped or steeped in warm milk before being eaten. My aged and toothless maternal grandfather dipped bread in warm milk every night before bedtime and Nana always said, "Norrie is having his sops." The bread may have had scant effect but the tryptophan in the warm milk certainly acted as a mild relaxant and soporific and thus helped Gamp's snoozing. Science now knows that the amino acid tryptophan increases the body's production of 'the happiness hormone' serotonin which assists our beddy-bye selves to climb aboard the bobbing skiff of sleep and propels us over the shallows of early night toward the benthic depths of REM.

Infusion

In my father's vocabulary, and so in my own word hoard as a child, the most common meaning of infusion was 'a hot, steeped drink.' Tea was an infusion. Herbal tea or camomile was an infusion in which hot water was poured over plant leaves to extract their useful properties and drink the resultant liquid. There are other meanings, medical, even philosophical, but I never knew or used them in my speaking life. Infusion entered English from French *l'infusion* < Latin *infusio, infusionis* 'a pouring upon < Latin prefix *in-* 'on' + Latin *fundere* 'to pour.'

And so, whether you plan to coddle an egg or cuddle a chauffeur, I feel I have here delivered data sufficiently remedial to quell the itty-bittiest qualm.

Chapter 30

A Note Concerning the Pejorative Simile "Whited Sepulchre" Meaning 'Hypocrite' or 'Impostor'

The *locus classicus* or chief site of this still-in-print insult is the King James Version of the New Testament, in Matthew 23:27, where Christ rebukes the high priests and exalted mucky-mucks of Judaism: "Woe unto you, scribes and Pharisees, hypocrites! for ye are like unto whited sepulchres, which indeed appear beautiful outward, but are within full of dead men's bones, and of all uncleanness."

Even today, in high-flown or rhetorical English, whited sepulchre means a dissembler who looks pure on the outside but inside hides foul malice, to wit, a fallacious phony with a virtuous exterior but with an interior rotten with deception, a dissimulator who states beliefs he does not hold in order to conceal his evil motives — like most modern politicians.

First question: Why is the sepulchre *whited*?

It is not merely, as less informed Bible websites proclaim arrogantly, because tombs were painted white. Duhhh. No. They are whited sepulchres because they were made of or daubed over with limestone plaster. As well as drying to a reasonable white hardness, limestone plaster as it disintegrated in the rain and soil moisture released lime which quickened the putrefaction of corpses. Also, Jews of biblical times often whitewashed tomb entrances as a warning to visitors not to touch tomb parts, for such an act defiled a pious Jew. After a visit to a necropolis, crypt, ossuary cavern or graveside, religious Jews might seek a ritual cleansing.

The word *sepulcher* and the phrase *whited sepulchre* grew familiar in English bibles, as a translation of the New Testament Koine Greek *taphos* 'tomb,' which root we still see in English words like *epitaph* 'words written on a tombstone' and the interesting *cenotaph* from classical Latin *cenotaphium* from Hellenistic Greek adjective *kenotaphion* = *kenos* 'empty' + *taphos* 'tomb.' A cenotaph, an empty tomb, is a memorial structure raised to honor a person or persons who are buried elsewhere, hence the tomb is empty. Such a monument was required even in ancient times when, for example, a brave general was killed in battle far away from his home whose citizens yet wished to pay tribute to him, although his body lay abroad under a foreign field.

How the Phrase Came into English

The full Greek phrase *taphos kekoniamenos* literally 'tomb whitened' was first rendered into popular English by Bible translators like John Wycliffe (1330 -1384) as *sepulcris maad whijt* literally 'sepulchres made white' (around 1382) and *sepulcris whited* 'sepulchres whited' (1388). William Tyndale (1494–1536) translated it as "paynted sepulchres." By the publication of the *Rheims Bible* of 1582, it had become 'whited sepulchres' and the scholars who gave us the glory of the King James Version followed Rheims.

Dust to Dust in Unsure & Uncertain Hope

of Lazarus Day Yet to Come

Kekoniamenos is a passive past participle whose literal meaning is 'dusted, whitened over with plaster, whitewashed' ultimately from Greek *konia* 'dust, powder, ashes, white plaster, lime.' St. Paul in Acts 23:3 used the same adjective to denounce an uppity bishop. Paul called the offending prelate in a vivid Greek vocative *toiche kekoniamene* 'you whitewashed wall!' Paul meant that under the shining robes of piety of this prince of the church lurked duplicity and sham.

Etymology of Sepulchre

Latin *sepulcrum* arises out of *sepultus* 'buried,' a past participle of *sepelire* 'to bury,' cognate with Greek *hepein* 'to care for' and with Sanskrit *saparyati* 'he honors.' The Latin etymon appears in several English words now mostly sunk into the swamp of desuetude near the bog of obsolescence. How many now know that a gentleman sepult is one buried? Occasionally some sniffish author will seek a synonym for burial and find sepulture. But his editor will red-pencil the rarity as obscure and therefore offensive to readers. Said editor would never have met Alexander Pope's delicious Englishing of *The Iliad* (1720) "The common Rites of Sepulture bestow, / To sooth a Father's and a Mother's Woe."

As I wend, chapter-completing, softly down the aisle toward the cathedral door, I think it not unjust to remark that there are enough whited sepulchres in modern Christian churches that the Vatican could open a Good Used Casket Lot near St. Peter's Basilica, operated by a friar named Sincere Sid.

Chapter 31

Cord versus Chord:
Hypercorrection & Archaism

Surprisingly, BOTH words, cord and chord, are from the same French word derived from Latin derived from Greek. Cord/chord's etymological pathway looks like this: English *cord* later *chord* < French *corde* < Latin *chorda* < Greek *chorde*. In classical Greek, *chorde*'s prime and sensuous meaning was 'piece of gut from an animal, a rope or stricture made from such dried gut.' A natural semantic expansion, even in ancient Greek, was *chorde* to signify 'string of a musical instrument,' like a harp or lyre, since many such stretched musical strings were made of dried animal gut.

Also a bit of a shock: **cord** was the first spelling in English, not *chord*. We have a printed record of the word in Middle English, from the year 1305CE "Bynde him honde and fet... With stronge corden" 'Bind him hand and foot with strong cords.'

Hypercorrection

But the spelling **chord** does not appear in English print until the sixteenth century. It is what some linguists used to term "learned overcorrection," while today the word *hypercorrection* is preferred by scholars. Some fussbudget knew the original Greek word commonly transliterated as *chorde*; so he deemed it appropriate to alter the English word by adding an unnecessary aitch. Aitch is the name of the

English letter /h/. This tendency to return to an ancient word form is called archaism.

The current *Oxford English Dictionary* calls that long-ago change of good plain English *cord* to fancy-schmancy *chord* "a refashioning." Ha! Such a euphemism is only a modern word snob agreeing with the first meddler who altered the spelling by adding the pompous /h/.

This foolish and spurious alteration of a modern English-spelled word to resemble its ancient Greek roots is indeed hypercorrection, a noun whose pseudo-medical sound reflects the diseased misunderstanding of linguistic evolution shown by the archaist who first respelled simple, clear *cord*.

Archaism

As there exists in paintings, architecture and many forms of art, there dwells in language an archaizing mode, in which the self-appointed guardians of a language insist that, in word forms, older is better. This is patent nonsense. The chief proof that a language is alive is its constant renewal and onward change. Yet, because these Pecksniffian nitpickers are ubiquitous, it behooves every careful, literate reader to avoid their dicta and consign their silly *pronunciamientos* to that special dungeon of words reserved for smarty-pants nigglers.

Among the surest signs deposited by hypercorrectors are double adverbs. Their rather dim cognitive processes consider:

(1) All adverbs terminate in –ly, such as deeply, clearly etc.

(2) Therefore it is correct to use forms like muchly*, doubtlessly*, seldomly*. All three of those words reek of a glutinous pleonasm. They are redundant, tautological, *de trop*, supernumerary and prolixly palaverous. I descend into redundancy myself only because the forms are so annoyingly useless. *Much*, *doubtless* and *seldom* are already adverbial forms!

They don't need the –ly suffix. But the grammarless archaists don't know that. Join not their dismal throng!

This wee essaylet does not discuss the variety of meanings assigned through the centuries to the words *cord* and *chord*. Any good dictionary will list their nuanced significations, their semantic multiplicity. I merely wanted the attentive word-lover to be aware of the scant historical reason for the snobbish aitch that lurks like a word tumour, a logoma*, in *chord*. Thank you, and good afternoon, class.

*Logoma is my coinage for a swollen, bloated, useless word form growing like a cancer in the midst of our healthy English word hoard, from Greek logos 'word + Greek word-forming suffix –oma 'a tumor, a swelling, benign or malignant but chiefly malignant, seen in many English medical terms like carcinoma and melanoma.

Chapter 32

"The Sun is God," said J.M.W. Turner

The English Romantic painter, water-colourist and light-worshipper, the great precursor of Impressionism, J.M.W. Turner was asked what religion he followed. Turner said "The sun is God."

So did the religious revolutionary of pharaonic Egypt, Akhenaton, sweeping away all the cow-headed and jackal-necked deities of the Nile delta, to introduce an early Egyptian monotheism. French monarch Louis XIV said the king is the sun and dubbed himself *Le Roi-Soleil* 'the sun king.' Napoleon Bonaparte said, "If I had to choose a religion, the sun as the universal giver of life would be my god."

Solar Etymology

Our ancient mother tongue, Proto-Indo-European, appears to have had two roots for sun, *sāol and *sāwol. Sol, luminiferous orb of day, round which our loving planet Earth revolves, is a solar name related to the word *sun*. Sol is sunny Latin *sol solis*, its adjective *solaris*, its sun-filled chamber: a solarium. An early Germanic translation of a Latin day name, *dies solis*, was *sunnon-dagaz* 'day of the sun' or Sunday.

From Latin descend all the Romance language suns: Spanish and Portuguese *sol*, Italian *sole* and French *soleil*. One of my pet sunlit phrases is Italian: *un posticino al sole* 'a little place in the sun.' The umbrella that protects your skin from harsh heavenly rays began in French as *parasol*, borrowed from Italian *parasole* = Italian *parare* 'to shield' + *sole* 'sun.'

The Latin reflex is cognate with Sanskrit *suvar* and other Indic sun words like *suar, sura* and *surya*, Lithuanian *saule*, Old Norse and Icelandic *sol*, modern Norwegian, Swedish, Danish *so*, Welsh *haul* Polish *slonce* and classical Greek *helios*, which gives us many scientific words in English like *heliocentric*, and the flower that turns toward the sun, the *heliotrope*, and the point at which a planet is farthest from its sun, its *aphelion*.

Also on board this etymological train are the West Germanic n-forms from the older etymon *sunnon: Old English *sunne,* Old Frisian *sunne*, Old Saxon *sunna,* Dutch *zon*, Afrikaans *son* and High German *Sonne*.

Country Name

Two common names for Japan are Nippon and Nihon, both meaning 'sun origin, sun rise' that is, land of the rising sun, but from a easterly Chinese perspective! Indeed the very terms originated in Chinese documents of the Sui Dynasty.

A Little Skyful of Solar Citation & Sun-splashed Poesy

Below shine a few of my favourite sunny citations from poetry and prose. In *The Tempest*, Prospero's great speech, renouncing his magical powers, throbs with the potent word music of Shakespeare's English:

> ". . . I have bedimm'd
> The noontide sun, call'd forth the mutinous winds,
> And 'twixt the green sea and the azured vault
> Set roaring war : to the dread rattling thunder
> Have I given fire and rifted Jove's stout oak
> With his own bolt;"

As Antony's star falls near the conclusion of *Antony and Cleopatra,* Antony bemoans his approaching fate:

> "O sun, thy uprise shall I see no more:
> Fortune and Antony part here;"

In *Hamlet*, Shakespeare has Polonius, that senile Aunt Blabby of advice-givers, keep giving it:

"Polonius
> Good madam, stay awhile. I will be faithful.
> [Reads.]
> 'Doubt thou the stars are fire;
> Doubt that the sun doth move;
> Doubt truth to be a liar;
> But never doubt I love."

And, in *Romeo and Juliet*, one of the simplest, starkest and most wondrous of lover's compliments is spoken by Romeo.

"Romeo
> [JULIET appears above at a window]
> But, soft! What light through yonder window breaks?
> It is the east, and Juliet is the sun.*"*

And elsewhere in the same play *sun* references proliferate.

"Juliet
> Give me my Romeo; and, when he shall die,
> Take him and cut him out in little stars,
> and he will make the face of heaven so fine
> That all the world will be in love with night
> And pay no worship to the garish sun."

Buddha said: Three things cannot be long hidden: the sun, the moon, and the truth. William Blake, England's most adept mystic poet, said: If the Sun and Moon should ever doubt,/they'd immediately go out.

But now, the fiery steeds who draw the four-horsed chariot of the sun across the daytime sky, flee toward Phoebus' stable of the night, and even yours sunnily, your kindly sage, *moi*, in whatever bestowing mood I be, must fling my book upon the straw, and in hay-pillowed repose, await the sleep kiss of the evening star.

Chapter 33

Noise & Confusion
rare Honks in the Sonic Repertoire of English

English offers choice noise-making terms that, in their aptness, go well beyond uproar, racket and clamour. In this little chapter I share with you some noise and confusion terms which were new to me.

Tohu-Bohu

Infrequent in extant English is our chance to use a phrase of biblical Hebrew lifted almost holus-bolus from the opening passage of Genesis. But here it is, tohu-bohu, a synonym for chaos or utter confusion. Here are the first two sentences of the Bible in the 1611 King James version: "In the beginning God created the heaven and the earth. And the earth was without form and void. The Hebrew of the last phrase is *thohu wa-bohu* 'emptiness and desolation' borrowed and used in English prose as early as 1619 by Samuel Purchas, an Elizabethan writer of early travel guides. Current American usage often omits the hyphen, as in this twentieth-century quote from the journalist Walter Lippmann, *"bringing order out of the tohubohu of human relations."* Tohu-bohu has made its way into French *tohu-bohu*, German *Tohuwabohu*, Estonian and Hungarian *tohuvabohu*. The great French symbolist poet Arthur Rimbaud, for whom the very syllables of modern French were delectable, liked tohu-bohu and used it in his *Poésies* collection in the poem *Le Bateau Ivre* 'Drunken Boat:'

Dans les clapotements furieux des marées
Moi, l'autre hiver, plus sourd que les cerveaux
d'enfants,
Je courus ! Et les Péninsules démarrées
N'ont pas subi tohu-bohus plus triomphants.

My translation :
  In the furious clankings of the tides
  I, last winter, deafer than infant brains,
  I ran! And unmoored peninsulas have not
  Undergone a chaos more victorious.

Tintamarre

Here is another French word still vibrantly alive in Acadian French and rarer in English but still causing the occasional ruckus and hubbub. Tintamarre is a fifteenth-century French word of uncertain origin that meant first an unholy racket of noise and uproar. One writer says she experienced it at a theatre where she disapproved of the play but the audience cheered and raved "in a tintamarre of enthusiasm." The word gained new life in the midst of the twentieth century when Acadian French revived another old meaning and tintamarre came to mean 'raising a ruckus by marching with horns and drums through a neighbourhood to celebrate some occasion by making the most noise the group can make.'

Nowadays in Acadian French communities a *tintamarre* is held to commemorate the expulsion of the Acadians by the British, a nearly genocidal banning that drove Acadians into exile out of Nova Scotia into Louisiana territory where they continued their race and culture as Cajuns, colloquial for Acadian.

The tradition of tintamarre is related to a charivari, any noisy group whoop-up to beat the drum, make merry and be jubilant about some reason to rejoice. A charivari is a wandering, cacophonous serenade of noisemakers like kettles, pans, tea-trays, and the like, used in France in mockery and derision of incongruous or unpopular marriages, and of unpopular persons generally. But in America the tradition softened, becoming more amiable. In Mississippi Valley French *charivari* metamorphosed into *shivaree*, a friendly but raucous celebration of a local wedding. As such there is an excellent example of a shivaree in the Rogers & Hammerstein musical "Oklahoma!" where the cowboys gather to make a grand noise outside the wedding-night bedroom of Curly and his new bride.

Noisy Verbs Needing Revival

Consider to latrate, to yawp, to ululate, and to tintinnabulate! Some noisy verbs describe animal sounds. **To latrate** is to bark like a dog, from Latin *latrare* 'to bark.' The other forms of the word all existed in English but have become obsolete. You however, dear and inquisitive reader, may decide to recall to life these verbal zombies. The agent noun is still apt. I myself have toiled under the loud voice of a boss who was a latrator. He barked orders at all his workers. He was flagrant in his latrant nastiness.

To ululate is another Latin borrowing. The Romans heard owls utter ululant night hootings.

To stridulate is to produce sharper, higher-pitched noises like the chirp of a cricket or the late-summer whirr of a cicada. Such sounds are strident indeed.

Bees buzz, of course. But bumblebees may **bombinate**, a lovely hum-buzz of a word worthy of wider use, borrowed first into French and then into English from medieval Latin *bombinare*, a variant of *bombilare* 'to buzz like a bee,' itself borrowed from ancient Greek *bombyliazein* 'to buzz, to hum,' from Greek *bombos*, the same source as our upblowing bomb.

Our final animal-noise word shall be an adjective, mugient. It rhymes with the surname Nugent. *Mugire* in Latin is a verb 'to low like cattle, to bellow, to moo like a cow." This verb too is onomatopoeic.

To tintinnabulate is 'to make a sound like a bell ringing' and is an excellent example of onomatopoeia or imitative harmony in Latin. Onomatopoeia (Greek for 'name-making') is part of word making where speakers imitate the sound of something in nature by trying to spell it then say it in letters, e.g. gurgle, murmur, hiss, trickle, gush and perhaps rumble. We in modern English hear a bell as ding-dong. The ancient Romans heard a bell as tin-tin. So their verb was *tintinnabulare* 'to ring like a bell.'

Therefore, lectors, taint not the verbatorium with stale words, overused, clichéd, obscenely smooth vocables sandpapered to oblivion by repetition. But seek ye rather those polysyllabled gems sequestered here in the worders' trunk, in the bountiful trove of English verbal treasure. Then let your sesquipedalian yawp be heard!

Chapter 34

Rootching Around:
Canadian and American Dialect Phrase

This is a word my late father used frequently. But first, before we get to rootching around, a very brief offering of personal history. My father was descended from German Lutheran immigrants who arrived in America in 1710 as Kasselmanner, today Casselman and Castleman. At the end of the seventeenth century, my family fled Roman Catholic persecution in the German state of Hesse, probably amidst vestigial skirmishes of the Counter Reformation.

You'll remember, as part of the Counter Reformation to "get" Martin Luther and his Protestant heretics, the Roman Catholic Church reviving, among other gifts to humanity, the papal Inquisition in 1542 in order to seriously combat Protestantism, chiefly by burning Protestant heretics alive in a bonfire while tied to a central stake. Such burnings of human beings were always open to the public. Why? Let me quote from one of the torturers' guide books, the *Directorium Inquisitorum*, a dandy little handbook for inquisitors, printed in 1578. In this passage the kindly authors explain the purpose of inquisitorial penalties: *...quoniam punitio non refertur primo & per se in correctionem & bonum eius qui punitur, sed in bonum publicum ut alij terreantur, & a malis committendis avocentur* '...for punishment does not take place primarily and *per se* for the correction and good of the person punished, but for the public good in order that others may become terrified and weaned away from the evils they would commit.'

Is this abomination, said to have burned alive over its evil course of its history more than one million women as witches, still alive? Its modern version (1965) resides at the Vatican, robust and kicking, as the Congregation for the Doctrine of the Faith. They don't turn as many virgins on a spit over a slow fire as in the good old days, but who knows what devilment they get up to nowadays?

To return to my more innocent family memory, well do I recall Dad giving advice when my brother or I had lost a toy. Said he, "Just rootch around in the toy chest and you'll find it." Or "I'm going out to the garage to rootch around for that lost hammer."

To rootch is a Pennsylvania Dutch (Deutsch or German) word meaning 'to be restless in one spot, to be fidgety, to squirm, to sort through in a rough manner, to search for something lost, etc.' Teacher to restless pupil: Quit rootching around in your chair, it's disturbing the class.

The German etymon is the common noun *der Rutsch* and its reduced-forms verb *rutschen* as seen in the common, modern German New Year's Greeting: *guten Rutsch!* 'have a good Whoop-Up!' As a German noun *der Rutsch* means 'a slip, a slide, a fall, a rock-slide, a trip, a travel outing.'

Some idiomatic German expressions are:
in einem Rutsch 'in one go.
rutsch dem Brontosaurus den Buckel runter wie Fred Feuerstein 'slide down the back of a brontosaurus like Fred Flintstone'
Rutsch auf den Fahrersitz und lass den Wagen an. 'Slide into the driver's seat and start the car.'

So, if you are ever rootching around for a nifty bit of residual German-American slang, rootch no further!

Chapter 35

School is a Leisure Word!

I am a writer and a pretty apt coiner of locutions. The choicest phrases of my invention, bountiful though they be (he said with all due lack of humility), have come to me while lulled in the comfy slippers of repose, alone in my tidy abode of study, hamlet-bound, snug in my town bungalow. The telephone has been disconnected, Twitter silenced, Facebook closed, obtruding email unread, the yammer of unlettered peasants for a moment squelched.

The slippered ease of quiescence is pleasing to body and to brain. It was, in fact, during contemplative musing I first perceived how bare yawns our English cupboard of leisure words.

After ease, repose, vacation and free time, the scanty list dribbles away to naught. Nowhere in English, for example, is Cicero's ample Latin formula of *otium cum dignitate* 'leisure made useful with the dignity of thought and intellectual work.' Oh, we English-speakers have a few exotic, rare leisure words. One is *requiescence*, a state of peace and quiet. The root is familiar to graveyard-wanderers in the common epitaph, a post-classical Latin subjunctive sentence: *requiescat in pace* R.I.P. 'May he (or she) rest in peace." A threadbare, a shabby apopemptic if ever I read one!

Absent from English — except as a loan word — is the lovely Italian concept of *villeggiatura*, a rest period or vacation passed at a country-seat; a rural interval in the country where the daily music of life's sweet flow is marked *adagio* 'at ease.' *Durante una villeggiatura*, one might saunter slowly past all the splashing fountains singing frothily in the grounds of the Villa d'Este at Tivoli. And one might spend several days in doing so, under the warm brown heat of Italian summer, sheltered betimes 'neath a bower of Roman pines.

Stern Anglo-Saxon forefathers of English had little use or regard for leisure. No Brit coined *dolce far niente* 'sweetly to do nothing, to do sweet nothings.' How did the English urban elite frame a rural sojourn? Why, sir, going to the countryside in Britain was a punishment! Consider that time-worn Oxford verb *to rusticate* which means to send someone down from the university for untoward student behaviour. Such a collegian is banished, dismissed or suspended for activities such as painting a don red. Now, if you have encountered even a small number of Oxford dons, you will realize at once that being painted bright red is often exactly what an Oxford don most needs.

Long ago the verb *to rusticate* had an initial English meaning which was positive. To rusticate first meant "to live a quiet country life," derived as the word is from the simple Latin term for countryside, *rus, ruris* which gives us our common adjective *rural*.

Rus in Urbe

Appropriate here is a brief gloss on the phrase *rus in urbe* 'the country in the town,' coined by that master of Latin epigrams, the classical poet Martial (*circa* 40 CE to *c.*104). Nowadays *rus in urbe* usually signifies trying to bring a bit of the countryside into an urban environment, such as a city park where designers attempt to recreate a small forest setting. The phrase is also used as a pejorative against a person whom the insulter views as a clod, a rube, a country hick, who belongs in a hayfield and not perhaps at city hall where the insulter encounters him.

Greek & Roman Perspectives on Leisure

Ancient dwellers under bright Mediterranean skies held views about leisure quite distinct from glummer, cloudier northern races. One attitude shows up in the Latin word for 'doing business', namely *negotium*, which renders forth our solemn English words of commerce and polity: negotiate and negotiations. *Negotium* is a compound Latin noun made up of Latin *nec, neg* 'not' + *otium* 'leisure.' Business to the citizen of early Rome was, above all else, NOT leisure. *Negotium* in Latin also meant trouble or bother. Latin *otium* partook of sterner Roman significance for it also meant resting up, recovering from the rigors of labour.

But did the sour, aggressive Romans invent such a concept? They did not. *Negotium* is what we call in linguistics a loan-translation, in which a foreign term is broken up into constituent roots and each of these foreign, non-Latin roots is then translated into acceptable native Latin roots. Romans filched their sneering idea about common business from an ancient Greek word for business, *ascholia* = *a* 'not' + *schole* 'leisure, hobby, pastime.' To the Greeks, *schole* was leisure to pursue knowledge rather than befouling free time with idle moping, sex, or drunkenness. That's why our English word *school* comes directly from *schole* through its Latin form *scola*, whence too *scholar* and *scholium* 'learned footnote.' A school, to Aristotle, was a place where there was leisure to study philosophy and theology, the written and spoken arts, music and the beginnings of science. At school one sought truth not profit. How educational times have changed! Today one gets an education to learn a trade to make money to live.

Three words give us the truest importance of leisure: time to learn. Leisure time is not to be jammed with amusements and play. "The first principle of all good action is leisure." Aristotle concluded that leisure is necessary for the development of excellence and the performance of political duties. The English word *leisure* derives from French *loisir* from the Latin verb *licere* 'to be permitted,' its original and prime but now obsolete meaning in English was 'freedom to do a specific task.'

Calmness in Greek Philosophy

I have seen leisure translated into Attic Greek as ataraxy. Wrong! Ataraxy is not leisure. The Greek roots are *a* 'not + classical Greek *taraxia* '*trouble, agitation.*' It is a technical term in Greek stoicism meaning literally "not being excited or stirred up by life events," from *a,* a negative prefix denoting 'not' or 'no,' sometimes called "alpha privative" since it deprives the root of meaning, for example, in the word *acephalic* 'NOT having a head, headless,' used in neonatal medicine to describe a still birth in which the fetus has no developed head. By the way, mass acephaly may be observed in any wide-angle TV shot of fans at a soccer game.

Chapter 36

Punch-drunk
Punch *and* Pentateuch *Share a Common Cognate*

Punch properly prepared — several literate alcoholics have sworn — is a quaffable potion fit to sluice the larynx of a god.

Nowadays this reputed elixir is a party drink made from a mixture of ingredients: usually wine or spirits mixed with water, fruit, spices, and sugar, and often served hot.

My reference to its suitability to soothe divine palates is no idle kudos. The very word *punch* was borrowed into English from an ancient language of India, where in Sanskrit *panca* or *panc* is the numeral five, the term short for *pancamṛta* 'five nectars.' The libation or infusion was said to be confected of the five nectars of the gods, because of the ancient traditional ingredients: milk, curd, ghee butter, honey and molasses. In the seventeenth century, British visitors returning from India made the drink a sensation, a potable intoxicant of sweetly pleasing savour whose tonsil-tickling repute spread quickly across Europe. Look at the dates of the first uses of the word: French *punch* (1674), Spanish *ponche* (1737), Portuguese *ponche* (second half of the eighteenth century), Dutch *punch* (1721), German *Punsch* (c1700), Swedish *punsch* (1710 as *poins*) and Danish *punch* (first half of the eighteenth century).

Not related to any of the words below is our English verb *to punch* which begins as *puncheon* possibly from a Late Latin form *punchus* 'piercing tool.'

Noted Military Domicile & HQ

Lest the Sanskrit word for five appear irretrievably odd, recall its close cousin in classical Greek *pente* 'five,' from which English drew many derivatives. Consider that five-sided, five-angled building near Washington, the Pentagon (Greek *pente* 'five' + *agon* 'angle, corner, wall, side').

Attention, Demons!

The little devils in our puritan midst may know the magic pentacle, a five-pointed star, supposed to have mystical significance, formed by five straight lines connecting the vertices of a pentagon and enclosing another pentagon in the completed figure. The word is the gift of medieval mumbo-jumboists who knew the Latin *pentaculum*, literally 'little five-parted thing,' a Greek root *pente* 'five,' and a Latin diminutive suffix.

Attention, Christians & Jews!

The first five books of the Old Testament are called the Pentateuch. These same five holy books comprise the Torah in Judaism. Hellenistic Greeks dubbed the opening five books with this moniker. Originally the nickname was Greek *pentateuchos biblos* 'book of five books,' but that seemed redundant and it was soon shortened to a singular noun *pentateuchos. Teuchos* in its prime sense meant 'thing made' then 'vessel, implement, tool, scroll' and much later in Hellenstic Greek it came to name the protective case in which a scroll of Holy Writ was safely kept. Then finally it meant 'book.' The Greek verbal root is *teuchein* 'to make, to confect, to manufacture.'

View Maps of Nether Ind

Another instance of a *punch* cognate signifying the numeral five appears in the name Punjab referring to five rivers that course through Punjabi territory. The now Urdu name is composed for two Persian words *panj* 'five' + *ab* 'waters,' since this region of northern India and Pakistan is irrigated by five rivers: the Jhelum, Chenab, Ravi, Sutlej, and Beas. All are tributaries of the mighty Indus River.

Namaste, Kama Pita!

Also cognate are a few technical terms in Hinduism and Hindu medicine (ayurvedic) which appear occasionally in English text like *panchakarma*, a five-part therapy for cleansing the body of toxins and restoring a balance of humours, the compound word from Sanskrit *panca* + Sanskrit *karman* 'action, treatment.' Think of karma, in Buddhism and Hinduism, personal actions that determine future reincarnations, as well as less formal meanings in modern English like destiny, fate, one's lot in life and afterlife, one's kismet.

A Buddhist phrase like *panch shila* from Sanskrit is made up of *panca* five + si*la* 'character, disposition, good conduct.' These are the five no-no's of basic morality in Buddhism, namely that one does NOT take life, not take what is not given, not commit adultery, not lie and not get drunk.

What a little roundup of five! So, word dudes, gimme a high-five and let's blow this punch stand!

Chapter 37

Some Laughs & Smiles

a modest compendium of verbal merriment

Cachinnate

How many of us know the English verb *to cachinnate*? Damn few is my bet. Its etymon or word source, Latin *cachinnare,* is probably reduplicative and onomatopoeic. Let me explain. Modern English speakers represent laughter as *haw-haw.* We often double or duplicate sounds from which we make simple words. Dodo, doo-doo, poo-poo, ka-ka. Modern English hears laughter as haw-haw. Ancient Romans, I surmise, heard the sound of laughter as *cah-cah.* So one Latin verb was *cachinnare* 'to laugh.' Onomatopoeia or imitative harmony is forming a word to sound the way it does in nature.

After we borrowed the root into English, *to cachinnate* came to have a pejorative semantic taint; it evolved in English signifying 'to utter immoderate, loud or vulgar laughter.' A cachinnator at milady's elegant evening formal meal was a tablemate to eschew, a vulgarian, a repulsive toad, a verminous rotter, who might slap your back just as you attempted to sluice a juicy oyster down a slippery gullet. Instead the obscene oyster might end up in one patchless eye-socket of a startled half-blind grandmother sitting across the table from you! Such a misfortune would brand the backslapper and cachinnator as a mere *campesino,* an uncouth rustic, a misinvited guest to be avoided for the rest of the evening, as a necklaced dowager might shun a dung beetle or seek to elude a person of low breeding.

Insouciant

In current English this adjective borrowed from French has acquired a negative hue. *She left the meeting with an insouciant shrug.* In other words she showed an unwelcome indifference to what was being discussed at the meeting. But, in its earliest days in English, insouciant was bright and breezy and buoyant and carefree, as befits its literal source in French, namely, *sans souci* 'without care, carefree.' Compare a common name given to many European county cottages and villas by the seaside "Sans souci" or carefree. The most famous such residence is Sanssouci, former summer palace of the King of Prussia, Frederick the Great, in Potsdam near Berlin, often claimed by Germans to be a rival to France's Versailles. An elegant abode it indeed is, but that Kraut shed holds not one wax-clogged candelabra to the coruscating glory of Versailles.

Insouciant to me describes a blithesome mood of easy-going mellowness, in which, as a happy day unfolds, a person carries on, untroubled, serene of mind and countenance, while bothersome care has been put away and locked up in the Cabinet of Concern, a strong cupboard the key to which has been lost with purpose and deliberation.

Jocund

An insouciant person will be perhaps jocund. I see in the current *Merriam-Webster Unabridged Dictionary* a very dodgy etymology where the learned word scribe tells us that the Latin adjective *jucundus* stems from *juvare* 'to help.' Does that mean that jocund's prime and sensuous meaning is 'full of help'? Maybe. How about *io-, jo-* ancestors of the same root found in our English word *joy*, to which the suffix of abundance *–cundus, cunda, cundum* has been affixed, so that *jucundus* means 'abounding in joy.' Think of Cicero's pithy little apophthegm: *"Acti labores jucundi sunt* 'Work done abounds in joy.' Does such a word as *io* exist in classical Latin? It does. *Io!* is an interjection of joy invoking a god. The Greeks used the same exclamation, io. Now English borrowed our word *joy* directly from French *joie* which itself descended, with Gallic transformations, from Latin *gaudia* or *gaudium* 'joy, delight, gladness, happiness, physical or sensual delight.'

As Late Latin turned into early French, transformations occurred. For example, to increase the speed of saying words aloud, intervocalic dentals sometimes disappeared. That puts paid to the *d* in *gaudium*. Latin declension endings dropped away. Bye-bye to the *a* of *gaudia* and the *–um* of *gaudium*. Then the hard Latin *g* softens leaving us *joie*. My question is: did some of these alterations in pronunciation occur earlier in street Latin and Roman soldiers' slang, long before a French language was even conceived? Of course they did! How else to explain sound shifts piling up to produce all the Romance language changes that evolved into Spanish, Italian and Portuguese as tongues quite separate from Latin yet deeply related. Here are the words in Romance: French *joie*, Provençal *joia*, joi, Spanish *joya*, Portuguese *joia* 'jewel', Italian *gioja* 'joy, jewel.'

We ought not to leave *gaudium* without a brief quote of its verb from the most famous of medieval student drinking songs in Latin: *"Gaudeamus igitur, iuvenes dum sumus."* 'So let's rejoice and whoop it up, while we are young!'

Jape

Seldom written or spoken nowadays is this expressive monosyllable, whether noun or verb, *jape*. A synonym for jest, joke or merry tale, sadly it repines in the dank grotto of neglect. Known in English since the fourteenth century, its source is obscure.

To revive it, we could praise sportive behaviour by adding to the wonderful phrase from Dickens' novel *Great Expectations* "What larks! What japes!" There is, of course, a melancholy undertone to the original in the novel where the simple blacksmith Joe visits Pip in great London. But the two men are now grown apart by circumstance and are awkward together. Whenever Pip comes home for a visit, Joe promises "What larks, Pip! What larks."

Ribald speech may be put down by branding it as mere japery, using the now obsolete longer noun of jape.

Innocent Merriment

One of my favorite words in the entire English language is *merriment* and its adjective *merry*. The adjective lingers in our familiar seasonal greeting of Merry Christmas! But, aside from that festive use, merry is considered too quaint, too Dickensian, too *raffinée*, much too sophisticated or much too corny for modern use. I could not disagree more.

Gilbert and Sullivan bid the murderous Mikado sing of "innocent merriment," mocking his horrid goal:

> *"My object all sublime*
> *I shall achieve in time —*
> *To let the punishment fit the crime —*
> *The punishment fit the crime;*
> *And make each prisoner pent*
> *Unwillingly represent*
> *A source of innocent merriment!*
> *Of innocent merriment!"*

Surprisingly the word *merry* is of Germanic provenance. Yet the honey of its gliding sweetness effuses all happy times.

Come, let us make merry! That should still be a command one can pronounce without embarrassment. But it is not! Has any toy of revolvable infants ever been better named than a merry-go-round?

In all his extant plays Shakespeare uses the word *merry* 175 times. In *A Midsummer night's Dream*, I like Puck's self-intro: "Thou speak'st aright; I am that merry wanderer of the night." Would that we all might be. In *As You Like It*, Amiens sings:

> *"Under the greenwood tree*
> *Who loves to lie with me,*
> *And turn his merry note*
> *Unto the sweet bird's throat,*
> *Come hither, come hither, come hither.*
> *Here shall he see*
> *No enemy*
> *But winter and rough weather."*

And so, what better toodle-oo can I offer than this: God rest you merry, gentlewomen, gentlemen, gentlepersons all.

Chapter 38

Reft, to reave, rift, riven, bereft, to rive

are these parts of verbs on their way to obsolescence in spoken and written English?

I launched a word search after seeing this sentence in a 2015-written newspaper report: "There was a reft in his web of deceit." I knew rift meaning 'split, fissure, rip' and discovered that the noun *reft* was a now rare variant of *rift*. Both monosyllables ring with a terse, enunciatory displeasure in shredded hope and fissured dream.

As well as its noun meanings, reft is also the past tense and the past participle of the verb *to reave* 'to tear, to split, to cleave.' To reave is a variant of the more usual *to rive*, although both verbs are rare or of confined use.

To rive 'to divide, to split' is a borrowing into English of a verb brought to the British Isles by Viking raiders speaking Old Norse. Compare Old Icelandic *rifa*, Norwegian *rive*, Old Swedish *riva* and Old Danish *rywae*.

Nowadays in English the verb *to rive* is seldom used except in woodworking where it means to split wood along the grain with an axe in order to make laths and shingles.

Still in wider English use is *to rive*'s past participle, riven. Torn, rent, split, cloven, cracked are meanings for riven. "The distasteful rise of racist illiterates has riven this once benevolent political party."

A variant of *to rive* is *to reive* 'to tear, to split, to cleave." If you tear something away from another person without their permission, you may be a thief, a stealer, or a reiver.

Typical of the Oxford English dictionary's pro-British bias and partisan snottiness is the OED's omission from mention of the only acclaimed, best-selling novel in English using the word, William Faulkner's 1962 comic novel *The Reivers,* winner of the Pulitzer Prize for Fiction in 1963. *The Reivers* is not even mentioned in the hundreds of exemplary passages quoted in the OED. Oxford editors then wonder why so many of us North-Americans would like to give OED editors a solid kick in their snooty limey arses. The title refers to "thieves" or reivers, some feisty southern farm hands who steal their employer's turn-of-the-century classy automobile, a yellow Winton Flyer, and light out for a wild, lewd weekend in 1905 Memphis. The story is wonderful, warm, light-hearted Faulkner and thus the novel is often dismissed by literary snobs who hold that Faulkner is only worth reading when he is meditating on the deep character flaws of southern "white trash."

A related verb is *to bereave* whose prime sense is 'deprive of something valuable, rob, plunder, steal' with its more familiar past participle *bereft* and its past tense *bereaved.* "The bereaved of the family arrived at the funeral home and onlookers could tell they had indeed been robbed of a beloved family member."

Here's hoping future selectors of illustrative quotations at the *Oxford English Dictionary* can bring themselves to include exempla from American authors. Several American authors could actually spell!

Chapter 39

Hiemal, Brumal, Algid: Wintry Adjectives Worth Knowing

Winter's root is wet, literally. The same Germanic root that gives our words *water* and *wet* makes the first vowel nasal and so adds an 'n' to obtain a putative root *ued > *wet > *went > *wint > winter. Thus winter is closely related to other English words like *water* and *otter*!

Druids' Winter

An alternative origin suggests that our word *winter* may stretch all the way back to a root form in Proto-Indo-European *ueid that gives Celtic words for 'white'; compare for example Old Irish *find* 'white' and many other Celtic cognates like Welsh *gwyn* 'white' and perhaps even the Druids 'people of the white oak' from *dru-ueid or oak-white. Dru means 'oak tree' and there are two PIE morphemes represented as *ueid. The second *ueid means 'know, see.' One of its reflexes in English is the word *wit* with its prime meaning of insight. In Latin, PIE *ueid produces the reflex *videre* 'to see.' Take *dru and *ueid compounded to make the word Druid, and the Druids could be the 'oak-knowers' based on their veneration of the oak tree and its mistletoe.

Classical Winter Words

English borrows Latin and Greek words for coldness and winter to obtain both poetic and medical words. The most common Latin word for winter is *hiems*, from which English derives a learned adjective *hiemal* 'taking place in winter, pertaining to winter.' Latin *hiems* is cognate with these Indo-European relatives: Greek c*heimonas* 'winter', Greek *chion* 'snow', Sanskrit *hemanta* 'winter' and Russian *zima* 'winter.'

Rare in modern English, the word *hiems* is used memorably as a poetic personification of winter by William Shakespeare in the opening scene of Act 2 of *A Midsummer Night's Dream*. Titania, queen of the fairies, tells her husband Oberon that even the moon is displeased with their quarrels and consequently the very seasons of the year are changed.

TITANIA
"Therefore the moon, the governess of floods,
Pale in her anger, washes all the air,
That rheumatic diseases do abound:
And through this distemperature we see
The seasons alter: hoary-headed frosts
Fall in the fresh lap of the crimson rose,
And on old Hiems' thin and icy crown
An odorous chaplet of sweet summer buds
Is, as in mockery, set. . ."

Brumal

Brumal, a Latin-derived wintry adjective I like, bears a blustery, blizzard-riven sound. Brumal chills freeze and peel the very skin from your shivering bones. In classical Latin, *bruma* referred to the shortest day of the year. The word is contracted from a superlative form of the simple Latin adjective *brevis* 'short,' *brevima*, itself a contraction of *brevissima*, a feminine superlative adjective nominative, possibly from a phrase like *dies brevissima* 'the shortest day' [of the winter solstice].

Secondarily in Latin, *bruma* meant midwinter but was nowhere near as common as *hiems*. Ancient winter feast days named Brumalia are mentioned in Roman literature. Winter sea fogs are brumal. They tumble across frosted docks and cling to the matted felt of pea jackets.

French borrowed *bruma* too, first as *la brume* 'short winter day' but in modern French it means haze, sea mist or fog. In 1938 director Marcel Carné made a beautiful film of poetic realism called *Le Quai des brumes* starring three of the great early actors of French talkies: Jean Gabin, Michel Simon and Michèle Morgan. The film title is usually translated as "Port of Shadows," but that is pallid and tepid beside its much punchier literal meaning which I translate as 'Wharf of Fogs.'

Just after the French Revolution, when French monthly names of the calendar were altered by law, February for a brief time was rechristened *Brumaire* 'month of wintry fogs.'

Boreal

All Hail, Boreas, god of winter, winged wind deity of the north. Hair and beard spiked with ice, he blows down from cold mountains of Thrace, chilling the air with his hiemal breath. To the north, beyond (Greek *hyper*) his mountain home, lay Hyperborea, a land of eternal spring never touched by, and thus beyond the god's brumal blast. In mosaics, Boreas often is depicted as a gust-blowing face with air-bloated cheeks up among the clouds. This image survived into post-classical art and cartography, and is frequently found in the upper and lower corners of old maps."

An ancient Greek rural belief was that fecund winds Boreas and Zephyros would sweep down upon early spring pastures where mares in heat waited to be fertilized by the horses of the spring wind, ghostly stallions but full of equine vigor. Horses thought to be born from these mystic couplings were considered best of breed.

Afterwinter & Back-Winter

Both these terms name a return to winter temperatures after spring weather has already begun or simply cold, muddy weather leading up to real spring.

Robin Storm: A Canadian After-Winter Phrase

You've opened the cottage, primed the pump, set the summer chairs on the new cedar deck, shared a christening goblet of *Château Qui Sait?*, and, just as you settle into the hammock to imbibe the piney brio of it all, a thick snow squall blows in across the lake to welcome the start of June. It's a late-in-the-season storm familiar to most Canadians, and some call it a robin storm, in an attempt to lessen its chill by invoking one of our cheerful spring birds, the robin.

Lapwing Winter

To birders in Denmark and Scandinavia, a cold snap in the spring is a lapwing-winter or a lapwing-snow, because it arrives just as lapwing birds return.

Blackberry Winter

In the southern United States, a period of cold weather late in the spring is a blackberry winter, because it happens often just as the blackberry bushes set buds or bloom. *Blackberry Winter* is the title of a wonderful 1946 novella by American novelist Robert Penn Warren who captures rural Tennessee slang and a young boy's innocence, depicting it as well as any American writer ever did.

Hibernate

English supplies verbs to describe what critters do seasonally. To hibernate is to pass the winter in a state of torpor. *Hiberna* is a Roman military word for 'winter camp,' related to *hiems* 'winter.' To estivate is to the pass the summer in suspended animation. But we need a verb to describe what many do all the year round. With due humility, I suggest totannate from Latin, *totum* 'all' + *annus* 'year' meaning 'to pass the entire year in a state of torpor.' To observe the phenomenon visit Washington or any state capital.

Algid

Rarest of the cold synonyms, poor, tiny, freezing wordlet *algid* crouches furtively in the less read pages of medical literature where it means 'very cold,' from Latin *algidus* 'cold' from *algere* 'to be cold.' One may still read of algid cholera where the patient is damp and clammy instead of moist and hot.

I do like its noun *algor* which has a distinct wintry chill about it. She treated his begging for forgiveness with utter algor. In Victorian medicine, algor referred to the chills that often mark the onset of a fever.

To Inwinter or Not

Finally, a neat English verb, to inwinter, is to protect sheep or other domestic animals by sheltering them inside barns or other structures during viciously cold inclemency that might kill them. Inwintering breeding ewes is safe farm practice.

Now bleak Jack Frost may still make cheek raw and red, but at least we are two or three winter words up on the rimy rascal.

Chapter 40

Eyot, Brae, Ghyll, Tarn, Toft & Co.
being short landscape words in English

Let us summon a pony and trap, gentle persons, and set off at trotting pace down leafy lanes of British countryside.

Ait

This word meaning 'a little island, islet' is perhaps an Old English diminutive form of Old English *ieg* 'island' with *–eth* a diminutive suffix appended, to give a probable but unattested form like *egeth. Several small islands in England's River Thames contain the root in their names, e.g. Middileit, Boreseyt, Dockeyte (now Dog Ait) and Neyte Hill (now Neight Hill).

Eyot, a word still in English use, is a more common variant of ait. Here's a 2010 quote in a New Zealand newspaper: "a two-hour paddle away through the labyrinth of eyots and sandbanks." An eyot is often a small island in a river. A similar though rare English form *islot* came from a French diminutive for little island, namely *îlot*. The OE etymon *ieg* appears in our word *island*, originally Old English *ígland* or *íegland*.

Beck

In parts of Britain invaded and conquered by Vikings, beck is a still common name for a little stream or brook, from the language of the Vikings, Old Norse, where *beckr* is a rivulet, a creek, a rill. This Germanic etymon also shows up in the modern German word for stream, *Bach*. It's the source of the famous surname of the great family of composers, where a founding ancestor dwelt beside a stream and was thus, during the infancy of surname use, once dubbed perhaps, for example, *Fritz am Bach* 'that Fritz who lives beside the little creek.' To be at the beck and call of another person is an entirely different word root.

Brae

Now chiefly Scottish, *brae*, this word for the brow of a riverbank, brings a surprising bit of Viking poetic metaphor into Old Norse that we think of customarily as a dour, sour, glumly practical language like the Viking marauders who spoke it. In fact Old Norse *bra* meant eyebrow or eyelid. It is cognate with English *eyebrow*. Thus a brae was the eyebrow of a riverbank, the part that heaved up, swollen beside a flowing stream. Familiar in Robbie Burns "Ye banks and braes o' bonnie Doon" and the fine Scottish border ballad "Braes of Yarrow" where the braes are also called "the dowie dens" meaning in Scottish dialect "the dismal wooded valleys."

Fell

Hills in the north of England bear names often given these heights by Viking raiders. In Old Norse *fiall* and *fjall* and even today, in modern English *fell* in some northern British dialects, the word refers to a hill, mountain, moorland, upland pasture, wood thicket or highland plateau. So we meet Bowfell 'bowed or curved hill' and Seathwaite Fell. Some upland breeds of Scottish and northern English domestic animals have names like Rough Fell sheep and Fell ponies. In the Coniston Fells, slopes carry names like Tilberthwaite High Fell, Low Fell and Above Beck Fells. In the Lake District occur sports like fell running and fellwalking. Hiking or hillwalking are commoner terms.

Old Norse *fjall* is cognate and akin to modern German mountain words like *der Fels* 'rock' and *die Felsen* 'cliffs,' used in a large number of German alpine flower names, like the delightful name of one of the sedums, *Felsen-Fetthenne* 'mountain fat-hen' a cute little blue stonecrop for rocky soils.

Ghyll or Gill

Yet another Viking gift is the British geographic label, met frequently in Kent and Surrey, namely gill or ghyll, to name a short, narrow gully or valley, a wooded cleft forming the course of a stream, a ravine. Place names like Gillamoor might be a ravine on a moor. Dungeon Ghyll and Garrigill also lurk on the landscape. So do Troller's Gill, and Cowgill and Masongill, which rendered forth an English surname, Massingill, that became famous for the manufacture of douches.

Hythe

Queenhithe is a tiny street in London (EC4). Queenhithe trundles down to the north bank of the River Thames. Once it led to an important landing place where cargo-laden barges and small ships dropped anchor to bring food into the city. As old as Anglo-Saxon times, the London harbourage is mentioned in one of the charters of King Alfred the Great as early as 898 CE.

For five hundred years Queenhithe was the most important London wharf for the unloading of food, chiefly corn and fish. It was not called Queenhithe until early in the twelfth century when it became the property of the wife of King Henry I. Queen Matilda thus began a tradition that British queens could charge an unloading toll at Queenhithe (Queen's dock) and so they did for centuries. A few hundred years after Queen Matilda pocketed her last pence, the name was transferred from the pier to the little street leading down to and away from the landing.

Hyth is an Old English word for 'landing place,' now obsolete and surviving only in place names like Hythe Bridge at Oxford and Rotherhythe in southeast London, originally the site of a dock from which cattle (Old English *hryther* 'cattle') were put on barges and shipped across the Thames to the great market at Smithfield.

Hurst

Old English *hyrst* cognate with Old High German *hurst* 'wooded hill with sandy soil, thicket, sandbank with brushwood,' appears in dozens of British place names. Does an early visitor spot birds of prey circling over the heights of the hill? Perhaps a sound name would be Hawkhurst? Chislehurst names a wooded prominence with gravelly sand (Old English *cisel* 'gravel'). Ferniehirst may beckon with fresh green fern fronds lacy and feather-billowing in spring shade. Amherst might be 'near the hill' with Welsh *am* 'near' tacked on as prefix or with Gaelic *am* 'the,' Amherst might be THE Hill.

Tarn

American spookster scribe, Edgar Allan Poe, liked the ink-steeped tincture of the word *tarn*, as in these gloom-ridden lines of his poem "Ulalume."

"The skies they were ashen and sober;
The leaves they were crisped and sere—
The leaves they were withering and sere;
It was night in the lonesome October
Of my most immemorial year;
It was hard by the dim lake of Auber,

In the misty mid region of Weir—
It was down by the dank tarn of Auber,
In the ghoul-haunted woodland of Weir."

A tarn is a little lake, at some considerable elevation, with no tributaries leading to or out of the lakelet. It's yet another Viking gift to northern English from Old Norse *tjorn*. England's Lake District has a tiny body of water named Tarn Hows 'hills with tarns,' originally owned by the famous children's author Beatrix Potter and bequeathed by her to the National Trust as a park. It is open for tourists to visit and is one of the most scenic spots in "the Lakes." But do attend when clustered peasants of a simian persuasion are not gobbling Wimpyburgers, tossing Marmite cans into the lake or trading soccer scores as they swing through the smaller trees. Yes, I'm a dirty, rotten snob who loathes soccer yobbos. Sue me.

Toft

A toft is the site of a house including nearby fields and outbuildings, a Viking word, Old Norse *topt*, *tuft*, *tyft* meaning 'ground surrounding a house.' A British real estate and housing phrase 'toft and croft' once denoted an entire homestead, its main home and any adjoined arable land. It is frequent in British place names like Langtoft, Habertoft, Huttoft, Knaptoft, Lowestoft, Newtoft, Scraptoft, Sibbertoft, Stowlangtoft, Wibtoft, Yelvertoft. The last, Yelvertoft, means 'a home surrounded by elder trees.'

So let us now bring to cheerful stoppage our pleasant amble through the British countryside, imagining perhaps that we have been conveyed, if not by pone and trot, then by a dapper chestnut mare prancing sportively in front of our wicker *char-à-banc*, open-topped, leather-upholstered, with our fine selves lulled by champagne, say a Veuve-Clicquot Ponsardin Rosé, as well befits the pilgrimage of a summer afternoon.

Chapter 41

O Tenebrous Night, Descend not!

My first, personally important use of the noun 'night' occurred in Grade Seven, on an early dance date with a black-haired Russian girl, Natasha Noctambulovich. Rather a stern damsel she was, even for a champion female athlete (Grade Six Large Girls' Wrestling Queen). As we entered the school gym festooned with riant cardboard Santas and merry swags of red and green crepe paper, with Guy Lombardo's mucilaginous saxophone chorus of "White Christmas" playing on endless repeat for the Christmas upper school dance, I asked Natasha if we might get to first base that night. "*Nyet*, weasel!" she shoot back severely. "You, pipsqueak, will not even be permitted in stadium." It was only the next day that I learned Natasha's nickname among the other guys in Grade Seven was "She Who Walks by Night."

So early was a boy's somber murk of moonless night begloomed by sexless luck. So early did I learn that *nox pars obscura diei est* 'night is the doubtful part of the day.'

Night is an ancient Proto-Indo-European etymon, a usually monosyllabic husk of a word, Germanic in its inherited English form, but widely cognate throughout PIE language groups. Compare German *Nacht*, Old Swedish *natt*, ancient Greek *nyx, nyktos*, Latin *nox, noctis*, Sanskrit *nakti*, Old Church Slavonic *noshti*, Russian *noc'*, Lithuanian *naktis*, Albanian *nate*, French *nuit*, Italian *notte*, Spanish *noche*, Portuguese *noite* and Romanian *noapte*.

Vespers

Among the less frequent gems of nocturnal similitude (partial synonyms for "night") one of my favorites is Vespers. Vesper in the singular was first in English a simple classical name for the planet Venus when it appears after sunset during early evening hours in the westering twilight of nightfall. Vesper is the Evening Star, the one we wished upon in the familiar childhood nursery rhyme:

> Star light, star bright,
> First star I see tonight;
> I wish I may, I wish I might,
> Have the wish I wish tonight.

In the plural, Vespers is the Roman Catholic and Anglican sixth canonical hour, the time of evensong, a service of prayers, psalms and canticles, sometimes called choral evensong. Vesper is the Latin word for evening star or early evening or early in the night, cognate with the Greek *hesperos*.

Its lovely if uncommon adjective is vespertine 'coming in the evening, taking place at eventide.'

Zoology also boasts a derivative I like, namely the Latin word for bat, *vespertilio* literally 'little creature of the evening,' but today in modern zoological nomenclature *Vespertilio* (pl. *-iones*) is one of the many batty genera of Cheiroptera (Greek 'arm-wing').

Tenebrae

This Latin plural noun means 'darkness,' the many blacknesses of deep night. Pompous, silly, rare, obsolescent, but one of my pet night adjectives is tenebrous, with the stress on the first syllable as TEN-e-brus. Said aloud tenebrous has a felt-soft feel of velvet shrouds, of the matte dark of night. An even rarer agent noun is pure Latin and quite obscure in

English where *tenebrio* means 'lurker in the shadows of the night.'

Crepuscule

The crepuscular hour is twilight time when in the lyrics of The Platters' big 1950s hit song, "heavenly shades of night are falling." The founding etymon is Latin *creper* 'dark, dusky, twilit' so that the diminutive noun *crepusculum* is 'the time of little dusk,' that is twilight that precedes the lowering curtain of nightful nightfall.

To Lucubrate

Those of us who have written many books know this verb. To lucubrate is to work at night by means of artificial light, for the Romans perhaps a candle or small oil lamp, for us today electric light. I like one *Oxford English Dictionary* definition "to produce literary compositions by laborious study." The Latin verb *lucubrare* may indeed have *lux, lucis* Latin 'light' as its prime root but I am certain the verb appealed to ancient upper-class Roman ears because it appeared to contain both *lux* 'light' and some form like *cubital* 'little cushion for leaning on, propped up on one elbow, as one dictated prose to a copyist slave.'

And so, with that elitist vision of composing prose before us, I shall board the bobbing skiff of night, guide my little boat over nocturnal deeps and trust that a dawn wind shall spur the wee vessel into welcoming shallows along the shores of morning.

Chapter 42

Are They Culpable? Then, Guards, Seize Them!

English words and phrases from Latin culpa

Culpa meant in ancient legal Latin 'blame or fault.' Ecclesiastical Latin found the word in the classics and introduced it into the Roman Catholic Latin mass. There the priest, admitting sins, strikes his chest and calls out *"Mea culpa, mea culpa, mea maxima culpa"* 'By my fault, by my fault, by my most grievous fault.' The *mea culpa* is part of the *Confiteor* used at the beginning of Holy Mass and given at the end of this little note.

Also from the theological word hoard is a Latin phrase still in use: *felix culpa* "fortunate or happy fault" an apparent tragedy that yet ends happily.

Actions or persons worthy of legal blame or fault are still culpable, blameworthy, highly deserving punishment. One can almost see the vengeful spittle of magistrates gathering at the corners of mouths as judgment is pronounced. Does the amount of saliva secreted vary directly with the heft of the judicial chastisement? I imagine so.

Exculpatory

This adjective is still in wide use wherever the law is delivered in English, particularly in the common phrase "exculpatory evidence," that is, statements that intend to clear from legal guilt or blame an accused person, facts that vindicate an accused. The etymons are Latin prefix *ex-* 'away from, out of' + *culpa* 'blame,' hence 'delivering out of blame.'

Culprit

Culprit appears to be the ignorant error of a legal copyist who knew little Latin and scarcely more French or English. The word pops up suddenly in 1678 as an unlettered short form for culpable or Latin *culpabilis* 'guilty', abbreviated by some forlorn scribe as cul. prit. which in crappy Latin-French was supposed to mean 'ready to plead guilty.' To a prisoner indicted for high treason or felony, who pled not guilty, the clerk of the court said, "Culprit, how will you be tried?"

Coup

The many English uses of coup, like the word, were borrowed chiefly from French, where Old French forms like *cop, colp, coup* all descend from Latin *culpa* 'fault, blame, blow, strike.'

Coup d'état

Literally this French phrase means 'a blow of or to the state.' Such a coup is usually sudden, violent, illegal change to a legal government effected by persons outside the appointed or elected state powers.

Coup de grâce

More or less accurate movies about soldiers who desert ranks during war and are captured then shot by firing squad often show a "benevolent" executioner making his kindly way among the still-twitching, bullet-ripped and mortally wounded prisoners, taking out a revolver and shooting any still living wretch in the head. Such a pistol shot is called the *coup de grâce* or stroke of grace, stroke because at first the obliterative whack was a sword stroke several times on the dying person's neck. *Coup de grâce* is also used in the language of debate to describe an argument that settles with finality some disputed point.

Coup de soleil

This phrase is now obsolete but, once upon a queen, British writers of the Victorian era liked it in place of the — to them — infinitely more vulgar term "sunstroke." A peasant laborer might suffer a sunstroke, but a grande dame in her carriage and four would endure a much more cultured *coup de soleil*. Mind you, the duchess would still stagger into the parlour for a week or two with her upper-class brains fried to a crisp, but at least the cause would not be a malady of milady as lowly as prostration due to excessive physical work or inappropriate hot weather sent by God without consulting the gentry. How *infra dig.* that would be! And there's another Victorian fave phrase, pure Latin, an abbreviation of *infra dignitatem* 'beneath one's dignity.'

Coup de Foudre

This 'stroke of lightning' is rarer than the phrases already given. It refers to a sudden revelation, to surprisingly unforeseen happenstance, or even to love at first sight.

Chapter 43

What Vertigo & Impetigo
Share as Medical Words
a Latin suffix seen in English names of diseases

The technical names of diseases in English medicine are chiefly of Greek origin and thus their suffixation, for example *–osis* and *–itis*, is likewise of Greek provenance. Think of –osis, usually appended to a Greek word-root indicating a disordered condition. Arteriosclerosis has artery + Greek *skleros* 'hard'+ *-osis*, and means abnormal hardening or thickening of the walls of arteries. Nephrosis is any liver disease, but nephritis is any inflammation of the liver. *Thrombos* is a Greek word for blood clot. Thrombosis originally merely referred to the act of a fluid clotting. Then thrombosis acquired a strictly malignant sense. Thrombitis is the inflammation of a blood clot.

It will perhaps be useful to state the correct adjectives from these medical nouns, as they are often "ballsed up," even by learned doctors. Nephrosis denotes a nephrotic condition. Nephritis denotes a nephritic condition. In like manner, thrombotic and thombitic are the proper adjectival forms of thrombosis and thrombitis.

I Must Coin a New Medical Term

There is no current word in medical dictionaries that refers to the practice and science of making up names for diseases. Boldly I offer my neology: pathonym, of good classical Greek provenance from *pathos* 'disease' + *onyma* 'name.' The science of naming diseases would thus be pathonymy (pa-THON-i-mee). Thank you, O ghost of Hippocrates, father of medicine.

Latin Medical Suffix

Latin has a few medical suffixes too, but they are not as numerous in modern medical English as Greek suffixes like *–osis* and *–itis*. The most common Latin disease-indicating suffix is –igo as in vertigo, impetigo, intertrigo, porrigo and prurigo. Outside of medicine is a crop disease like rubigo and a disease of sheep called mentigo. *-Igo* tacked on to a Latin root usually implies physical weakness, deterioration, sickness. It is a marker of malady.

Vertigo

This is Latin for 'spinning around, feeling you are being twisted against your will, losing your balance in spite of how earnestly you attempt to walk upright and straight head. Vertigo names a symptom that may indicate any or several of a large number of adverse medical conditions. Vertigo is one of the Latin nouns from the common verb *vertere* 'to turn, to twist,' a verb that gives dozens of words in modern English. A vertex or a vortex may be the action or the spinning object itself, perhaps water. If we turn back to some abandoned practice, we revert to it. If you take up a new practice, we convert to it. If we go against normal practice, we pervert it. If we avoid the practice, we avert it.

Vertere Latin 'to turn' is a very old and very widespread root in Proto-Indo-European languages. Consider a language of ancient India where in Sanskrit *vartayati* means 'he turns.' In modern Russian *vertet* means 'to rotate.' German *werden* 'to become, to happen' is a related word or cognate. So is the English noun *worth*.

Impetigo

In wide use in medical English, impetigo names several usually mild diseases of the skin in which pustules arise. In general impetigo is completely manageable and without serious effects. But there is contagious impetigo, a once common malady of school classrooms, where high fever and other worrisome symptoms may occur. Impetiginous outbreaks and their indicia respond well to topical antibiotics. The Latin root is the Roman verb *impetere* 'to assail, to attack,' which gives English the adjective *impetuous*. So the malady was originally 'an attack of skin pustules.'

Lentigo

This is a Latin word for freckle. To the Romans, whose upper classes avoided the sun, a modest freckle was the size of a small bean or lentil. The Latin word for that tiny bean is *lens, lentis*. This also appeared to be the common size of the focusing part of the human eyeball, the lens. The little bean eventually took a diminutive of lens as its name in early French, hence *lentille* 'small bean,' from an unrecorded but supposed popular Late Latin form like **lenticula* and so today we have healthy lentil soup. Lentigo as a malady is usually a plethora of freckles on the face and hands. Only *lentigo maligna* may develop into cancer. Most freckles of a lentiginous nature are benign.

Shun the Sun, Honey Bun

I offer here a short note about the avoidance of the solar rays by upper-class Romans. One NEVER saw a Roman senator with a sun tan. Persons in the Roman empire who had a tan were slaves who worked in open fields. The wives and mistresses of rich freemen even applied a thick makeup made of white lead to give them a totally white face. This plumbous goop, together with lead water pipes from the aqueducts, caused thousands of ancient Romans to die young of lead poisoning.

Intertrigo

This word is rare but still used in the modern language of dermal pathology. It is a disorder, a skin inflammation caused by the rubbing of surface skin against other skin, for example the chafing of a man's scrotal skin rubbing against the skin of his fat thighs or pudgy legs. The supposed Latin verbal root is *interterere 'to rub against each other,' with the Latin prefix *inter* 'among, in between, closely aligned.'

Prurigo

A truly nasty-sounding medical word in English and in its native Latin, prurigo has a basic meaning of itching, wanting to scratch, even of a sexual itch to copulate, hence our English adjective prurient 'appealing to sexual interests, dirty'. However, in English medical terminology, prurigo is a dermatosis, a chronic skin disorder with very itchy papules and nodules, sometimes filled with pus. The common malady is pruritus mitis, a mild type; the rarer form is the very severe pruritus ferox. The therapies for pruriginous afflictions are complex and do not always give relief. In some cases, antihistamines and emollients offer temporary benefit. Other trickier drugs like Doxepin and Mirtazapine may be more helpful. *Prurire* is a Latin verb meaning 'to itch.'

Porrigo

This affliction denotes a number of scaly, flaky conditions of the scalp, like ringworm. But even the scurf of common dandruff is porriginous. The word is a direct borrowing from classical Latin where *porrigo* means 'scurf, scaly flakes in the scalp hair, dandruff.'

Furfur

However a much better 'scratchy' Latin word for dandruff, also still in English nomenclature, is *furfur* Latin 'bran' or 'bran-like bits of epidermal scurf flaked off as symptoms in crusty afflictions of scalp skin.' Should a satirist want to refer, perhaps in a comic manner, to someone suffering obvious dandruff, the satirist could do worse than referring to a person's "furfuraceous noggin."

Mentigo

Now we attend to animal diseases. Mentigo is a disease of sheep where symptomatic scabs, sores and eruptions cluster on the lips and mouths of infected sheep. The word meant exactly the same thing to ancient Roman farmers and it is mentioned in one of the few agricultural handbooks in classical Latin still extant, *Res rustica* 'Country Matters' by Columella. It may be derived from the Latin word for chin *mentum* + *-igo*, the disease-naming suffix we are discussing here.

Rubigo

Plagues of planted fields now concern us as we touch upon botanical blights and contagions of greenery. Rubigo means 'crop rust' or 'crop blight' in classical Latin. In the English vocabulary of plant diseases, rubiginous fungal infections include smut and mildews, particularly of cereal grains. The root is the common Latin adjective for the color red: *ruber, rubra, rubrum*. That etymon gives us the word that names sentences printed in red ink to make them stand out from the ordinary text of a printed page, and that term is *rubric*.

Tentigo

We must not neglect sexual terms. Nor may we fail to appease those of my readers who want a truly obscure word to test their verbivore friends. Literally *tentigo* means tenseness, from the Latin verb *tendo, tendere, tetendi, tentum* 'to stretch, to extend, to erect.' But there is a specific reference, namely tenseness of the human penis, that is, an erection. Tentigo means priapism, an erection that lingers too long. You've probably seen and heard the TV ads for drugs that treat erectile dysfunction. One of those ads has a helpful voice-over that says "For an erection lasting longer than a few hours, see your doctor." I always think the ad should add: "And, for God's sake, men, see your tailor!"

Chapter 44

Siren

One Word's Many Changes of Meaning through History
from Singing Fish to Cop-Car Horn to Fire-Truck Alarm

The Sirens (Greek *Seirenes*) first lure sailors to their briny doom by enchanted singing in the Homeric hexameters of the Greek home-quest poem, *The Odyssey*. The Romans borrowed the word to give the Latin *Siren* and subsequent Romance-language derivatives like Italian and Spanish *sirena,* French *sirène*, and Old French *sereine* and *seraine*, the source of the earliest English forms like *sereyn, serayn, serayne, seryne* and *syraine*.

Seiren, as the word first appears in Homer, may be derived from Greek *seira* 'rope' (Ionic Greek *seire* 'rope') from an Indo-European etymon *sei 'to bind' as in the Sanskrit *syati* 'he ties, he binds.' So siren might mean 'binder', she-demon who ropes men into her spell. She's a spellbinder.

Vocalizing Evocatrix

From first naming a vocalizing evocatrix, descanting doom to naïve mariners, the word *siren* came to mean enchantress and then, in the nineteenth century, it named a French musical instrument used in acoustic measurement. From there the semantics leapt to a high-pitched foghorn used on steamships to give warnings. Hopping back to land in the twentieth century, siren named piercing air-raid warning horns and the sirens on police vehicles and fire trucks.

The Founding Story

The "Sirens" passage in Book 12 of *The Odyssey* by Homer is short. Here's the set-up translated by Samuel Butler. Odysseus (Ulysses) quotes the good/bad witch Circe, as she gives Odysseus tips on surviving forthcoming perils: "'So far so good,' said Circe, when I had ended my story, 'and now pay attention to what I am about to tell you—heaven itself, indeed, will recall it to your recollection. First you will come to the Sirens who enchant all who come near them. If anyone unwarily draws in too close and hears the singing of the Sirens, his wife and children will never welcome him home again, for they sit in a green field and warble him to death with the sweetness of their song. There is a great heap of dead men's bones lying all around, with the flesh still rotting off them. Therefore pass these Sirens by, and stop your men's ears with wax that none of them may hear; but if you like you can listen yourself, for you may get the men to bind you as you stand upright on a cross piece half way up the mast, and they must lash the rope's ends to the mast itself, that you may have the pleasure of listening. If you beg and pray the men to unloose you, then they must bind you faster."

Possible Meaning of the Incident in the Poem

During the ordeal, Odysseus almost goes crazy pining, lusting, to follow the sirens' obscene melodies of death. So there it is, one of the best known episodes in *The Odyssey*. The wise poet Homer puts focus on a simple human truth: mankind will always struggle when he desires something whose appeal is fatal but almost irresistible. Homer here also seems skeptical about searching too ardently after divine and otherworldly things. True, the siren song may be a musical passageway to a titillating new plane of existence. But such pathways ooze danger for the heedless neophyte and are worth avoiding. What if, new-found paradise gained, tasted and rejected, the sated newbie turns to go back and finds the gate to home forever locked? As the Greeks always said, even in their folksy everyday sayings: "The middle way is best." Over the entrance to the temple of Apollo at Delphi loomed this wise advice: *Medèn agan* "Do nothing in excess."

James Joyce's Sirens

Many artists and writers throughout western history have borrowed Homer's *femmes fatales.* Among other tropes and memes, James Joyce's novel *Ulysses* employs a satiric and symbolic scene of Sirens. Befitting Joyce's proletarian schema, his sirens are two Dublin barmaids who partially seduce the hero and his companions.

The Coen brothers' 2000 film, *O Brother, Where Art Thou?* was loosely based on Homer's *Odyssey* and featured a scene of sirens, in this cinematic case a trio of provocatively clad southern laundry women cooing lustfully as they laved their lusciousness in a summer stream.

Symbolism in the Homeric Tale

The story was very common on ancient painted Greek vases where Odysseus is shown tied to the mast of his ship as his companions row. The rigid phallic mast bound with tight leather straps symbolizes the penile restraint Odysseus must adopt to survive, as sirens, in vulture swoop, flit about him, crooning allurement in lullabies of moribund lust. Of course, in the original Homeric poem, the sirens do not fly at all or go out to sea. Instead, hissing oblivion, they crouch in blood-damp meadows singing amidst the rotting corpses of the yokels whom they have lured to soggy, gut-ripped death.

Chapter 45

Woods Words

To paraphrase that well-known nursery song: if you go down in the woods today, you'll find a bounty of equivalence in wood words. Indeed, were I not a quasi-Quaker-like devotee of plain speech and unadorned verbal simplicity, I might say you will encounter a plethoric copiosity of sylvan synonymy.

Most pertly shall I treat these less than customary words for woodland, terms like spinney, frith or firth, bosk, weald, dingle and chaparral. If you know all these ligneous lexemes well, then, *mes élèves*, you may leave the classroom and play with utter abandon upon the margins of that sinkhole out in the recess yard.

Bosk, Bosky, Boscage, Bosquet

The basic etymon here arose in the speech of Roman soldiers posted to defend Rome's northern Gallic territories, where they used a Late Street Latin adjective, the commonly spoken adjective meaning 'wooden' or 'made of wood,' *boscus, bosca, boscum*. This is an example of Latin borrowing a term from a foreign language that was not Greek. *Boscus* is a Latinizing of a Frankish (a Germanic language) word for woods or forest *busk related to a much later Germanic form, namely our English word *bush*.

Perhaps the most interesting derivative is one of our English verbs whose prime and sensuous meaning is 'to spring out of wooded cover and attack someone from a hiding place," that is, *to ambush*.

A bosk is a thicket of underwood. Bosk, busk and bush are still in vibrant use in various English dialects. Boscage is merely the Old French term from a recorded Late Latin extension, *boscaticum*, still lurking in modern Italian as *boscaggio*. Bosket and bosquet are French borrowings from *boscetto*, an Italian diminutive of *bosco* 'woods.' The two diminutive forms usually named a plantation of trees within a garden or arboretum.

Chaparral

My acquaintance with this word began with a TV western titled "High Chaparral," broadcast between 1967 and 1971, starring Leif Erickson and Cameron Mitchell as members of a family with a ranch in Arizona. Chaparral as a word arose in Spain to describe tangled brushwood of almost impenetrable dwarf evergreen oaks, bramble-choked thickets so dense with thorns and briars that a man on horseback could not ride through the poor, dry scrub. *Chaparro* is Spanish for a kind of dwarf, evergreen oak. Castilian Spanish borrowed the word from Basque where *txapar* 'little thicket' is a diminutive form of Basque *sapar* 'dry heath, scrubland.' The suffix *–al* is common in Spanish to name a grove of trees, e.g. Spanish *almendral* 'almond tree grove,' Spanish *parral* 'vinyard,' Spanish *cafetal* 'coffee plantation.' Parts of the northern Mediterranean littoral are chaparral and so are areas of Mexico's northern Baja peninsula, and parts of California, New Mexico, Texas and Arizona. Chaparral is highly subject to summertime, drought-induced wildfires.

Chase

From the verb *to chase* animals while hunting them, a noun arose naming a hunting-ground or unenclosed land for breeding then hunting wild animals. The most known to English history is Chevy Chase, in a Border song entitled "The Ballad of Chevy Chase." The story takes place on stretch of hunting land in the Cheviot Hills, hence Chevy Chase. The owner of the land, the Scottish Earl of Douglas, had forbidden the English to hunt there. But English Percy, Earl of Northumberland, rode out to hunt and was caught in the banned venery. In the ensuing *mêlée,* dozens of combatants had their noggins cracked open by claymores or were disemboweled by the deft slice of a honed halberd.

The American comedian Cornelius Crane Chase uses, as his showbiz moniker, Chevy Chase.

Coppice & Copse

Coppice and its later syncopated form *copse* stem from Old French *copeiz* 'cut wood' from the Latin verb *colpare* 'to cut with the stroke of an ax, to chop down.' A copse is a small woodlot where the trees are planted specifically for later harvesting.

Dingle

The word is best known to readers of Charles Dickens first loose novel, *The Pickwick Papers* (1832) as the residence of the spinster Rachael Wardle who lives at Dingley Dell manor. Dingle meaning a deep dell with trees appears in the thirteenth century with that meaning but any earlier root is quite unknown.

Firth was First; Frith Second

Firth, an Old Germanic root apparently meaning 'deer-forest, hunting-ground' appears first in English. Then firth suffered a slight, metathetic, vowel-consonant interchange to frith. Today it is chiefly met by students and scholars encountering general woodland phrases in older poetry: "in firth and fell, through firth and field, o'er firth and fold." Firth meaning a body of water stems from a quite different word borrowed from the Vikings.

Spinney

A spinney was a small clump of trees planted or set aside on a landed estate to protect game-birds raised to be slaughtered for the lords' and ladies' hunting delight and sometimes for their nourishment. The word arose in Old French as *espinei* (modern French *épinaie)* 'thorny place, bramble bush,' from Latin *spina* 'prickle, spine.'

Weald

Weald is an Old English word for forest. Today it is chiefly a specific British place name. The Weald is the name of a large tract of once-wooded countryside comprising parts of Sussex, Surrey and Kent lying between the North and South Downs.

Wold

Wooded upland or general forest land, wold is a direct descendant of Old English *wald* 'forest,' utterly Germanic. Compare the modern German word for forest, *Wald.* The term is frequent in British place names: The Yorkshire Wolds and the Cotswolds' delightful market village, Stow-on-the-Wold in Gloucestershire.

As a suitable exitus from this sylvan scene, I summon the entire family to gather at the edge of the oak grove which begirds stately Casselman manor, there to recite in unison the opening verse of Henry Wadsworth Longfellow's *Introduction to Evangeline* (1847).

"This is the forest primeval. The murmuring
pines and the hemlocks,
Bearded with moss, and in garments green,
indistinct in the twilight,
Stand like Druids of eld, with voices sad and
prophetic..."

Hey, you! Yes, you druid of eld, I see you trying to slip
away to avoid the Longfellow recitation. Is that purloined
mistletoe hidden in your robe? You won't reach the portcullis,
dude. Guards, seize him!

Chapter 46

Tarragon: Its Spicy Word Origin

Over many swards of the awakening world, spring, the bud-tide, the flood tide of shy green, bids us pot up herbs and spices and look to grow them on sun-warmed sills. A wee sprig of potted tarragon may beckon us at the greenhouse, as it did me. When I looked at tarragon's official botanical name, I saw a little dragon and was charmed.

Tarragon the spice belongs to the wormwood family of plants, whose genus name is *Artemisia*. Tarragon's botanical binomial is *Artemisia dracunculus* 'the little dragon of the Artemisia family.' I'll explain that name below.

This "plant of Artemis" bears the name of the Greek goddess of hunting and chastity, equivalent to the Roman divinity of the hunt, archer-queen Diana. Artemisios was the name of a spring month in ancient Sparta and in Macedonia, the time of the year when good hunting could once again be resumed after the rigor and scarcity of winter. The species of Artemisia native to Greece bloomed as hunters returned to the woods and mountains, after a prayer to the goddess of the hunt, Artemis.

Is Tarragon a Mourning Herb?

A secondary possibility is an origin of the plant in the name of the mourning wife of King Mausolus of Caria. Her name was Artemisia and she so loved her dead husband that she superintended at Halicarnassus the building of an elaborate tomb for him, which became one of the seven wonders of the ancient world, known as the Mausoleum. This story was widely known in antiquity, quoted by Cicero and Pliny, from older Greek sources. Some species of artemisia look distinctly droopy and mournful, particularly in bloom. Most species have a silvery-whitish coating on the leaves. It may be recalled that a frequent token of mourning in many ancient Mediterranean countries was for members of the funeral party to pat flour on their faces and not remove it until the burial or cremation had occurred. Could such people have seen in these old Greek "Dusty Miller" species, a sign of floury mourning ritual?

Tarragon and other species of Artemisia belong to the largest plant family Compositae, the daisy family, named from the Latin adjective *compositus* 'placed together,' referring to the compound flowers of its members. Small florets of individual flowers make up large clusters or heads.

Etymology of the Word *Tarragon*

That most essential herb of French cookery, known as French tarragon, is *Artemisia dracunculus*. The specific means 'little dragon,' a reference to the complicated etymology of tarragon. It seems to be something like this: Greek *drakon* 'dragon' > Arabic *tarkhon* 'dragon' and this herb > Medieval Greek *tarkhon* (the word borrowed back into Greek) > Old French *tarchon* > Modern French *estragon* > Modern English *tarragon*. Fascinating, but why is the plant associated with dragons? Did ancient herbal folklore think a nosegay of tarragon leaflets would fend off those nasty fire-breathers? Perhaps. But I can find no cogent source.

Other Artemisia Species

From *Artemisia absinthium* a green French liqueur flavoured with oil of wormwood was once distilled. So potent and addictive was absinthe its manufacture was banned. It is made today in France but is only a pallid ghost of its original.

A common garden plant of silvery-powdered foliage is Dusty Miller, known in the greenhouse as *Artemisia stelleriana* named after Georg Wilhelm Steller (1709-1746), a German collector of botanical and zoological specimens who discovered the species in Siberia.

Along the Sagebrush Trail, *Pardner*

Another of the Artemisia tumbles through cowboy movies as sagebrush, pesky weed of the West. Well, it used to be an Artemisia but has been redubbed, reclassified and given its own little genus and now bears the splendidly upscale moniker, *Seriphidium tridentatum. Tridentatus* is botanical Latin for three-toothed, said of the leaves.

The unlovely-named mugwort is also an Artemisia. Mugwort was *mycge-wyrt* in Old English, that is, 'midge-plant,' hence a vermifuge, a plant that keeps away midges, tiny gnat-like insects. This yellow-flowered *Artemisia vulgaris* (Latin not vulgar but 'common') is native to Eurasia but has been naturalized in North America where it is often a troublesome weed.

But now I head for my kitchen to toss freshly crinkled tarragon leaves into a mortar and pestle, grin them up to release their savour and mush them into a slab of butter. Later I shall slather tarragon butter on whole grain bread hot from the toaster!

Chapter 47

Water in Motion: Words like Tide

Good Tidings

In Old English the rise and fall of the sea was NOT called tide. The rise of tide was called *flod*. Consider the later compound *floodtide*. The fall of tide was called *ebba*. Consider its later compound *ebbtide*. Following its Germanic cognates, one of which is the modern German word *die Zeit* 'the time,' the Old English word *tíd* meant 'a point in time, due time, fixed time.' Only later, by about 1340 CE, did the English word *tide* come to signify the inflow and outflow of moon-and-sun-drawn waters. Possibly English borrowed the meaning from a Middle Low German form like *getide* or Middle Dutch *ghetide*.

As to neaptide, the origin is lost. *The Oxford English Dictionary* offers however one of the clearest definitions of neaptide "Designating or relating to a tide occurring just after the first or third quarters of the moon, when the high-water level is lowest and there is least difference between high- and low-water levels."

A Favorite Verb of Mine

One of my pet water-in-motion words is sluice. One of America's best comic writers was S. J. Perlman, a word master who once described taking a drink of whiskey as "sluicing the larynx." Perlman liked the evasive, placid slippage implied in the verb, with its quasi-onomatopoeic sound. But in fact *sluice*, noun and verb, is not an imitation of water rushing out of a gate, but is ultimately from the Latin past participle *exclusus* 'shut out, cut off' referring to the gate or valve in a sluice which permits the held-back or cut-off water to flow through the gate at a rate determined by the operator of the sluice-gate.

A sluice is a water dam with an adjustable gate, used particularly in irrigation and in gold mining. Its trip from Latin into English featured a sojourn in Old French as *escluse* (modern French *écluse*). When it was borrowed into the Germanic languages, the word usually lost its hard /c/ and became Middle Dutch *slues,* Dutch *sluis,* West Frisian *slus*, Low German *sluse,* modern German *Schleuse,* English sleuss, sleuse, slewse, slowese, slus, sluice and finally sluice.

The Most Obscure Water-Movement Word

As we climb the sheer cliff face of new-word acquisition, sometimes we must look down and cast a rope back into the cave of obsolete terms and rescue a word from the oblivion of desuetude. Desuetude means 'passing into a state of disuse, lack of use' from Latin *desuescere* 'to not use anymore' = *de* Latin negative prefix + *suescere* 'to do customarily.' Such a cast-off gem is the verb *to disembogue*.

Disembogue? Said of a river or lake, to disembogue (dis-em-BOAG) means 'to empty itself into' or 'to flow out of the mouth of a river into the sea or some larger body of water.' The verb may reverse direction also and be used of the sea disemboguing into a narrow creek or as tidal wash flowing up a rivulet.

Yes, I admit that disembogue is now obsolete. Today writers might use the verb *to debouch* 'to issue forth from a confined space into a wider space,' as a river at its estuary might issue forth into a larger body of water like a lake or sea. It's French from *déboucher* which contains *la bouche* 'the mouth;' other meanings include unblock, uncork, unstop, break cover.

Disembogue was borrowed into Elizabethan English around 1595 CE from Spanish *desembocar* 'to come out of the mouth of a river,' its Spanish etymology consisting of *des, a* Spanish intensive, privative prefix that takes the Spanish verb *embocar* and as *desembocar* makes it mean 'flow out of the mouth greatly.' *Embocar* 'to put into the mouth' = Spanish *en* 'in' + Spanish *boca* 'mouth' from Latin *bucca* 'cheek, mouth' as in the English medical and dental adjective *buccal* 'pertaining to the cheek.'

Originally pertaining to rivers, disembogue's meaning was broadened and generalized by some writers during the 18th and 19th centuries. They used the verb to mean 'pour forth' and 'emerge' and 'empty into.'

We kissed goodbye to this cute little verb in 1871 CE, when, according to the Oxford English Dictionary, it made a last appearance in print in a poem by Robert Browning. But disembogue merits revival because it aptly imitates the discharge of some polluted, sluggish, semi-liquid glop into a vast receptacle. One might think of Canada's polluting tar sands as they disembogue into pipelines that used to carry ecotoxic Canadian sludge toward American refineries. Thick cough syrup may disembogue into a spoon held up to the revolted face of a croupy child.

Maelstrom!

This great word, in modern Dutch *maalstroom*, now in English *maelstrom* once referred to a specific whirlpool located off the coast of Norway on Dutch shipping maps. Its origin features the Dutch verb *malen* (German *mahlen*) 'to grind up, to turn around quickly (said of roiling sea currents and even of millstones grinding wheat) combined with Dutch *stroom* 'stream.'

Bill Casselman

The Maelstrom was a funnel of doom, sucking into its pelagic vortex all vessels who sailed too near its ship-splitting constrictor gyres.

Now our water words trickle into defunct eddies and in pools disperse. Long combers of oblivion now carry this verbal spate far out to sea.

Chapter 48

Sheriff: Medieval Etymology of a Modern Word

From old western movies, how well we know the hornswoggler, the lily-livered, yellow-bellied sheriff, a stumblebum drunk, a pissed-his-pants, chicken-hearted fraidy-cat, his mustache twitching in fear and greed. Yeah, it's that new lawman fresh off the boat from Holland, that new sheriff, one Perk van der Graft, who is in league with the cattle baron who rules the town of Horse-Puke Gulch, Oklahoma Territory.

Nor, in movie oaters, are sheriff's deputies cut from cleaner cloth. His helpers include the always dodgy Mel E. Factor and his Mexican helper Porcito Sánchez de Payola. The baron's theme song might be a take on that old Bob Marley/Eric Clapton hit. The baron might sing "I *bought* the sheriff." To a man the copper badges of these proud do-badders are tarnished with that commonplace green-black patina, the verdigris of malfeasance.

Tarnished tin stars or not, partners, we may not know that the word *sheriff* is a grammatical contraction of the Old English compound agent noun *scírgeréfa* 'shire-reeve.'

The reeve of a shire was the king's representative who carried out royal orders in ancient British counties including executing the law and supervising the collection of punitive taxes.

Shire stems from Old High German *scira* 'official charge, care of an activity,' probably cognate with Latin *cura* 'care.'

Reeve was *geréfa* in Old English, possibly related to Old English *rof* 'number, row,' but otherwise of obscure origin.

Shires

British historian Peter Ackroyd offers a succinct introduction to shires in his *Foundation: The History of England from its Earliest Beginnings to the Tudors* (St. Martin's Press, NY, 2012), 71-72. This excellent new panorama is the first of Ackroyd's upcoming four-volume history of the nation. By the tenth century "the country was divided into shires, hundreds and vills or townships, precisely in order to expedite taxation. The shires of England were unique, their boundaries lasting for more than a thousand years... The earliest of them date from the late seventh and early eighth centuries, but many of their borders lie further back in the shape of Iron Age tribal kingdoms. . . Each shire had a court . . . and was ruled on behalf of the king by a shire-reeve whose name became sheriff."

Disambiguation

The English word *sheriff* has no connection with sharif, shareef, an Arabic adjective meaning 'noble.' Shereef is a Sunni honorific noun in Islam naming a descendant of the prophet Muhammed through his daughter Fatima. Ashraf (masc. plural of sharif) are entitled to wear a green turban or veil. The verbal root of the word is expressed as *sharafa* 'to be exalted, to be high-born.' The western sheriff is usually pronounced [CHER-if] while the Arabic sharif is usually pronounced [shaw-REEF].

Now, vamoose, git, you varmints, else — I warrant — I'll have Deputy Abner see if the sheriff's sober. And — I swan — sheriff'll mess you up!

Chapter 49

Words of Wonder

"WHY! Who makes much of a miracle?
As to me, I know of nothing else but miracles."

— Walt Whitman

Has a moment of the miraculous ever befallen you? I don't mean a wonderment as prodigious as tall tales from the ancient Near East, such as people arising from the dead, such as when Uncle Ned sits up from the coffin at his wake and starts singing "Take me out to the ball game." No, nothing so vulgar. I mean a day, an hour, a mere breath-stealing second when scientific conduits of daily life plug up and the pleasing flow of "common-sense" experience is clogged.

You, a sceptic about ghosts, suddenly see a long-dead friend buying his favourite scotch at the liquor store. A second look shows you the person bears only the faintest resemblance to your dead friend. But, for those milliseconds of phantasmal similitude, dread constricts your heart. Lubb-dup. Lubb-dup.

We undergo life marvels often, more than are comfortable to acknowledge. Suddenly we perceive a mis-stitching in the fabric of our universe. All the twirlings, neural and subatomic, which revolve to produce the illusion of our lives go suddenly awry. The spindle slips. Its axis skids askew. There occurs a perturbation in the diurnal vortices, when all the little revolvings and spinnings and elliptical orbits are suddenly out of their ordained order. The weft and warp that weave our life-loom fall into misalliance. Bobbins wobble. Skeins of existential yarn unravel. The everyday tapestry of comfort wears thin. A tachycardia of fear out-thumps calm normalcy.

Pondering such thaumaturgical instances made me begin to wonder about the very word *wonder* and its synonyms.

Wondrous Etymology

The old Proto-Germanic and Scandic noun appears first in Old High German as *Wunter*, Low German *wunner*, from its Proto-Indo-European etymon **wundra*, its PIE verbal stem **wen* 'to wish for, to strive for, to win.' Reflexes appear as Old Norse *undr*, Danish and Swedish *under*, Old English *wundor*, modern English *wonder*, Dutch *wonder*.

Modern German loves the sound, and it is still productive in new countless compounds, and old ones: *bewundern, Weltwunder, wunderbar, Wunderheiler, Wunderkind, Wunderland* and *Wunderwaffe*.

The lucky ones among us can say with Miranda in William Shakespeare's *The Tempest*:

> "O, wonder!
> How many goodly creatures are there here!
> How beauteous mankind is! O brave new world,
> That has such people in't."

Miracle

This word is in Old French and Anglo-Norman by 1050 CE from its classical Latin form *miraculum* 'object of wonder' used by Christian writers extensively from the thirteenth century onwards. Its ultimate etymon is the Old Latin adjective *mirus* 'wonderful, whence also the common deponent verb *mirari* 'to wonder at, to ponder, to examine.' Modern Romance reflexes include Spanish *milagro* and Italian *miracolo*.

Surprisingly *miraculum* is rare in the great Latin version of the Bible, St. Jerome's Vulgate, where the Latin words *signum* (a sign*)*, *prodigium* (a prodigy) and *virtus* are employed to translate New Testament koine Greek words like *semion* 'sign, *teras* 'wonder', and *dynamis* 'power' or 'mighty work.'

Quiet, Please! Thaumaturge at Work

Also rare in the Greek version of the Bible is a common Attic Greek word for marvel or wonder, namely *thauma, thaumatos* literally 'something to gape in astonishment at,' considering its source in the Greek verb *thaumazein*. Thus a thaumaturge is a miracle-worker, a doer of wonders and matters thaumaturgical.

Rachel Carson, the great writer who helped awaken us to the earthly threat of pollution, also wrote a keen little volume entitled *The Sense of Wonder*: "If I had influence with the good fairy who is supposed to preside over the christening of all children I should ask that her gift to each child in the world be a sense of wonder so indestructible that it would last throughout life, as an unfailing antidote against the boredom and disenchantments of later years, the sterile preoccupation with things artificial, the alienation from the sources of our strength."

Marvel

This word stems from the same Latin roots as miracle. Marvel entered English with the Normans by 1050 CE from some Old French form like *merveille* or *marvaille*, itself from a classical Latin plural *mirabilia* 'things to wonder at, miracles' from the verb *mirari*.

Wonderful Quotations

"Wonder is the beginning of wisdom."
— Socrates

"The invariable mark of wisdom is to see the miraculous in the common."
— Ralph Waldo Emerson

"I would rather have a mind opened by wonder than one closed by belief."
— Gerry Spence, *How to Argue & Win Every Time: At Home, At Work, In Court, Everywhere, Everyday*

Chapter 50

Ridiculous Words like Ridibund & Rident

Risus Sardonicus

The phrase is Late Latin and means 'sardonic laughter.' The term arose in seventeenth-century descriptions of the symptoms of tetanus, specifically the rigid smirk caused by a spasm of the facial muscles in tetanus and other diseases and sometimes seen post-mortem in the faces of the deceased.

Sardonicus is a Latin adjective borrowed from a Greek adjective meaning 'Sardinian, from the island of Sardinia,' which in later Greek was confused with a similar adjective *sardanios*, descriptive epithet of bitter or scornful laughter. The motive of the substitution was the notion that the word had primary reference to the effects of eating a 'Sardinian plant' (Latin *herba Sardonia* or *Sardoa*), which was said to produce facial convulsions resembling horrible laughter, usually followed by death. So says *The Oxford English Dictionary.*

Ridibund

This frolicsome tidbit of adjectival rarity means 'abounding in smiles and laughter.' It might be useful in a stern putdown of undue frivolity by some sour-cheeked killjoy teacher. "Class, the hilarity shall cease. Let us now rid ourselves of all that is ridibund." *Ridibundus* 'laughing' is an adjective of abundance from the Latin *ridere* 'to laugh' and the verbal- adjective suffix *–bundus* 'abounding in, characterized by.'

193

The Laughing Gull

The word is also seen in the specific part of the ornithological name of the black-headed gull, *Chroicocephalus ridibundus*, also called the black-headed gull. This is a noisy species, especially in colonies, with a familiar "kree-ar" call. In the exquisitely written animal fantasy *Watership Down* by Richard Adams, one of the characters is Kehaar, a black-headed gull. Author Adams coined his name based on one of the bird's familiar calls. In the animated film Kehaar was voiced memorably by Zero Mostel, the original Tevye in the Broadway musical "Fiddler on the Roof." The gull's genus name *Chroicocephalus* is derived from Greek *chroa* 'color' + Greek *cephalus* 'head.' The Latin shows up in the French name of this gull species: *Mouette rieuse*. *Rieux* is a French adjective meaning 'laughing.'

Rident

This adjective means 'radiantly cheerful,' from the Latin present participle *ridens, ridentis* 'laughing' from *ridere* 'to laugh.'

Ridicule

This is a diminutive form seen in classical Latin as *ridiculum* 'little object of derision or laughter, a jest, a joke, with its later developed senses of 'a thing mocked' or 'the action of mocking someone or something.'

The Anatomy of a Smile: The Risorius Muscle:

In its original anatomical Latin coined in 1724 as *musculus risorius*, the name stemmed from the classical Latin agent noun *risor* 'one who laughs, laugher.' Humans usually have two risorius muscles, one at each corner of the mouth. When we smile the risorii draw the mouth laterally, to stretch the cheek flesh and pull the smiling mouth apart in a customary grin. The risorius is a muscle that varies in size and may even be absent at birth, forecasting a rather glum-faced visage for the human who lacks it.

And we'll grin our way out of this note with a wreath of 'smile' sayings:

In *Othello*, Shakespeare wrote "The robbed [person] that smiles, steals something from the thief."

"Don't cry because it's over, SMILE because it happened." – Dr. Seuss

"She gave me a smile I could feel in my hip pocket." – Raymond Chandler. This same writer-dispenser of oinky tough-guy lines wrote "She had a chassis that would make an archbishop kick a hole in a stained-glass window."

"The man who smiles when things go wrong has thought of someone to blame it on." – Robert Bloch

"Start every day with a smile and get it over with." – W.C. Fields

"The teeth are smiling, but is the heart?" African Proverb

Chapter 51

Swag, Pelf, Lucre & Raven:
words for dishonest gain & ill-gotten goods

Swag

I love the sound of the word *swag*, with its sonic burden of heavy golden boodle distending a thief's fat sack as he scurries away under the muffling quilt of night. Farewell, my silver teaspoons!

This bold word for plunderer's booty seems Scandinavian in origin. Actually it is an instance of two separate words blending. Swag is directly related to *sway* which verb contains echoes of other verbs, namely both weigh and sway. Swag weighs down a thief's coin-rich bag and makes it sway? Possibly. There are Norwegian dialect words like *svagga* and *svaga* 'to sway.' And most English speakers know Australia's national song, "Waltzing Matilda" and the happy hobo of its opening lyrics, who packs his sleeping bag and total worldly belongings in a swag and hits the road:

> "Once a jolly swagman camped by a billabong
> Under the shade of a coolibah tree,
> And he sang as he watched and waited till his billy boiled
> 'Who'll come a-Waltzing Matilda, with me?'"

Pelf

It means 'stolen goods, obscene riches, filthy lucre." This terse relative of the words *pilfer* and *pilferer* is one of my cherished monosyllabic nouns. The clawed hand of a miser's clutch grasps the word itself. Yes, I hold it to my word-heart as a toothless beldam, alive but embalmed in black bombazine, might press a defunct lapdog to her withered dugs and force a niece to pry it from yellowed fingernails. Pelf has been lurking in English since the Norman Conquest. In Anglo-Norman it was *pelfre* 'ill-gotten boodle,' perhaps an altered version of *felpe, ferpe, frepe,* ancient French words for 'old clothes, rags.'

Happily do I quote a Canadian poet, E. J. Pratt, who wrote in "Towards the Last Spike": "At least they knew His personal pockets were not lined with pelf, Whatever loot the others grabbed."

Two Obsolete Synonyms for *Plunder*

1. Direption came into fifteenth-century English from its proximate etymon, a French form, *la direption*, itself borrowed from a classical Latin noun *direptio, direptionis* 'a laying waste, a tearing down.' At first in English, direption was a military term that meant 'sacking a town;' then, like many nouns of destruction, it gained semantic amplitude, and came to refer to pillaging on a broader scale, such as laying waste an entire country.

2. Reiving and to reive are active and frequent in current Scottish English. The agent noun was given briefly renewed life in World English by its use in the title of William Faulkner's last novel, published in 1962, *The Reivers*. It was made into a fair-to-middlin' movie starring Steve McQueen.

To reave is related to the commoner English verb to rob, itself cognate with Modern German *rauben* and Dutch *roven* 'to steal, to plunder, to despoil,' their ultimate

Proto-Indo-European etymon the same base as Latin *rumpere* 'to break' and Sanskrit *rupyati* 'it really hurts.'

The Oxford English Dictionary cites this tasty March 1999 quotation from a Scottish newspaper, *The Glasgow Herald*: "To have a team called the Edinburgh Reivers is nonsense, as nobody from Edinburgh ever reived."

Reive is a popular verb to use in rhyming verb phrases, verbs coupled for semantic intensification, e.g. to rob and reive, to reive and ravage, robbed and reft and left for dead.

To Raven

Although nowadays in current English we only know its present-participial adjective in phrases like 'ravening hunger' and 'ravenous greed,' to raven is a very old verb which flourished in sixteenth-century English (and perhaps two hundred years earlier) as a commonplace in legal documents, for example, from 1513 CE "his movable goods were spoiled and ravened among the King's officers." To raven meant to seize property and divide it as spoils among other people. For two or three hundred years, a cliché was the double verb phrase 'to spoil and raven.'

Etymology & Semantics

Some form of raven's root appears to have arrived from France during the Norman invasion of England (1066 and all that). In twelfth-century French, we find *raviner* 'to stream, to rush' and later in Middle French *raviner* means 'to furrow the earth with gullies,' hence our English borrowing *ravine*.

To raven has a secondary meaning of 'to plunder.' The soldiers swept over the countryside ransacking everything, marauding, ravening for plunder. This seems a cogent expansion of meaning: from furrowing by gully to robbing and rampaging for booty like violent floods of water.

The current most common usage of *to raven* is likewise old. It meant to feed greedily, to eat and devour like an animal, by the sixteenth century. The clustering sharks ravened on the dead whale. Wolves raven passive sheep.

But note that the raven which is a large black crow is from an entirely different root word.

Other Terms, Similar But Not Necessarily Synonymous

Boodle, bootlegging, booty, burglary, contraband, counterfeiting, despoiling, dough, gain, goods, graft, hot goods, haul, loot, marauding, pickings, pillage, piracy, plunder, poaching, rapine, raven, ransacking, ravaging, robbery, sacking, smuggling, spoils, spoliation, swag, the take, takings, theft and trafficking.

Lucre

In current English, with a depreciative meaning, lucre is immorally obtained profit, obscene gain at the expense of others. Entering English from French *lucre*, our word began as Latin *lucrum* 'wages, reward,' cognate with Greek *apolauein* 'to enjoy the fruits of conquest' and with the modern German noun *der Lohn* 'wages, pay.'

Let me now employ the word in an illustrative sentence I wrote: Once upon a more profitable time, a tar-sands oil executive wallowed in the greasy lucre of his wealth, bobbing upon the surface of his Calgary Hills swimming pool like a bloated porpoise, a smirk of smug contentment crinkling his lips, as poison clouds drifted past, toxins so far above the pleasantly buoyant mogul as to be not worthy of his observation.

One Really Obscure Booty Word

It is my wont to provide loyal readers with the occasional gem of true verbal rarity. Among the swag-pelf words, the rarest of all is the adjective *manubial*, a word blistered in wrongful conduct, a word sticky with the mucilage of iniquity. You just know that any object introduced into one's yawning coffers by manubial acquisition was obtained by evil.

Manubial

The adjective *manubial* describes booty taken in war. Manubial enters English directly from classical Latin *manubiae* 'a general's share of the spoils of war.' With blunt greed, the Latin word literally means "what one can get one's hands on,' because the compound term is made up of Latin *manus* 'hand' + some shrunken suffixal morpheme of Latin *habere* 'to have, to hold.'

Surprisingly this rare word is still in print and used by classicists writing in English about the Roman republic and the early days of the Augustan empire.

As a stylist always on the *qui vive* for a fresh word of abuse, I would not be above slipping the noun itself into some analysis of do-bad bankers, as they finger their manubiae aboard a two-hundred-foot yacht bound out for Fiji. May the Good Ship Larceny founder — with all hands on cash.

Chapter 52

Siesta: Awaken to its Origin

Stir not the slumberous droop of sleepy noon. Obey slug-slow limbs sweetly heavy with numbed fatigue of siesta. Stop not the drone of languid indolence, nor lassitudinous ponderosities of listlessness. Torpid as a sloth, sink down; succumb to feathered duvet and snoozing lethargy. Be Hamlet to his father's ghost and to your inner ghostly self say, "Rest, rest, perturbèd spirit."

Siesta

To approach a meaning of siesta, take a sandaled step backward, shod like slippered Venus or buskined like Adonis, back into the temporal abysm of ancient Rome and learn how they divided their day. Latin *dies* 'a day' had twelve hours of light, Latin *horae,* and twelve hours of night, Latin *horae noctis.* From Latin *hora* descend many modern words naming the twenty-fourth part of a day: English *hour*, French *heure*, Spanish *hora*, Italian *ora*. The Latin word was cognate with the ancient Greek word for 'time of day,' namely *ora*, from which derive words like English *horoscope* and modern French *horologe* 'clock.'

And in the Watches of the Night

Because no guards could stay alert for twelve hours, the night was split up into four watches, Latin *vigiliae*, hence our word *vigilant* 'remaining on careful watch, keeping a vigil.' I like this use of watch, resonant in the title of Hugh MacLennan's 1959 bestselling novel *The Watch that Ends the Night,* all about a noble, Norman-Bethune-like doctor and his ill wife.

Resonant too is Psalm 63:6 (ESV) "when I remember you upon my bed, and meditate on you in the watches of the night . . ." Later the psalm was used to form the lyrics of the 1799 Anglican hymn written by Isaac Watts:

> "Twas in the watches of the night I thought upon Thy power,
> I kept Thy lovely face in sight amidst the darkest hour.
> My flesh lay resting on my bed, my soul arose on high:
> My God, my life my hope, I said, bring Thy salvation nigh."

Siesta's Etymology in Sunny Spain

The Roman day began at midnight for some religious observances, but at dawn for most ordinary, civil occasions. Counting then from a rosy-fingered 6 a.m. dawn, the sixth hour of the day would be noon, hot noon in countries like Italy situate on the Mediterranean littoral. In Latin that 'sixth hour' was *hora sexta.* In Spanish, whose mother source was the vulgar street Latin brought to ancient Iberia by Roman soldiers, *hora sexta* became *ora siesta* 'the sixth hour.'

After a midday meal and a goblet of the fermented grape, a wee nap was often in order. The siesta accomplished several good things. It kept the Mediterranean noggin out of the hot, melanoma-causing sun. A siesta quenched the drowsiness instilled by a good lunch. Human beings experience tiredness twice a day, the heaviest impulse at nightfall, the lightest at midday. Science now tells us nodders-at-noon that a short, fifteen-minute nap is indeed restorative and preventative of heart disease, given other healthy factors obtaining in the individual napper. One of the truest, cleverest metaphors in literature about sleep's remedial property first dropped from Shakespeare's nib.

Macbeth, Act 2, Scene 2:
Methought I heard a voice cry, "Sleep no more!
Macbeth does murder sleep"—the innocent sleep,
Sleep that knits up the raveled sleeve of care. . ."

To conclude, here is the most delightful internal rhyme of the word, in Noel Coward's lyrics to his song "Mad Dogs & Englishmen."

"Mad dogs and Englishmen go out in the midday sun.
The Japanese don't care to, the Chinese wouldn't dare to,
Hindus and Argentines sleep firmly from twelve to one,
But Englishmen detest a siesta . . ."

International Naps:

In South Asia a post-lunch nap is common. In Bengal, the word which describes the concept is *bhat-ghum*, literally meaning "rice-sleep", a nap after lunch.

In northern India a colloquial term *sustana* literally means 'taking a small nap,' possibly of Persian origin.

In some southern German-speaking regions, the *Mittagspause* or *Mittagsruhe* is still customary; shops close, and children are expected to play quietly indoors.

Afternoon sleep is also a common habit in China and Taiwan after the midday meal. This is called *wujiao* in Chinese.

In Islam, it is encouraged to take a nap before midday. It is called by some *qailulah*.

Chapter 53

Phyllo, Butter-Kissed Nutriment of the Gods

Phyllo, a word borrowed whole from modern Greek, is simply their term for 'leaf' or 'dough rolled out to be as thin as the leaf of a tree.' It's the flaky, butter-brushed enclosure for apple strudel and for baklava. Often commingled with perfumed almond paste, honey-swathed bands of phyllo in a lovingly ovened pastry may induce the total abandonment of dietary stoicism. The New Testament parable of the Gadarene swine may be invoked, metaphorically, to describe one's demolition of the baklava tray. The devil lurks in each calorific, sugar-starred, twinkling slice. Alas, no saviour, save self-control, lurks behind the plate of baklava and no herd of 2,000 piggy-wigs is in attendance to receive the saving transfer of satanic hunger-madness.

Mille-Feuille

Other languages have other words for this type of dough. In French pastry, it's known as *mille-feuille* 'a thousand leaves or sheets' and is sometimes the wrapping for such a scrumptious confection as Napoleon pastry. Puff pastry in French is *pâte feuilletée* literally 'sheeted paste.' Although modern Greeks have the perfect name for this pastry in phyllo, a Napoleon pastry in current Greek is a mere transcription of the French term, that is, milfee-yuh.

Kataifi

A popular Middle Eastern pastry, especially in Palestine, a treat made with a special form of phyllo dough cut into small strips is kataifi, used to make sweet pastries with pistachios, almonds, walnuts, sugar syrup, cloves and orange zest, the strips of kataifi rolled up into little logs, baked to a golden brown, then brushed with honey. The word originates in Ottoman Turkish from Arabic *qata'if*, literally in Arabic 'not able to be counted,' presumably because the vermicellioid dough striplets are so teeny-weeny.

In ancient Greek, Homer knew the word as *phyllon* 'leaf.' Note that it is cognate with Proto-Indo-European *fol/ful which gives Latin its word for leaf, namely *folium*, with its many related English borrowings like foliage (the leaves of trees), folio, exfoliate, cinquefoil ('five leaves'), foil (a leaf-thin layer of often metallic sheeting like aluminum foil or gold foil) and portfolio (originally a container to hold or carry (*portare*) many leaves (folia) of drawings on paper).

As phyllo-, a combining prefix in modern English scientific vocabulary, we find it in the name of the biochemical that makes leaves yellow in the autumn, namely phylloxanthin, whose suffix contains the Greek adjective for yellow, *xanthos*. It is one of the few scientific words that is also commonly used with the two Greek roots interchanged; and then it is xanthophyll, a derivative of chlorophyll, now known to be the same chemical as lutein.

There is a tiny night creature called the nose-leafed bat, one of whose defining scientific adjectives is phyllophorous 'bearing a leaf.'

Enough then, let us edge with stealth-stayed tred towards the kitchen, following an odorous tendril of ovened almonds and fresh-poured honey which lures us onward to the crisp, flaky phyllo on the cooling board.

Chapter 54

Going Potty with Ceramics, Majolica & Faience

Majolica (earlier, still extant form *maiolica*) began as a simple Italian adjective denoting the island of Majorca (Maiorca in Italian). It named lusterware pottery made with a glaze of tin, the technique brought to Italy from Spain, and in turn brought to Spain by the invading Moors, such glazed ware being imported from Baghdad starting in the ninth century CE. Crusaders may have also brought back to Europe some Middle Eastern examples, to brighten the stone walls and wooden shelves of Renaissance Italy.

Majorca, today a tourist resort of wanton repute where erotic tumult of bacchanalian excess would bring a nightly blush even to Cleopatra's cheek, is the largest of the Balearic Islands lying east off Spain in the Mediterranean Sea. Other islands in the group include Ibiza (O fen of iniquity!) and Formentera. Very early Majorca's Latin name was *insula maior* 'the bigger island' and its smaller Balearic neighbour was *insula minor*, today Minorca.

Italian majolica is tin-glazed earthenware made opaque by adding tin oxide to make a white cover upon which decorative motifs are easily painted.

Faience

Faience is a catch-all term that names several types of glazed earthenware pottery and some porcelains. It takes its name from a city in Italy, Faenza, from the sixteenth century onward a major center of ceramic manufacture. The French form of the town name was Fayence. So it is the appellative use of a place name, not rare in European languages.

The French word *faïence* keeps the dieresis over the letter /i/. Dieresis (or diaeresis) is a pronunciatory mark, two dots placed above a vowel to show that it is sounded, often placed over the second of two adjacent vowels to make clear that it is a separate syllable, as in the word *naïve*, or above a single vowel, as in the British literary surname Brontë.

Ceramics

Ceramics 'making pottery' is plural in its English form but grammatically collective, that is, it often takes a singular verb, e.g. "Ceramics is the course I'm taking this autumn." The root is one of the ancient Greek words for pottery clay *keramos* 'potter's earth' The adjective, namely Greek *keramikos* 'of or for pottery' gives us words in most European languages. One of the common phrases in ancient Greek was *keramike techne* 'the potter's art.' There was a city district in ancient Athens near the Dipylon Gate, Kerameikos 'the potters' quarter.'

And those are the shards of pottery vocabulary I selected for the kiln of our examination.

Chapter 55

Bible, Paper & Their Ancient Sources
& A Page of My Personal History
in which the author lashes out against
an early teacher who tried to change his nature

Bible

The word *bible* depends for its present meaning on early Greek merchants trying and failing to pronounce the name of a Canaanite port. It was a failure of scant significance, for throughout the long, garbled interchanges of translation history, strangers hearing a word foreign to themselves have attempted to make that odd word familiar by altering it into sounds they find comprehensible in their own language.

That Canaanite port was Gubla or Gebal, composed of the Phoenician word for water well *gb* + *El* 'God' hence 'the well of God." If a well brimmed with a bounty of water, it was customary in days of biblical yore to dub it with the name of any local deity, hence God's well probably betokened plenty of water. Ancient Hebrew was, like Canaanite, a Semitic language and the town's name in Hebrew was Gabol. The modern Arabic name for the port Jubayl or Jbeil also stems from its Phoenician or Canaanite name. Archaeology has proven that Gebel is more than 5,000 years old. Some claim it is the oldest, continuously inhabited place on earth.

Docking in the Port of Byblos

But Greeks heard Gebel as Bubl, then added one of their noun suffixes and called it Bublos or Byblos. There was a reason for such a naming. The little port was the chief shipping conduit to Greece for paper made from Egyptian papyrus and from some local reeds too. Papyrus in Greek was *byblos*. Paper was made from the inner pith of the papyrus reed and its name in ancient Greek was a diminutive form of *byblos*, namely *biblion*. The plural of that word was used to name early scrolls, parchments, folded book pages, and the manuscript of any important writings such as canonical religious texts. That plural form is *ta biblia* 'the books.' In later Koine or Hellenistic Greek, early Christian writers so dubbed the Christian scriptures, for them "the" books, and therefore eventually in English: The Bible.

The Greek *biblia* of course provides the word for Bible in dozens of European languages like French *la bible*, Provençal *bibla*, Spanish *biblia*, Portuguese *biblia*, and Italian *bibbia*. One famous instance is German *die Bibel* and Martin Luther's renowned *Bibelübersetzung* 'translation of the Bible' into German.

Biblus or Biblos

Both forms of the word had a three-hundred year run in English meaning pith-like innards of the paper-reed, the part of the papyrus that was wetted and pressed into Egyptian reed-paper.

At a French Library

La bibliothèque, the French word for library, is worth a mention here, because it was the original word for bible in Old English for centuries, *bibliotheke*, its prime etymon being Greek *bibliotheke* literally 'place to put books, book-case, then library' from *biblion* book + *theke* 'place to put something, repository, lid, cover, box, chest, vault' a noun related to the common ancient Greek verb of putting and placing, *tithemi* "I place, put, set.'

Paper

The ultimate known etymon of our familiar English *paper* is a Greek word *papyrus*, an abundant reed of the Nile River from which the ancient Egyptians made both textiles and a material upon which to write their cursive hieroglyphics. The Egyptians cut the inner pith of this reed into long thin strips, laid the sticky strips crosswise and then pressed the transverse layers under heavy rocks until it stuck together. The composite of papyrus layers was then allowed to dry in the Egyptian sun for about three weeks. The gum-like sap of the stems acted as an adhesive that held the layers together. Sometimes these sheets were sanded or otherwise abraded to render them smooth enough to receive ancient inks.

Greeks likely borrowed the word *papyros* from some now lost Egyptian term. It is difficult to believe no mention of this important and boast-worthy Egyptian invention of reed-paper can be found in any extant pharaonic literature. But such is the sneaky jest of that elusive trickster, history.

From Greek, the word entered Latin as *papyrus* and wound up in Anglo-Norman French in forms like *papir* and *papere* whence English grabbed it, as did almost every other European language.

Cyperus papyrus

Papyrus is a 10-foot tall aquatic sedge which thrives by central African waterways and along fertile Nilotic river banks. The Greek historian Herodotus wrote, with apt concision: "Egypt was the gift of the Nile." The entire civilization of ancient Egypt depended on the annual flooding of the upper Nile. Papyrus belongs to a large plant family of sedges which are perennial, grasslike herbs found over most of the world. Over 3,500 species reside within the Cyperaceae family whose name stems from Greek *kypeiros*, an aromatic sedge called galingale in English.

Shocking True Confession of an Author's Time of Trial!

While I luxuriate in feeling the flexuous textures of handmade papers, lovingly squeezed and teased from vats of pith and pulp, I don't miss writing on paper with pen and ink. In public school, learning my cursive letters, the gracile stroke of the calligrapher's nib was not mine. Penmanship came not nigh unto Little Billy. My writing looked like scratches by an arthritic crow.

Part of this was my naturally jittery hand, the palsied pen-clutch of a youth already an infidel at eight. But my marred longhand arose as well from the chirographical fascism of a teacher I shall call Miss Mandible, the iniquitous Medea of Grade Three. She hated all males, but reserved her highest, liver-curdling opprobrium for that monkey hoard, little boys.

"Jesus is a big poop?" cried Miss Mandible, quoting my recess rebellion. "Bill Casselman! You said that out loud on school property?" Stand in the corner and wear the dunce cap. O Cone of Shame, hide now his ungodly brow." Or words to that effect. For I doubt that Miss Mandible, even in the throes of lad-loathing odium, could rise to anything resembling Victorian oratory.

I was not helped as a child by being ordered to write with my right hand, when I was a born lefty. Pupils were not to write with their left hands. Wham! Down came the hickory yardstick on my little fingers, wielded by Miss Mandible with a boy-hating smirk on her dried wine-sack of a face. Pupils must try to write with their right hands. Wham! This time a leather strap blistered my little fingers and turned them screaming red. "Your letter *m* is not even!" Wham! sounded the oak paddle on my bottom. Even padded by my thick corduroy breeks, it stung.

How's the old ditty go? "Readin' and 'ritin' and 'rithmetic/ Taught to the tune of a hickory stick."

Oh, how Miss Mandible hated male issue. Boy children were anathema. None had ever splorped from her withered innards. Nor would sullen male spawn begot of macho member ever befoul her uterus.

I recall clearly being told that, after all, the very word *sinister* came from the Latin for left-handed. If you were left-handed, it was the mark of the Beast. Satan had seized thy tiny wrist. Bedouin wiped their nomadic asses with sandy left hands. Left-handed, my future was doubtful. I was certainly unemployable. Potential bosses would ban my deformed pencraft. Possible spouses would toss black cloth over my sinning hands. Quakers would shun my shabby scrawlings as not plain.

During penmanship period I did envy classmates who bent with zeal over foolscap to inscribe longhand of such perfection that monks at their scriptoria, upon viewing it, would swoon into their inkwells and bedaub their tonsures in pigment dark as raven's wings. And always nearby perched pertly a prim, purse-lipped coterie of smooth-pubed teachers' pets. Dirty little sucks. Next to me in class sat wee Gail Twinkleclaw who could dash off, seemingly with no effort, vast reams of Carolingian minuscule, flush-rowed hand screeds of medieval calligraphy whose apt shape and comely form would cause a bishop to shred his Book of Hours or nail up a rare codex in the cloistral privy.

A beneficent Fate did rescue me. One night, Miss Mandible was apprehended in the school janitor's tool shed, interfering in an untoward manner with the knob of a wood plane. The school board voted immediately to rusticate her to a distant asylum for sexual obsessives, *so in tiefste Provinz*, that is: so far out in the boondocks, that not another moan was ever heard from Miss Mandible. Then, some years later, to my joy and salvation, computer keyboards arrived.

Thus you will never find me, a moping Niobe, softly weeping for the passing of handwritten work.

Chapter 56

Lord and Lady, Take a Verbal Bow

There are modest truths of etymology that give pause to beginners, such as: 60% of English words of two syllables or more are likely to be derived directly from French. Consider these random examples:

despair - from Old French *desespeir* from Latin *desperare* 'to lose hope

geography - from French *géographie* from Latin from Greek *geo-* 'land, earth' + *graphia* 'writing about...'

gentleman - loan translation from Old French *gentilz hom* 'man of good birth'

parent - direct borrowing from Old French from Latin present participle *parens, parentis* 'having children'

Here's another axiom of everyday etymology: Most modern English words have been borrowed into our language and not altered excessively, so that, if we know French, Latin, Greek, German, and perhaps a few other European languages, we can recognize the language from which English borrowed a word.

Remember too that English is the great thief of tongues. Among the major world languages, English has the largest vocabulary of any language. We have borrowed more words from more languages than French or Arabic or Russian or German or Chinese. We have merrily filched words from every foreign language ever encountered in our scamperings across this earth.

My Lord and My Lady, Be Welcome!

But some English words have undergone extensive changes. The words *lady* and *lord* are two such inconstant changelings.

The terse roots and monosyllabic husks of English are Germanic. The basic Old English word stock, all those simple Anglo-Saxon words, have survived into Modern English reasonably intact. True, these old words have not rolled down through the centuries untouched. But the majority of them have not suffered an obscuring metamorphosis. *Lord* and *lady*, on the other hand, are words mightily altered by historical condensings and shortenings. Linguistics applies scientific names to these word-changing processes, names like crasis, elision, and vowel gradation.

A Wondrous Metamorphosis

Now and then English offers up a word so seemingly simple but so altered by age as to be startling when we discover its roots. Such a word, I deem, is *lady*. Lady begins in Anglo-Saxon or Old English as *hlafdige* 'bread-kneader' being compounded of *hlaf* 'loaf of bread' + *dige* 'female kneader.' So the first lady was she who kneaded the bread. Lord is what is left from Old English *hlaford* from *hlaf weard* = *hlaf* 'bread, loaf' + *weard* 'keeper, guard.' Think of *ward, wardrobe, guard,* and *garden* (place where you keep or guard plants). So the lady kneaded the loaf of bread and the lord guarded the bread as master of the household.

How did the Old English word *hlafdige* become the Modern English word *lady*? The precise details of all its transformations need not concern us here, except to state that Old English intervocalic /g/ tended to soften to a short 'yuh' sound and then disappear. Let's illustrate this process happening in another common English word. Compare our very English flower word *daisy*. Daisy began as an actual

Anglo-Saxon phrase *dæges-eage* 'day's eye,' that is, the eye
of day, a name both lovely and apt, referring as it does to the
sun-like yellow center of the flower that closes its white ray
petals each evening and opens them anew each dawn. This
word of course refers to an English daisy of the *Bellis* genus.
But the point worth noting is the disappearance in the phrase
of both intervocalic /g/ sounds. Thus all that remains of the
Old English word for eye *eage* is the final /y/ of daisy.

By the way, compare Old English *eage* with its modern
German cognate, *die Auge* 'the eye.' An interesting related
compound word came into English from the Vikings who
brought with them when they raided and conquered parts of
Britain, the Old Norse word *vindauga* literally 'eye of the
wind,' (from Old Scandinavian *vindr* 'wind' + *auga* 'eye').
A *vindauga* was a hole in a Viking dwelling to let in air. This
gave us our English word *window*.

Returning to *hlafdige* 'loaf-kneader' becoming lady, we
note that the /f/ sound in *hlaf* softened first to a light /v/ and
then went bye-bye too. When two vowels lose an interposing
consonant (like the /g/ dropping out of *–dige* and the /g/s
dropping out of *dæges-eage*) those vowels often blend together
in a process called in linguistics crasis (from Greek *krasis*
'a mixing, a combining'). The two vowels blend into one
long vowel or a diphthong (Greek *di* 'two'+ Greek *phthoggos*
'sound' hence 'made of two sounds.'

Origin of The Word *Crater*

Our English phrases 'lunar crater' or 'meteor crater' or
'volcanic crater' have the word *crater* borrowed from Latin.
The Romans borrowed it from Greek where *krater* was a big
mixing bowl (related to that Greek word *krasis* 'mixing' in
the last paragraph), usually for mixing water to lessen the
dreadful, acidic taste of most ancient wine. The Romans
regularly added honey to their revolting wine so they could

drink it. In extant Latin literature there are no long lists of tongue-teasing vintage wines. You'll read about wines like Falernian. But keep reading, to discover what the Romans had to add to their rough ferment to render it palatable.

Lord

Lord derives from Old English *hlaford*, itself reduced from an earlier form *hlafweard* = *hlaf* 'bread or loaf' + **weard* 'keeper, guard, warder.' The lord guarded the larder and decided who ate bread at his table. The word lord's popularity and persistence in English was guaranteed once early Bible translators decided to use it as the translation of the Vulgate's Latin term for God and Jesus, *Dominus* (Latin *dominus* 'head of the *domus*' Latin for 'house'). To dominate meant originally is to lord it over other members of the household.

A Sample of Old English

This brief quotation is from about 893 C.E. found in writings attributed to King Alfred the Great:

> Old English: *Ohthere sæde his hlaforde, Ælfrede cyninge...*
> Modern English: And Uther said to his lord, King Alfred...

Hlaford as a type of compound word was common in Germanic and Scandinavian languages. Consider one Old English synonym for servant, *hlaf-æta* 'bread-eater.' Modern German still has *Brotherr* = *Brot* 'bread' + *Herr* 'master, lord' meaning literally 'bread-master' but referring to a man who employs others so that they can earn their daily bread. Swedish and Danish have a word that servants used when referring to their mistress of the household, *matmoder* 'meat-mother.' The term is probably of Old Norse provenance since it persists in Icelandic *matmothir*.

Don't Let Your Bread Loaf!

The English word *loaf*, as in loaf of bread, has relatives in all the Indo-European languages. It derives from Old English *hlaf* 'loaf of bread.' Related are:

- Modern German *Laib* 'loaf of bread'
- Modern Russian *chlyeb* 'bread, loaf' pronounced / chlyeb/ and probably borrowed into Old Slavic from Proto-Germanic
- Old Norse (language of the Vikings) *hleifr* 'loaf of bread'
- Latin *libum* 'a sacrificial cake'
- Ancient Egyptian *hebnen-t* 'sacrificial cake'

Its appearance among the hieroglyphs of ancient Egypt suggests that this word for bread predates even the arrival of the Indo-Europeans, and further hints that they arrived in the Mediterranean area to find the word and the baking of bread already well established. The fact that the common IE word for bread was borrowed and is not a native IE word suggests that the Indo-Europeans may have learned after their arrival to bake bread from the Mediterranean peoples who populated the littoral of the great sea.

And so, my Lady doth curtsy farewell and my Lord doth take his gentle leave of you.

Chapter 57

A Viking Mouse or Vole

word history of an unjustly reviled rodent

Poor little voles! It's a teeny rodent, a furry bundle called in Dutch *aardmuis* 'earth mouse.' Voles only live about 18 months. Most predatory birds and larger mammals eat voles. Kestrels, barn owls, turkey buzzards and hawks rend their voley flesh gleefully. But perhaps the most loathed word in all of voledom is—rodenticide!

And they're so cute. Voles are good parents. They vote Green. They brush their teeth after every meal and attend church regularly where they squeak hymns like "A Mighty Mouse is our God." Male voles don't drink, don't do dope, and they don't carouse with loose women. The eldest son in a pious vole family, if he is also the family idiot, is always sent into Voley Orders.

Yet voles are universally reviled by humankind, for where they most abound and do pullulate, these lacey-pawed scurriers nibble to death tree seedlings and chomp up food crops planted by humans.

The vole was first called by the now obsolete term *volemouse* in English, probably from Old Scandinavian **völlrmus* 'field mouse.' Volemouse appears to have been scampering its rodent way through English dialects for centuries before it reached print. The earliest entries seem to be at the start of the nineteenth century. While it is true that the Old Scandinavian form **völlrmus* is not attested in surviving print, a very probable descendant of such a form occurs in the Icelandic word for vole, *vallarmús*. Compare the Dutch *woelmuis*.

There are dozens and dozens of species of voles. A wee Canuck pest is the prairie vole, *Microtus ochrogaster* or—to translate, in order, the Greek roots in its name — 'little-eared, brown-bellied creature.' The tundra vole (*Microtus operarius*) is important prey for arctic foxes and other carnivorous mammals of the world's Far North.

Ratty, the animal character in Kenneth Graham's children's classic *The Wind in the Willows*, is in fact a water vole. In Britain, voles are not endangered but their population has declined precipitously in recent decades.

Dingwall: Place & Surname

We begin to explain the etymology of the Viking word *völlr* with the story of a Scottish surname. The surname Dingwall is part of the influx of Old Scandinavian words into English and Scottish Gaelic that began with the first Viking raids on northern Britain in AD 787. From that time until almost 1000, Scandinavian words like *sky, egg, law, thing, them, their, riding, skin,* and *whisk* were all borrowed into Old English. Old Scandinavian is our modern label for the language spoken by the Vikings. It used to be called Old Norse. Dingwall is a direct borrowing into Scottish Gaelic of the Viking word *thingvöllr*, which means 'meeting field.'

A *völlr* was a field or meadow set off by round wooden stakes, several of which were hammered into the ground to mark off the field in which Vikings convened to squabble about their next raid, to divide booty, even to wax petulant about plunder ("That mead bowl is mine, Ragnar, you big poopie!"), and to vote about matters political and judicial. They were sea raiders after all, and many of their first settlements were mere temporary camps. *Thing* meant assembly, and the same root is the origin of our English word *thing*—an example of a shift common in the semantic history of individual words, namely, the development of a word's meaning from the particular to the extremely general.

Brief Etymology of the Word *Thing*

The Old Scandinavian word *thing* had a semantic breadth of these sorts of meanings: judicial assembly, get-together, business deal, matter, legal affair, any affair, thing, object. This range of meanings for a 'thing' word is quite common among Indo-European languages. Look at the Classical Latin word *causa* which begins its semantic life meaning 'lawsuit.' It was Roman superlawyer Cicero's word for any episode of litigation. Latin *causa* could also refer to any judicial process. Now those are *causa*'s meanings among the upper-class of ancient Rome's ruling elite. But, in the street, in soldiers' slangy Street Latin *causa* meant 'thing happening, cause, object, thing.' When Soldiers' Latin began to transform into early Romance languages like Old French and the earliest Spanish, it was the 'street' meaning of *causa* that made eventual words like Spanish *cosa* 'thing' and French *chose* 'thing.' In any of their evolved Romance forms, the *causa* derivatives have always liked vagueness of reference. Consider that once sly Italian synonym for the Mafia, *la cosa nostra* 'our thing.'

Look at the range of meaning of a Dutch word like *zaak* 'affair, thing, orig. strife, dispute, lawsuit, cause, charge, crime.' Finally, look at the semantic spread in another Latin 'thing' word, *res* 'affair, thing, case in law, lawsuit, cause.' Why, indeed, *res ipse loquitur* 'the thing speaks for itself.'

Thingvöllr All Over The Place

We know the piratical Norsemen liked to hold meetings in temporarily staked fields. In Iceland shivers the little town of Thingvellir. Of the same origin are the Scottish place names Tinwald in Dumfriesshire and Tingwall in Shetland. All of them are named after fields where Viking invaders eventually settled and then convened open-air political meetings. Icelandic emigrants to Saskatchewan, Canada named the town of Thingvilla 'place where the local council meets.'

On the Isle of Man in solemn conclave sits the Tynwald, the Manx legislative assembly that meets once a year to proclaim new laws. Founded by Vikings who invaded the Isle of Man, the Tynwald consists of a governor, a council, and an elected assembly called the House of Keys. Tynwald is the Manx version of the Old Scandinavian *thingvöllr*.

Just north of Canada's Cape Breton Highlands National Park lies the little Nova Scotia village of Dingwall. Scottish emigrants to the Canadian Maritimes brought the name to Cape Breton Island and other Gaelic-speaking settlements of Nova Scotia. Once in 'New Scotland' (Nova Scotia) these emigrants were remembering Dingwall, a town in the Scottish county of Rossshire, often also cited as the origin of the family name. But evidence in ancient deeds and wills shows that Dingwall existed as a surname before the Scottish town was founded. So how did a person come to have a surname like Dingwall? Well, someone who dwelt beside a field where Vikings once met could be called Angus of the dingwall, and eventually Angus Dingwall.

Modern Norwegian Surnames

A reasonably common Norwegian surname is Vollan which implies that the founding ancestor of the family lived near 'a tilled field or farmstead.' Voll is also a Norwegian surname named from an ancestor who was perhaps a farmer who lived beside his *völlr*.

Remote Scottish Place Name

There is a deserted highland village named Rosal and a Scottish surname Rossal, both Viking names, from Old Norse *hross-völlr* 'horse-field.' The root *ross* is still riding around in modern German. 'A knight on his steed' in modern German might be *'ein Ritter auf seinem Ross.'* Etymologists used to assume that the same root lurked in the ancestry of the English word *walrus*, that walrus evolved from some form like *hval-hross*, that is, whale-horse, that its form traced far back to a confusion between two Viking words, *hross-hvalr* a kind of whale and *rosm-hvalr* a walrus. But the *hross* component now seems doubtful and the precise origins of walrus are perhaps forever obscured.

Cognates of Völlr

The Old Scandinavian *völlr* is cognate with the German word for forest, *Wald*, with Swedish *vall* 'field' and with Old English *weald* 'forest' which produced the English word *wold*, now confined to poetry and older British place names like Stow-on-the-Wold or The Yorkshire Wolds or The Lincolshire Wolds. Wold now generally means high land long cleared of its original forest. A famous tourist destination in Britain, the Cotswolds were originally the high forest lands of an Anglo-Saxon named Cod, that is, *Codes woldes*. When Brits say 'The Wolds' they are almost always referring to the ones in Yorkshire which have their very own long footpath called Wolds Way. Wold hides in other British place names like Walton-on-Thames and Waltham Forest.

Weald is still seen among English place names and meant a forest or wooded area. Weald too could mean now open land cleared of forest. A well-known area in southern England still bears its ancient moniker, The Weald, shortened from its Anglo-Saxon name, *Andredesweald* 'the forest of an AS bigshot named Andred.'

The Vikings were dominant in Britain for only a few hundred years but they left fascinating, persistent mementoes within modern English, not least of which is our name for those unjustly persecuted moist-meadow-and-streamside dwellers called voles.

Chapter 58

The Peanut is Not a Nut?

Is There Nothing Left to Believe in?

The peanut is the bean of a legume enclosed in a fibrous pod. A filbert is a nut. A pecan is a nut. Dick Cheney was a nut. So – is 'peanut' an apt common name for the plant? No way. Ground nut is not much better. But, yes, the peanut is—by a bit of a stretch—a pea.

Fabaceae - Family Name Origin

But, to repeat, the peanut by no means a nut, botanically speaking. A peanut is the oval seed enclosed in the fibrous pod of a plant that is a member of the large bean family, whose botanical family name is Fabaceae. You have probably heard of a kind of broad bean called fava. Beans take their family name from that bean. The root is the Latin word *faba* 'bean.' On its way into the English word kitchen, faba passed through Italian and changed its /b/ to /v/, as did many other intervocalic plosives in Latin, to become Italian *fava*.

Let's offer another example of that sound change, common as Latin slowly morphed into its derivative Romance languages, like Italian and French. Consider the morphology of the Latin word for 'oak tree' *robur* becoming *rovere* in Italian.

Fans of Italian cinema will recall that word prominent in the title of Roberto Rossellini's 1959 film "*Il generale della Rovere*" where the Italian novelist on whose book the screenplay is based used the surname deliberately and ironically (English translation of the movie title: General Oaks). Vittorio De Sica plays a cheap hood forced by the Nazis to impersonate a leader of the Italian resistance during World War II and ordered to weasel out info after he is planted in a Milan prison full of captured resistance fighters.

English borrowed the *robur* adjective directly from Latin and so something as strong as an oak is likely to be ***robust***. Intervocalic /b/ in the Latin word for book *liber* became in French *livre*.

Just to add an annoying tittle of confusion, fava also is used as the specific epithet of the common broad bean, namely, *Vicia faba*.

The etymon or root seen in *fava* is ancient. Other Indo-European cognates of Latin *faba* are Old Scandinavian *baun*, Old English *bean* and Attic Greek *phakos* 'lentil.'

Growth of a Peanut

As the pod (peanut shell) ripens, it goes underground. Its flower is borne above the ground. After the flower withers, the stalk elongates, bends down, and forces the ovary underground. When the seed is mature under the soil, the seed coat changes color from white to a reddish brown. The entire plant, including most of the roots, is removed from the soil during harvesting. When harvested and mature, the beans are roasted to become the peanuts of commerce.

Antiquity of Peanut Cultivation

The peanut is native to South America. By the evidence of fossil remains, paleobotanists have determined that the peanut's domestication must have taken place 8,000 years ago in Argentina or Bolivia or Peru, where the wildest strains of peanuts grow today. Most pre-Columbian cultures depicted peanuts in their art. When the bullying *conquistadores* of Spain invaded Mesoamerica they found the Aztecs growing peanuts, called in Nahuatl, the Aztec language, *tlal-cacahuatl* and that's why the Spanish word for peanut is *cacahuate* and the French word is *cacahuète*.

Other Peanut Names

The most satisfying alternate name for peanut is goober. Black slaves brought that name from Africa, where, in one of the languages of central Africa, namely Kikongo, the word for peanut is *nguba*.

The peanut had a circuitous path to the American snack table. First, around 1800 C.E., Portuguese merchants took the plant from Brazil to Africa where it became very popular and widely grown in tropical climates. Later the peanut entered the then English colonies of North America as a favourite food of African slaves.

Peanuts are also known as earthnuts, goober peas, pindas, jack nuts, pinders, manila nuts, and monkey nuts; the last of these is often used to name the entire pod.

Botanical Name Origins

The peanut's botanical name is descriptive— *Arachis hypogaea*. Arachis was the name, among the ancient Greeks, of some leguminous weed, not the peanut. The precise ancient meaning of arachis is unknown but the components of the word suggest that arachis may have been composed of: /a/ Greek 'not' + *rachis* Greek 'spine, backbone' so that the flower of this ancient weed perhaps appeared to have no central support structure or axis or rib. In 18th-century Botanical Latin, rachis was the part name for the main axis of a leaf or the rib of a frond or leaf. Rachis is still used in botany with this meaning — but we don't know if the ancient Greeks used it in that sense.

Hypogaea: Etymology

The second part of a formal botanical plant name is termed the specific epithet. The first word in a plant name is the species names, in the case of the peanut, it's *Arachis*, explained above. The next part of a botanical name is an adjective describing some feature of the species, usually one that differentiates that species from other species in the same family. A Greek word for adjective is *epithetikos*. Just as the Latin *adjectivus* means 'thrown near' a noun, so the Greek *epithetikos* means 'put close to' a noun. Thus the name of this second part of the scientific name: specific epithet. In the case of this peanut, its specific epithet is *hypogaea*. The botanical names of plants are customarily italicized.

Hypogaea is the exact Greek counterpart of the Latin-derived adjective *subterranean* 'under the ground.' Hypogaea is Greek for underground, from *hypo* 'under' + *-gaia* Greek 'earth.'

Short, Intemperate Advisory to the Semi-Literate

Many of us who know words get weary of seeing the word *species* mangled. The singular of species is species. The plural of species is species. Why? Because it was a fourth declension Latin noun borrowed directly from Latin, where also the singular and the plural forms are identical: species.

Therefore please do not write sentences like this one from a famous greenhouse website: "Only one specie [sic] of cactus is native to this northern county." No! "One species of cactus is native . . ." is the correct form.

The word *specie* can mean "in gold coin" and has several other senses, but it is **not** the singular of species, not even in a Latin phrase like *in specie*.

Persons who commit the egregious solecism deprecated in the above paragraph are the same sloppy readers who think Charles Darwin wrote a book entitled "The Origin of the

Species." No such book exists. Darwin's short title was "The Origin of Species." He did not discuss only the origin of *Homo sapiens* but how evolution produces many different species. Darwin discusses speciation.

Be warned! If I catch any of you uttering either of these vulgar lapses, I shall have to fetch from the classroom cupboard my hickory correcting stick, ¾ of an inch in diameter, the one with the solid iron ferrule. Harrumph!

Little Peanuts of Trivia

1. The Peanut Gallery

As one elderly wrinkly who trod the earth when pterodactyls flapped their leathern wings across a sulphur sky, I am old enough to remember an early kiddie show on TV that featured a peanut gallery. Yes, I remember fondly Buffalo Bob with his Peanut Gallery of kiddies on "The Howdy Doody Show." A web note asks "Ever wonder where the term 'Peanut Gallery' comes from? The term became popular in the late 19th century and referred to the rear or uppermost seats in a vaudeville theater, which were also the cheapest seats. People seated in such a gallery were able to throw peanuts, a common food at theaters, at those seated below them. It also applied to the first row of seats in a movie or vaudeville theater, for the occupants of those seats could throw peanuts at the live performers on stage or at the cinema screen, showing their displeasure with the performance."

Of course, good old Buffalo Bob was using peanut because it was an early 20th-century affectionate nickname for children by their parents. "I love you, little peanut!" Much to the macho horror of young schoolboys, mothers would call out such a ghastly phrase as one set forth in manly manner for school of a morning, "Now, Peanut, careful crossing the road!" Boys would immediately check to see if any of their pals had been within hearing distance of the dread epithet. To be addressed as "Peanut" was a violation of boyish dignity almost as heartless as being forced by your mother to wear your sister's mittens to school because you had lost yours in a snowball fight the previous afternoon.

2. Mummified peanuts have been found in Inca burial sites.

3. Tom Miller pushed a peanut to the top of Pike's Peak (14,100 feet) using his nose in 4 days, 23 hours, 47 minutes and 3 seconds.

4. Dr. George Washington Carver researched and developed at The Tuskegee Institute laboratories more than 300 uses for peanuts in the early 1900s. Dr. Carver is considered The Father of the Peanut Industry because of his extensive research and selfless dedication to promoting peanut production and products.

5. Astronaut Allen B. Sheppard brought a peanut with him to the moon.

6. Peanuts are a good source of folate, which reduces the risk of certain birth defects in the brain and spinal cord.

And so, my wee goobers, we must put the lid on this particular jar of peanut knowledge.

Chapter 59

A Swarm of Bee Words

Recent science news items claim to have found causes for the devastating mass deaths of the Western honey bee, *Apis mellifera*—billions of individual bees—who simply flew from their hives and disappeared. Does this frightening, widespread and so far mysterious die-off of the honeybee vault the little pollinator into new admonitory status? Is the honeybee this decade's "canary in the mineshaft," warning us of a toxic incubus perching gently on humanity's bedpost and gazing down upon our innocently sleeping forms with a soft smile, much as a fed eagle might perch upon a treetop, plump and content, stuck to its beak: blood-flecked songbird feathers. May mankind yet save bees!

More than one third of the healthy natural foods humans eat, fruits and vegetables, depend on bees for pollination. Our honeybees' alarming disappearance bids us indulge an interval of concerned browsing and a few moments' buzz around bee words of the world, collecting some of the piquant stories about bee vocabulary. This is by no means a thorough etymology of the word bee, but rather a page scribbled in a word-nut's notebook.

Our English word bee has many Germanic and Slavic cognates and relatives:

Old English *beo*
Old Norse *by*
Modern German *Biene*
Dutch *bij*

Lithuanian *bite*
Latvian *bite*
Russian *pcela*
Polish pszczola
Old Church Slavonic *bucela*
Irish *bech*
Welsh *begegyr*

Greek & Jewish Bee Words Compared

Note that the Greeks named the honey bee *melissa*, after its honey (Greek *meli*). The Jews named the bee in modern Hebrew de-vo-RAH, after its sting. Deborah is a common Hebrew feminine name. Deborah means 'stinging bee.' The Semitic triliteral root is *d-b-r*, one of whose reflexes is *dabar*, a Hebrew word for 'word, sting, goad.' Compare Arabic and Proto-Semitic *dabar(a)* 'sting, ox goad.'

An interesting but utterly coincidental similarity exists in the Hebrew and Latin terms for 'word.' In Latin it is *verbum* (the Latin root *verb-* 'whip, lash, sting, cattle goad.' In Biblical Hebrew, word is *dabar* from the triliteral verbal root *d-b-r* - 'say, speak, prod, sting, goad.'

Hebrew scholars offer other possible Semitic origins of *devorah*, the modern Hebrew word for bee. They consider ancient cognates like the Aramaic for bee, *debarta*, and its Syriac cousin, *deboritha*, as well as the Hebrew word for honey, *debash*. There is another *shoresh* (three-letter Semitic word root) brought forth for consideration: the Mandaic Aramaic *dibra* 'back, tail, hence bee's stinger' to be compared with the Arabic *dubr* 'backside, tail.'

Sweet Isle of Honey

Is the Greek word for honey hidden in a well-known Mediterranean place name? The island of Malta, say some sources, was first *Melita* 'land of honey' (Greek *meli, melitos* 'honey'). But the preponderance of linguistic and historical evidence suggests that the place name Malta is Phoenician, the Semitic language of the Mediterranean trading people who colonized the six little islands which comprise Malta very early in history. The Semitic shoresh or triliteral root *m-l-t* carries the meaning of 'take refuge' or 'hide.' The Semitic verb form *malata* can mean 'one takes refuge.' Therefore it is quite likely that a later noun form *'malta'* may mean 'place of refuge' or 'isle of refuge.' If you examine the sea map and observe Malta's position south of Sicily, not too far from Tunisia, and think from the perspective of Phoenician traders sailing stout and yare vessels to and fro upon the Mediterranean, such an origin makes good sailing sense and good linguistic sense.

Medved, a Honey of a Russian Name

The common Russian surname Medved is an apotropaic circumlocution for 'bear' meaning literally 'honey-eater.' This is an old Slavonic periphrasis for bear. *Med* is Russian for honey, and the *ved* root means 'eat.' The *ved* and *yed* roots are related to *yest* (Russian 'to eat') and are cognate with other Indo-European verbs like Latin *edere* 'to eat' (which gives us the adjective *edible*) and even with English *to eat*.

Another Russian word containing this Slavic root is the interesting and racist Samoyed, the name of a people and a breed of dog. *Samo-yed* means 'self-eater' in Russian, a synonym for cannibal! Guess what? The Samoyed people do **not** call themselves by that name. They possess their own proper ethnonym, and it does not mean 'cannibal.' Inuit is an ethnonym; Eskimo is not.

In order to keep bears away and/or to placate the spirit of the totemic animal of his 'bear' clan, the tribesman never uttered the name of the animal, for fear that if one spoke aloud the word *bear*, then the animal itself might appear to devour one. For the same reason, the word *mother-in-law* is seldom said aloud in North America. Among many peoples of the world the imposition of taboo on certain words is still a prevalent superstition.

How did one avoid saying the word 'bear' out loud? One made up other names for the animal, and one old Slavic circumlocution was 'honey-eater' or *medved*. An almost similar type of periphrasis occurs in the monument poem of Old English, *Beowulf*. The hero Beowulf has a name that means 'bee-wolf.' That was a synonym, an Anglo-Saxon kenning for 'bear.' It was probably not because the word *bear* became taboo. Kenning was a feature common in Old English poetry. It added flavour and verbal brio and memorable word formation to the poetry, very much like the compound Homeric epithets of *The Iliad* and *The Odyssey*, for example Homer's reference to "the wine-dark sea" or to "rosy-fingered dawn." Both are Homeric epithets. Such poetic figures are also mnemonic devices. All these long poems were recited by a bard. Standard epithets and kennings, all with proper metrics, allow the reciting bard some help and allow the audience the pleasure of recognizing familiar tropes.

Other examples from the poem *Beowulf* are kennings, or poetically phrased synonyns, for the word *sea*. Compounds that meant 'sea' include *segl-rad* 'sail-road', *swan-rad* 'swan-road', *bæth-weg* 'bath-way' or *hwæl-g* 'whale-way' and *hronrade* 'whale-road'.

Under the rubric of Curious & Meaningless Trivia, we humbly place this nugget: the pig Latin word for bee is eebay.

St. Ambrose of Milan, Patron Saint of Beekeepers

Known as "the honey-tongued doctor," Saint Ambrose is often painted in episcopal vestments wearing a mitre with crozier in hand, while nearby sits his most frequent iconic symbol, the beehive. One delightfully spurious explanation of Saint

Ambrose's connection with bees recounts how bees deposited the honey of theological knowledge on his lips while he slept.

As usual with popular excuse-making, there is no suggestion that his eloquence was the outcome of many years of rhetorical practice and learning. Thus are illiterate *hoi polloi* forever spared from the possibly upsetting insight that their profound ignorance is the direct result of their profound laziness and ploppish do-nothingism. "Like, why should I study when I can nab my welfare check and smoke some primo crack?"

Source of Apis, the Classical Latin Word for Bee

The word for bee in the Romance languages stems from Latin *apis* 'bee.' French *abeille*, Spanish *abeja*, Italian *ape* — all descend from Roman buzzers. So do words like apiary and apiculture. This little note concerns the ultimate source of *apis*. Some scholars suggest that the Latin root and even the Germanic words for bee like German *Biene* entered Indo-European languages from ancient Egyptian. One of the Egyptian hieroglyphic words for honeybee is *bj-t*. The /t/ at the end of the Egyptian word is simply the marker in hieroglyphics for a word that is grammatically feminine.

A Few Obscure Bee Words

Apitherapy is the pseudo-medical use of honeybee products. Almost none of the claims of apitherapy have been proved scientifically. Apitherapy includes the true **bee**lievers who rub queen-bee "royal jelly" on their body parts while murmuring "Heal! Buzz! Buzz! Heal!"

Cleptoparasitic Bees

(*kleptes* Greek 'thief' + *parasite*)
Among cleptoparasitic bees, females lack pollen collecting structures and do not construct their own nests. They enter

the nests of pollen collecting species, and lay their eggs in cells provisioned by the host bee. When the cuckoo bee larva hatches, it consumes the host larva's pollen ball, and if the female cleptoparasite has not already done so, kills and eats the host larva. Many of us have human neighbours who, given a chance, would perform as efficiently.

Skep

Here's a word brought into English by Viking invaders speaking Old Norse. *Skeppa* was a Viking word for basket or bushel. By 1100 CE, in early Middle English, skep meant a basket-shaped beehive made of rope or bound twigs or straw. Early Anglo-Norman beekeepers made rustic skeps of dried and bound grapevines.

After so *bee*laboured a chapter, I'm sure some readers would like me to buzz off. I shall, but ever so briefly.

Chapter 60

Circus to the Max!

Our English word *circus* descends from the name of one building in ancient Rome, namely, the *Circus Maximus,* Latin, literally 'the largest exhibition space for public spectacles.' Chariot races, gladiatorial combats, athletic competitions, wild-animal spectacles, *Christiani ad leones* (Christian martyrs fed to starved lions) all took place within that stone oval surrounded by lithic tiers of seating.

The first use of *circus* recorded in English is in a work by Chaucer written around 1380 CE and probably refers to the Circus Maximus in Rome.

The Circus Maximus at its largest expansion under the emperor Trajan held more spectators than any other building ever built then or since; approximately 250,000 Romans crammed in. The Roman satirist Juvenal sourly but correctly saw that the blood-soaked sands of the Circus Maximus and the Coliseum were free entertainment conceived to distract a poor and starving Roman underclass.

Blood-Soaked Sand of the Arena

Our modern English word *arena* to describe large sports buildings is the Latin word *harena* 'sand,' referring specifically to the sand thrown down on the Coliseum floor to absorb the blood of wounded and slain gladiators, Christian martyrs and animal victims.

Juvenal dismissed the gladiatorial gore as mere *panem et circenses.* Although the phrase's literal translation is 'bread and gladiator shows,' today we might translate it freely as something like "free bread and wrestling matches," something to keep the starving masses happy for a few hours. Is reality-show television much different? A distraction for the unemployed dummies so they will sit still while the wealthy and the powerful pickpocket what's left in poor patched jeans for overpriced, high-markup toothpaste?

The Etymology of *Circus*

Latin *circus* 'circle, ring' looks like it was borrowed directly from the ancient Greek word *kirkos* 'ring' 'round area.' But it may be simply cognate, that is, sprung from the same Indo-European root as *circus*, that is, **kerk*. This Proto-Indo-European etymon itself may be an emphatic, reduplicated, then clipped form of the simpler root **ker* 'roundish, oblong, ovoid, curled, so that it appeared as **kerker* or **kirkir* 'truly round, hence circular, then was clipped to **kerk*. Just a guess, folks. But — an incredibly learned one! Other etymologists say the PIE root is the simple **(s)ker* 'to bend, to turn.' I prefer my hypothetical construct. Remember that reduplication in Indo-European languages often emphasizes the semantic force of the plainer, simpler root.

Also cognate with the Greek and Latin forms are such words as *krevas* Lithuanian 'crooked,' *krivoi* Russian '*curved, crooked*' and other akin Greek words like *korone* 'ring, crown, chaplet.' Latin *curuus* is cognate, giving English forms like *curved*. Another Latin word is probably cognate too, *cirrus* 'curl, lock of hair' which gives us cirrocumulus clouds, cirrate, and cirriform, most of the derivatives being scientific terms. Latin *circus* also gave rise to the preposition, originally an adverb, *circum* 'around' with all its dozens of English derivatives like circumstance, circumference, circumcise, circumspect and circumvent. *Circuire* Latin 'to go around' leads ultimately to English *circuit*.

Coliseum

Our English noun *coliseum* began as the nickname of The Flavian Amphitheatre, in classical Latin *Amphitheatrum Flavium* (begun around.70 C.E.). It was the name of a specific Roman building, based on a Greek adjective *kolossiaios* from *kolossos* meaning gigantic statue. The Greek historian Herodotus applied the adjective *kolossos* first when describing the Sphinx and other large sculptures in ancient Egypt. The Colossus of Rhodes was a statue that made the list of the Seven Wonders of the Ancient World. The Flavian amphitheatre may have gained its medieval name from a colossal statue of Nero that long stood nearby.

Interesting Words Related to Latin *Circus*

1. In Britain, circus may refer to a circular intersection of streets. Think of Piccadilly Circus in central London.
2. *Chercher* French 'to search' ultimately from *circare* Latin 'to go around, to go around looking for things'. Do it twice and it is *rechercher*. The French words were borrowed into English as *search* and *research*! English has borrowed a past participle from *rechercher*, so that recherché in English means 'sought out and thus rare,' 'too refined,' 'too elegant,' 'of studied elegance rather than naturally elegant,' 'researched rather than natural.'
3. Circle comes through Norman-French *cercle* from the Latin diminutive of circus, *circulus* root of English words like circulate, circulation, encircle and circlet.
4. Circadian rhythms endure through one day, from *circa* Latin 'around' + *dia* Latin 'day.'

My Favorite Word Story Related to a Circus

P.T. Barnum, the crafty salesman and originator of the three-ring circus, also opened what would evolve into the world's first department store. It was in New York City and Barnum called it "The American Museum (at Broadway and Ann Street from 1841 to 1865)." It was immediately wildly popular and visitors would spend all day gawking at the strange creatures and exhibits on its five floors. This caused clogging of the aisles, so Barnum had to find a way to get people to move along faster, in order to make more money from admissions.

Now one of his exhibits was a tigress, the first live tiger many New Yorkers had ever seen. Therefore, near certain doors, Barnum had signs put up that read "This Way to the Egress." Gullible visitors thought the egress was a rare female animal they had never heard of. In fact, egress is a fancy Latin-derived word that means 'the exit.' Once people had walked through the egress door that led outside back to Broadway, the door clicked locked behind them. If they wanted to complete the tour of "The American Museum" they had to walk around to the front door and pay the admission price again!

And now, Ladies and Gentlemen, as ringmaster of this prodigious, three-ringed display of philological prowess, I declare this circus performance to be complete, and I say to all readers, "This way to the egress!"

Chapter 61

Forceps

& the shocking personal revelation that
the author was a forceps baby.
O Shame, obscure thy blush!

Basic Etymology

Forceps is Latin 'tongs, pincers' from a possible unrecorded compound like **formu-ceps* literally 'taker of something hot' from Latin *formus* 'warm' + Latin verb *capire* 'to take.'

The first use of Roman forceps was by blacksmiths, then by teeth-extractors. But an alternate origin may lie in *ferrum* Latin, iron + *-ceps* < *caput* Latin, head, giving an early, unattested form like **ferriceps* 'iron-head' tongs or pincers.

Fussbudget Note about the Singular and Plural Forms of Forceps

Please note that there is in English NO SUCH SINGULAR FORM as **forcep, although I have heard this solecism from nurses and doctors. The singular is ***forceps*** (from the etymology above you can see why) and the common English plural form is also ***forceps***. If you don't mind sounding like a Cantabridgian priss-fart, a mincing precisian, you may use the obscure plural form *forcepses,* but it is awkward, rare, and more pompous than me at my worst. Even more recondite and show-offy is usage of the Latin plural *forcipes*. Do remember that, like the unknown *kudo as the singular of *kudos*, *forcep does not exist. Using *forcep brands you as a letterless, blunder-prone yutz afloat on the Cesspool of Ignorance.

Kinds of Forceps

Forceps originated as flattened blades with a handle in ancient ironmongery. Some ancient blacksmith thought of joining the blades by crossing them at their centers and fastening them with a bolt that permitted their movement. There are many kinds of medical forceps used to grasp, handle, compress, and join body tissues or medical equipment. Clamp forceps have an automatic locking device. Mosquito forceps are very tiny haemostats with fine points, used to clamp off blood vessels. Towel forceps clip towels to the site of a surgical incision or operative wound. Chamberlen forceps are the classic set of obstetric ones: high, mid, and low, used in forceps delivery, to shorten extended labor or to quickly deliver a baby in fetal distress. A baby's head may become lodged in the birth canal in an inappropriate transverse or posterior position. Often gentle rotation of the head by forceps solves the problem. There is of course no medical procedure that is free of risk, and this is true of forceps deliveries too.

Peter Chamberlen (1601-1683) was an English obstetrician and court physician to Charles the Second. Around 1665 he invented midwifery forceps, the original obstetrical forceps with no curvature. There have been many improvements to obstetrical forceps and these modern adaptations continue today.

Indications for operative vaginal delivery vary. In general, however, forceps or vacuum extraction may be called for during the second stage of delivery, when the fetal head is engaged and the mother's cervix is fully dilated and the labour is prolonged for hours so that the baby's health and life are threatened, or the mother's health and life are endangered.

Intimate Revelation of a Personal Nature

I found this caption beneath a photo of a new-born at a medical site written by doctors: "The semi-circular red mark on this infant's right cheek is a forceps mark. When forceps are needed to assist with a delivery, this type of superficial red mark can occasionally been seen on the sides of the infant's face. In most cases, the marks are small (2cm) erythematous streaks. These marks have no consequence and will spontaneously resolve. In rare cases when the skin is abraded, antibiotic ointment may facilitate healing."

Really? On the contrary, forceps marks don't always vanish as Snow White did, into the barn after palpating the Prince's schlong. No, indeed, kiddies, some forceps marks persist — as did those on my own forehead, visible dents I bear to this day. Doctors always say, "But they are so small, so insignificant." Then I am forced to point out that I have successfully grown geraniums in the forceps-made cavities of my forehead for forty years. Quite simple really. One begins by not washing one's forehead in springtime.

My prominent frontal indentations are a reminder of the doctor who attended my birth, a scalawag I shall obscure by giving him the false but apt name of Doctor Blurr who, drunk as a distillery janitor, delivered me at eight-bells under a New Year's moon, lo! these many eons ago. Those in attendance: two nurses, my father and, notably, my mother, stated that Dr. Blurr was, throughout my natal entrance, wreathed in an antiseptic fetor of Haig & Haig Pinch, a brand of Scotch whiskey. Spicily did it blend with the familiar nostril-curling reek of diluted carbolic acid used to wash down hospital delivery rooms in those long-ago days.

While clamping the wrong part of my reluctant-to-emerge forehead with Dubois obstetrical forceps (circa 1840 CE), Dr. Blurr sang heartily several well-known sea shanties, a song form he favoured over the somber Anglican hymns he was forced to conduct each Sunday as choir master of Saint Brit-Snot's Anglican Church.

You may perhaps sympathize with my infant hesitancy in entering a delivery room and a world, the only world I knew at that moment, filled with a forceps-waving, booze-sodden doctor loudly singing "A randy man was wee Jack Tarr/ when he roped a seal to the gunwale."

I rest my case, but not my creased forehead!

Chapter 62

Yo! Coach! Check This Out!

The word *coach*, as in basketball coach, began as a Hungarian cart. Here's the story. The coach was named after a small Hungarian village, Kocs, where superior wagons, carts and carriages were built. Kocs, in the Hungarian district of Komarom-Esztergom, lay on the main road along the Danube between Vienna and Budapest. These two great cities needed well-built, fast vehicles that would carry more than two people over the bumpy roads of the day in as much comfort as was then possible.

One of the best of these multi-horse carts was called in Hungarian *kocsi szekér* 'a wagon from Kocs.' In Kocs, one of the first successful, reasonably comfortable passenger coaches, a light, graceful, four-wheeled wagon with a strap suspension, was built. Its design was so compact, elegant and sturdy that this coach design spread throughout Europe in the 15th and 16th centuries. The German-speaking Viennese started to call this vehicle a *Kutsche*, which is how they heard Hungarians saying the name of the little carriage-making town. From Vienna these lively vehicles traveled to Paris and the French, adapting the Austrian word, called it a *coche*. In Rome it was, and still is, in Italian *cocchio*. Eventually the English borrowed the word and the vehicle and called it a *coach*.

How early did the little Hungarian town of Kocs gain renown as a place of excellent carriage-makers? There is strong evidence (printed) that when Anne of Bohemia married England's Richard II in 1382 CE, she brought carriages from Kocs, Hungary with her to England.

English words we borrowed from the Hungarian language include *goulash* (a stew made with beef or veal), *paprika* (a seasoning made from sweet red peppers), *coach*, and *saber* (a cavalry sword).

How Did a Hungarian Carriage Word Get Applied to a Basketball Coach?

Two theories have been offered, one suggesting metaphorical word use, the other bluntly descriptive of an action.

A coach was first a tutor who guided students through various fields of study or lessons. The coach carried the student through the course, as a coach and four might carry an eighteenth century English family to London. That is the commonly accepted theory.

I prefer the other British idea that wealthy squires had their literate servants read to them as they drove in coaches about the countryside on their business or on long trips into a nearby city. A private tutor might come along to assist their children or indeed read aloud to the children, who would thus be "coached" in their studies as they proceeded along the country roads in coaches. It was only a short jump in meaning from an academic "coach" to one who coached in sports like basketball or football, one who showed players, by virtue of his broader expertise and experience, some of the plays and tricks needed to excel in a particular sport.

How much we lost when the eco-friendly coach and the team of horses were lost to civilization, to be replaced by smelly, poisonous vehicles from Detroit propelled by one of the least efficient fuel-operated machines ever devised, namely, the internal combustion engine.

How much more calming it would have been to set off on a quiet summer afternoon at a modest trot in a slim yellow caleche.

About the Hungarian Language

Hungarian is an Ugric language of the Finno-Ugric subgroup of the Uralic language family. Originally from a large region in Central European Russia, Finno-Ugric peoples started migrating in different directions around 3000 BC. In the first centuries of the Christian era, the Ugrians began a slow migration westward towards present-day Hungary. They arrived in the ninth century, making contact with the Bulgar Turks and the Khazars. In this way, the largest Finno-Ugric nation came into existence. Constituting a unique enclave surrounded by speakers of Germanic, Slavic, Romanian and Turkic languages, Hungary was linguistically very isolated. The closest related languages are the Ostyak and Vogul languages of Siberia, spoken in a region more than 2,000 miles away.

Coaches & Their Horses in History

Coaches speeded up postal services which had been terribly slow and jolty before 1784. In that year the first English mail coach rumbled along its inaugural pebbly route. Not only was it the fastest, but also it offered the most punctual service in the world.

Postal coaches required sound horses. They were known as Yorkshire Coach horses and were unrivalled right up until the mid-nineteenth century when the Hungarian Jukker, an unbelievably nimble-footed breed, took the lead. Jukkers drew the carriages of monarchs all over Europe including the German Emperor William II and Tsar Alexander III. Even King Edward VII journeyed to Budapest to buy a carriage with Jukkers. One of the most spectacular Hollywood films ever shot featured four Hungarian horses. Ben Hur's chariot was drawn by Hungarian horses sired by the Esterházy family's Tata stud.

For me, a small child in the late 1940s and early 1950s, the most magic use of the term was in the compound word *stagecoach*, evoking bandanna-masked banditos riding cayuses as they charged up out of Dead Deputy Gulch and chased the stagecoach down a dusty trail. The noble cowboy hero, often John Wayne, would save the gold stored in trunks on the stagecoach by blasting the villains to smithereens with rifle and revolver. Who cared if you were likely to fracture your coccygeal vertebra as you jolted over rocky desert *pistes* in your Wells Fargo coach? You were clearin' the pristine, god-lovin' territory of no-good varmints! Makin' the West safe for bribe-accepting basketball coaches to come.

Chapter 63

"Funiculì, Funiculà": Rope Songs & Rope Words

Funis is the Latin word for rope or cord, and several interesting English and Romance Language words descend from it, including some medical terms.

Funis umbilicalis

The formal anatomical name for the umbilical cord is *funis umbilicalis*. Funic presentation in obstetrics sees the umbilical cord appear before the body of the fetus. Funic souffle (*souffle* French, a breath) is sometimes heard during fetal stethoscopy as a soft, muffled whooshing sound, the sound of blood flowing through the umbilical vessels in time with the fetal heartbeat.

Everybody Sing: "Funiculì ! Funiculà !"

Consider first the phrase "*Tirato con la fune*," Italian 'pulled by the rope.' *La funicolare* is Italian for 'funicular railway' from *funiculus* Latin, diminutive of *funis* Latin 'rope, cord.' The basic meaning of *funiculus* is 'little rope' from *funis* + *-iculus* common Latin diminutive suffix.

Time it is to share a pleasant memory from a trip I made to Italy thirty years ago. From the little harbour at Sorrento, a friend and I embarked on a sleek hydroplane with fifty other passengers on board. Motorized lacewings, we skimmed over the Bay of Naples to the Isle of Capri. Our fellow boat passengers were an entire class of Italian public-school-age kids on a holiday excursion from nearby Castellamare di Stabia, singing with gusto a song they had been taught from the cradle, for it was a Neapolitan folk song written and first performed where they lived: *"Funiculi, Funicula."*

The Song

Written in 1880 to celebrate the first funicular railway to ascend the slopes of Mount Vesuvius, the instantly popular song had lyrics by a local journalist Peppino Turco and music by his friend Luigi Denza. Funicular, in its first strict usage, referred to a cable car system in which the weight of an ascending car was counter-balanced by the weight of a descending car. An aerial funicular railway features cars suspended from pulleys that run on an overhead cable.

Here is the original first verse of "Funiculì ! Funiculà !" in the Neapolitan dialect of Italian:

> *Aieressera, oi' ne', me ne sagliette,*
> *tu saie addo'?*
> *Addo' 'stu core 'ngrato cchiu' dispietto farme*
> *nun po'!*
> *Addo' lo fuoco coce, ma si fuie*
> *te lassa sta!*
> *E nun te corre appriesso, nun te struie, 'ncielo*
> *a guarda'!...*
> *Jammo 'ncoppa, jammo ja',*
> *funiculi', funicula'!*

Do you know where I got on, yesterday evening, babe?
Where your ungrateful heart can't spite me anymore!
Where the fire burns, but if you run away, it lets you go!

And it doesn't run after you, doesn't tire you...
look at the sky!
Let's go on, let's go, let's go,
funiculi, funicula!

A Funambulist is a Tightrope Walker

Latin *funis* 'rope'+ Latin verb *ambulare* 'to walk'
A rare synonym is funambulator, rope walker. Also from *ambulare* is the English word *pram*, a shortened form of *perambulator*, a vehicle by which babies and infants are perambulated. *Per*, a Latin preposition and frequent prefix whose basic semantic function is to intensify the meaning of the verbal root, so that, if *ambulare* means 'to walk', then *perambulare* means 'to walk thoroughly.' Ambulance stems from *ambulantia* Late Latin noun 'the act of walking.' An ambulance was originally any vehicle that helped patients move about and spared them the possibly painful act of walking to proper hospital care. The first *ambulancia* was Spanish. Queen Isabella introduced a special wagon to carry the wounded at the Siege of Malaga in 1487.

Spermatic funiculus or spermatic cord

The spermatic funiculus (*funiculus* Latin, diminutive of *funis*, hence 'little rope') is a cord in males that suspends the testis within the scrotum, contains the vas deferens and vessels and nerves of the testis, and extends from the internal abdominal ring through the inguinal canal and external abdominal ring downward into the scrotal sac.

Funiculitis is inflammation of the spermatic cord. **Funisitis** is an inflammation of the umbilical cord, seen of course in newborns, and associated with congenital herpes virus infection of the mother.

There, I've given you enough rope to discourse yourself raw.

Chapter 64

Soap: A Bubble of Etymology

This modest inquiry foamed up when someone asked me what the Latin word for soap was. There was none! Soap was unknown to ancient Rome. The Romans bathed in water: hot water in a caldarium; lukewarm in a tepidarium and cold in a frigidarium.

Calidarium was a Hot Place

The word root in *caldarium* or its rarer, longer, older form *calidarium*, namely Latin *calidus* 'hot,' has a host of reflexes in later languages derived from Latin. Think of French *chaud* 'hot, warm'; Italian *caldo* 'hot' and Spanish *cálido* 'hot.' An interesting, partially hidden reflex shows up in the large boiling kettle or cauldron of witch stories and cannibal movies. Cauldron is from *calderone*, an Italian augmentative of a putative form like **caldario* 'kettle,' so that cauldron's basic meaning is 'big kettle.' The French word for kettle, *chaudière*, shares the same root.

Strigil and Aryballos (little jug of oil)

After the hot bath or after gymnastic exercise, Romans scraped off dirt and sweat with an instrument called a strigil ('STRIDGE-ul,' rhymes with vigil) that looked like a curved butter knife (Latin *strigilis* from *stringere* 'to touch lightly, to scrape, to strip off.' Without bathing at all, Romans also sometimes rubbed olive oil on their skin and scraped it off with a strigil.

The Romans probably borrowed olive-oil cleansing from their ancient neighbours, the Etruscans, who in turn borrowed it from the Greeks. Thousands of years before Caesar rose from the bath to have a slave draw a strigil down his torso to remove the oil and dirt, Greeks were using a similar instrument. The very ancient Greek word is a bit of a tongue-twister for us, stlengis. Its root is unknown and the word itself was replaced later in ancient Greek history with another word for oil scraper, *xyster* 'scraper' from Greek *xuein* 'to polish, to sharpen, to scrape.'

The early Greeks cleaned their bodies with blocks of clay, sand, pumice and ashes, then anointed themselves with oil, and scraped off the oil and dirt with a stlengis. They also used oil with ashes. Clothes were washed without soap in streams.

When Greek males set off for morning exercise on the palaestra, they or their slave took with them a tiny container of olive oil attached to their stlengis. Olive oil was rubbed on the body before the exercise began and then scraped off, with the sweat and dirt, after the exercise.

Greeks did their pushups 'in the rude,' as the prissier Victorian euphemists used to whisper. Our word *gymnasium* is merely a Latin version of the Greek *gymnasion* 'place of nudity' from *gymnos* Greek 'naked.' In botany, a gymnosperm is a plant which has naked seeds, like the pine tree and the hemlock fir. The generic name of the little oil container carried by exercising Greeks was *aryballos*. One of the most charming *aryballoi* can be seen by visitors to Paris. It's a little owl-shaped Protocorinthian aryballos or oil phial found in the Greek Antiquities Department in room 40 on the first floor of the Louvre museum.

Latin: Sapo, Saponis

The first true appearance in extant Roman literature of a 'soap' word is in the writings of the Roman encyclopedist

Pliny the Elder (23 -79 CE). His only surviving opus is *The Natural History*, an utterly non-scientific amassing of lore and ancient Roman knowledge riddled with folk error. It is a preposterous farrago of illogical nonsense but one of the most influential volumes in Latin. The reader gets to peek into the minds of first-century educated Romans and read what they believed about their world.

The word is *sapo, saponis* and Pliny tells us that Romans soldiers borrowed the word during the Gallic Wars: *sapo, Galliarum hoc inuentum rutilandis capillis* 'sapo, invented by the Galls to dye hair.'

Later, the Roman army found Germanic tribes like the Teutones using *sapo* (the same root as English soap and ancestor of the modern German word for soap, *Seife*) to dye their hair red, but not to cleanse themselves or their clothes. *Sapo* did not take on the meaning 'soap' in Latin for hundreds, perhaps a thousand years.

Of what ingredients did sapo consist? Animal fats were boiled with ashes and the resultant medium was mixed with whatever dye materials were being used. The Teutonic colour most desired was red and the chief colorant was a dyestuff that is with us still, henna. The Romans imported henna from the Middle East where it is extracted from the leaves of a tropical plant, *Lawsonia inermis. Hinna* is the Arabic name for this plant. Roman traders, who usually accompanied Roman armies in order to sell things to defeated enemies after the battle, took henna with them on all trips to the outer marches of the empire.

At the Wotanning Salon

To dye their hair red, Wotan-worshipping Germanic tribes used several other local plants in their *sapo* mixture, but not henna, since it is killed by temperatures below 15°C. Among the northern European dye-ingredients that could produce reddish hair were walnut-shell extracts mixed with powdered iron oxides. Why did those proto-krauts love red hair? Well, for one thing, their main god Wotan was usually depicted as a hypertrophic Viking on steroids with fiery red hair and a voluminous russet beard in which the entire mouse population of Prussia could hide.

History of Soap

From an internet history of soap: "A soap-like material found in clay cylinders during the excavation of ancient Babylon is evidence that soap-making was known as early as 2800 BCE. Inscriptions on the cylinders say that fats were boiled with ashes, which is a method of making soap, but do not refer to the purpose of the 'soap.' Such materials were later used as hair styling aids and hair dyes. . . The ancient Egyptian *Ebers Papyrus*, a medical document from about 1500 BCE, describes combining animal and vegetable oils with alkaline salts to form a soap-like material used for treating skin diseases, as well as for washing. . . At about the same time, Moses gave the Israelites detailed laws governing personal cleanliness. He also related cleanliness to health and religious purification. Biblical accounts suggest that the Israelites knew that mixing ashes and oil produced a kind of hair gel."

One question that arose when I was discussing the origin of the word soap: If the Romans borrowed the Teutonic or Gallic *sapo*, were the early Germans and Gauls washing with soap—just as we do—long before the Romans? One Germanophile who is always rootin' for the Teuton said yes. History says no! *Sapo* was goop that one rubbed into one's hair to dye it. While performing this capillary function over centuries, some unheralded shampooer discovered the goop rendered one all clean and lovely. Thus was born modern cleansing soap.

By the second century CE, the Greek physician Galen recommended soap for both medicinal and cleansing purposes. But, after the fall, collapse and shrinkage of the Roman empire, personal cleanliness took a major dive. Soapmaking, as a means of sudsing and cleansing the human body, was not practised during the Dark Ages. What do you suppose hastened the Valkyrie-like ride of incessant plagues, vectored by lice and mice and filth back and forth across the continent of Europe? High levels of personal sanitation? No! Soapmaking only became an established craft in Europe by the seventh century CE. Very gradually more varieties of soap became available for shaving and shampooing, as well as bathing and laundering. England did not have soap-making guilds until the 12th century.

Etymology of the Word Soap

The 'soap' etymon (a technical term in linguistics for 'word root') is widespread in Indo-European languages. Hittite is the earliest Indo-European language we have found, in records written in cuneiform on baked clay tablets. Hittite is an extinct tongue spoken by a people who created an Anatolian empire in the twentieth century BCE that lasted until the twelfth century BCE. The Hittite verbal root meaning 'to cleanse' is *sap*. *Sapiya* was grease mixed with ashes, possibly a Hittite hair-dye medium. The word occurs in some Tartar languages and so the hair-dyeing goop may have been an early import to Greece and Rome and to the Teutons, introduced by early trade from the East.

Modern English *soap* and Old English *sap* 'resin' are direct cognates of all the Germanic and Scandinavian 'soap' words. Modern German *Seife* is related, once we remember the Germanic /f/ for /p/ shift. One example: Latin *piscis* is German *Fisch*. Modern Dutch is *zeep*; Danish *sæbe*, French *savon*; Swedish *sapa*; Estonian *seep*; Finnish *saippua*; Modern

Greek *sapoúni*; Roumanian *sapun*; Swahili *sabuni*; Italian *sapone*.

As one might expect, scientific English retains the full Latin form, so that, for example, the Botanical Latin name of the soapwort genus is *Saponaria*. Still an important process in industrial chemistry is saponification, the hydrolysis of a fat by alkali with the formation of salts of the fatty acids together with glycerol — essentially what happens when soap is made from ashes and heated fats.

Now, dear reader, I wash my hands of this inquiry.

Chapter 65

The Sinuous Sinus of Medicine & Math

This little essay is denser with medical words than most in this book. But, if you read your way through it, many are its bounties, including one lithe nymph. All these words depend on Latin *sinus* 'a curve, anything hollowed out, the fold of a garment, a bay or gulf of water.'

Three Meanings of Sinus

1. In anatomy, the paranasal sinuses are cavities inside the bones near the nose (*para* Greek preposition 'beside, near'). Also called the accessory nasal sinuses, they are lined with epithelial mucosa and act to moisten, warm, and filter air and perhaps they act as resonators for the human voice. Compare music critics who rave about a singer's "head tones." Some head tones depend on exquisitely placed and bounteously spaced sinuses.

2. A sinus is also a channel for venous blood, for example, the aortic sinus is a widened part of the aorta or pulmonary artery opposite a semilunar valve.

3. A draining sinus is a pathological passageway formed to permit the escape of pus from an abscess.

Sinusitis

Sinus + *-itis* a common suffix of disease names from Greek now signifying "inflammation of [the organ named in the front of the word]." Compare appendicitis, neuritis and otitis media (inflammation of the middle ear from *medius* Latin 'middle, inner, inside').

Without proper drainage, a paranasal sinus may become blocked, due to viral or bacterial infection or allergies. In acute suppurative sinusitis (*sub/sup* Latin 'under' + *pus, puris* Latin 'pus'), pus, pain, fever, chills, and headache must be relieved by bed rest, possible antibiotics, extra fluid intake, and hot packs. In chronic hyperplastic sinusitis, polyps crowd the lumen of a sinus and surgical remedy may be necessary.

Lumen is a medical word from Latin denoting the hollow portion of any tubular structure, e.g. the lumen of a vein, the lumen of the intestine, the bore of a hollow needle, the lumen of a catheter.

Sinus Node or Sinoatrial Node

This small mass of nerve fibers and cells is the natural pacemaker of the human heart. Lodged in the muscles of the heart's right auricle it transmits 'contraction commands' through a remarkable network of Purkinje's fibers. It was named by early anatomists who did not fully understand the structure of the mammalian heart, and thought it was like the sinus venosus of lower animals, like the first chamber in the heart of fish and reptiles, a chamber which receives blood from the veins and contracts to pump the blood into a second atrial chamber.

Sinus Rhythm in the Heart

Sinus rhythm describes the normal beating of the heart impelled by electric impulses of the sinus node, detected by ECG or electrocardiogram.

Sinus in Latin

Perhaps the commonest use of the noun *sinus* in Latin referred to the loose hanging fold in the front part of that formal Roman attire called the toga. A small purse was sometimes carried in the fold of the toga and loose coins were kept within the sinus also. Columella, a Roman writer on animal husbandry, wrote *aere sinus plenos urbe reportare* 'to carry back to the city toga-folds filled with coins,' that is, to return home very rich.

The *umbo* is the knob-like protrusion at the front of the toga where one fold is tucked into the crossband. The Latin word also means the boss of a shield and is used in scientific vocabulary as the name of certain structures in botany and zoology. Umbo is related to the Latin and Greek words for belly button, namely *umbilicus* and *omphalos*. Consider the umbilical cord and the fancy term *omphaloskepsis* 'meditation while gazing at the navel,' a practice common in Washington.

Other Related English Words

Insinuate

In Latin *sinus* frequently meant 'the bosom' or the innermost part of a thing, the part folded in. The Latin verb *sinuare* 'to wind, to bend, to curve' has a compound form that gives our English verb *to insinuate*. I may insinuate in a sly, underhanded way the idea that our teacher is stupid so that I am not punished. Were I some government hack, I might also insinuate myself into the good graces of a Washington nuclear-power lobbyist, for I too would appreciate a bribery-financed summer place in Colorado.

Sinuous

A related Latin adjective is *sinuosus* 'full of curves' from which descends our modern English *sinuous*. A sinuous rill is a little stream with bends and curves. A sinuous nymph may dance around you in a foreign café displaying her bodily curves and agile flexions.

Derivatives in other languages

Most of the western languages use the Latin term as well: Spanish: *seno*, Turkish *sinüs*, Italian *seno*, French and German *sinus*.

Sine as a Term in Trigonometry

A sine is a function in trigonometry whose precise definition I shall not attempt. Look it up in an online mathematical dictionary, if you care. Here I'm interested to point out that Latin *sinus* which became English *sine* was used as a translation of a similar metaphor in the Arabic original where the trigonometric function was compared using the Arabic noun *jaib* 'inner fold of a garment,' (Arabic *jaib* equalling Latin *sinus* in meaning) all this when some of the original tenets of trigonometry were being introduced to European mathematics from original trig. treatises in Arabic. I do recall from my high-school trig class that 'the sine of an obtuse angle is numerically equal to that of its supplement.'

Sine Wave

In a sine wave or sinusoid, a signal rises and falls in a repeating pattern, which is wave-like. It's a sine from Latin *sinus* because the waves bend and fold rhythmically.

The Oxford English Dictionary tells us that a sine wave is "a periodic oscillation of pure and simple form in which the displacement at any point is proportional to the sine of the phase angle at that point." A sine wave is a wave or curve resembling a segment of this in form.

That's all, folks. Sine-ing off for now. I think a wave, mayhap a sine wave, is appropriate.

Chapter 66

Your Klaxon is Parping, Sir!

Every now and then I traipse past a British phrase that trips me up, flummoxes me, stops me dead in my polyglot tracks, and induces the onset of IWH (instant word humility). It happened today with 'parping klaxons.' How many North Americans, I wonder, would recognize that phrase? I certainly did not know what it meant when I read about the last night of the Prom Concerts at the Royal Albert Hall in London, England. The BBC Sir Henry Wood Promenade Concerts ("The Proms") are one of the most pleasant and civil of London traditions. Can an event be civil and raucous all at the same time? Indeed yes! Londoners who attend the last night of The Proms are given to tossing paper birds which drift by the dozens under the vaulted span of the great hall's ceiling. The audience also brings to the concert all manner of noisemakers and horns and they do stand up, shout, and "parp klaxons."

There are 70 concerts every year from July to September. On the last night of The Proms, sundry and variegated Brits flock together like clustering rooks to caw out in song all the old warhorses of the British inspirational hymnal. One anthem always sung is that glorious summons of mystico-patriotic effluvium, "Jerusalem," William Blake's mighty poem, set to music in 1916 by C. Hubert H. Parry, usually played at The Proms in a vibrant orchestration by Sir Edward Elgar. The last night of The Proms often concludes with the rafter-thwacking roar of a thousand people singing "Rule, Britannia." If you can't go, there is a superb EMI CD of "The Last Night of The Proms," on which you may listen in digital delight to a vast and happy crowd of distinctly unphlegmatic Londoners bellowing their joy. There is also a BBC DVD.

Please Parp Pleasingly

Parp first appears in print in 1936 as an interjection imitating the sound of a car horn. Parp! Parp! By 1943 it was a noun meaning 'a honking sound.' Soon afterward to parp was a verb meaning to speak in a loud, honking manner or to utter words abruptly. Parp also means to sound the horn of an automobile. In one developed meaning of the word *parp* it represents the sound of emitted flatulence, and is thus a synonym for fart.

Sound of the Klaxon: Ah-OOOOOO-Gah!

When I was a kid watching too much television, one of the early series was "The Silent Service," all about American submarines in World War Two. It began with repeated blasts of a klaxon: AH-OOOOO-GAH! AH-OOOOO-GAH! Then the submarine captain would bark an order, "Dive! Dive! Give me a five-degree down-bubble." My brother and I often tried to reproduce a down-bubble in the bathtub on Saturday evening. Neither of us drowned.

The Klaxon was a trademarked horn for automobiles, the electric version invented by Dr. Miller Reese Hutchison, an American inventor and an associate of the more famous inventor Thomas Edison. The Oxford English Dictionary has a charmingly old-fashioned and quaint definition when it refers to the klaxon as "the hooter on a motor vehicle." How very retro! Hooters in America are almost always a vulgarism for breasts. There was, and may still be, a chain of restaurants called Hooters where bare-breasted waitresses bring you your meal, their mammaries bobbling as they bound up to the table. One prays that nothing untoward has flopped into your vichyssoise on the way from the kitchen. Although one imagines—because it is a cold soup—that it would tend to erect the server's nipples. Perhaps that is a desideratum at Hooters? The idea of breasts stirring one's food is apparently erotic to Americans. No wonder psychiatry throve in the land of eagles!

Hutchison's electromechanical klaxon horn was eventually used on trains, ships, and model-T Fords. I'm going to review the etymology, but first here is part of the Wikipedia entry on the famous horn: "The Klaxon's characteristic sound is produced by a spring-steel diaphragm with a rivet in the centre that is repeatedly struck by the teeth of a rotating cog-wheel. The diaphragm is attached to a horn which acts as an acoustic transformer as well as controlling the direction of the sound. In the first klaxons, the wheel was driven either by hand or by an electric motor."

Etymology of Klaxon

F. W. Lovell, the founder of the American company, coined the name *Klaxon* from the Greek verb *klazein*, 'to make a loud noise,' one of whose forms is *klazon*. Akin is the Greek noun *klange* which meant 'a loud twang of the string of a lute' or other stringed instrument that accompanied the recitation of Homeric epics. So we can imagine this distant ancestor of the Klaxon car horn twanging loudly to represent some dramatic pause in Odysseus' adventures. Related to that Greek word is the Latin (and now English) noun *clangor* 'a loud noise.' Even more interesting relatives of the Indo-European root are German *Gelachter* and English *laughter*, both loud noises too. All descend from the echoic Indo-European **klak-* 'to make a loud noise.'

The word was also borrowed into modern French where *le klaxon* is still the common word for 'car horn.' To honk the horn of your car is *klaxonner*.

Bill Casselman

Jerusalem
by William Blake

"And did those feet in ancient time
Walk upon England's mountains green?
And was the holy Lamb of God
On England's pleasant pastures seen?
And did the Countenance Divine
Shine forth upon our clouded hills?
And was Jerusalem builded here
Among those dark Satanic Mills?
Bring me my Bow of burning gold;
Bring me my Arrows of Desire;
Bring me my Spear; O clouds unfold!
Bring me my Chariot of Fire!
I will not cease from Mental Fight,
Nor shall my Sword sleep in my hand,
Till we have built Jerusalem
In England's green and pleasant Land."

Notes on "Jerusalem"

A legend tells the faithful that Jesus, while still a young man, accompanied Joseph of Arimathea to the English town of Glastonbury. William Blake's biographers note that the mystic poet believed in this legend.

One particular line from the poem, 'Bring me my chariot of fire' inspired the title of a film "Chariots of Fire." Blake here drew on a passage from 2 Kings 2:11, where the Old Testament prophet Elijah is taken directly to heaven: 'And it came to pass, as they still went on, and talked, that, behold, there appeared a chariot of fire, and horses of fire, and parted them both asunder; and Elijah went up by a whirlwind into heaven.' A church congregation sings 'Jerusalem' at the close of the film. The song also appears in Tony Richardson's film

'The Loneliness of the Long Distance Runner,' as the Borstal hymn."

And so we bring this anfractuous essay to an end, as we utter a modest parp, a humble ah-OOOOO-gah!, and klaxon off toward the next chapter.

Chapter 67

Billet-Doux for Valentine's Day

Literally 'sweet note' in French, billet-doux means 'love letter' in English. In French, *billet doux* was once a phrase odorous with rococo luxe, like a voluptuous coquette painted by Fragonard, milady afroth in laced sleeves perched at her escritoire. With flowers and a note from her lover freshly arrived, milady turns, naughty imp, to cast a beckoning smile from her sumptuous apartment in the long-ago Paris of Louis XV.

Nowadays billet-doux bears the mocking taint of satire or is starkly archaic. Billet-doux mopes under an old-fashioned sense, like faded dentelle de Chantilly from a once-fresh jabot, but nowadays only yellowed lace folded away in a great-grandmother's rosewood coffer, an accessory never to be reworn.

But, in alert English expository prose (see modern magazine and newspaper citations below) billet-doux as a printed word is still popular. Even in French however, the phrase has been replaced by the literal, dowdy and prosaic *lettre d'amour*. When billet doux first appeared in French print in 1680 CE it already had synonyms like *billet galant* and *billet amoureux*.

Is the hyphen in billet-doux correct? It is the customary English form. There is no hyphen in the phrase in French.

Down the Etymological Pathway

Billet-doux's adjective is *doux, douce*, the French word for sweet, from Latin *dulcis* 'sweet.' All the Romance languages (tongues derived from Latin) have borrowed the Roman adjective. Consider Spanish *dulce de leche* (sweet of milk) a desert or sauce of boiled milk. Think of that Italian hymn to blissful relaxation, *dolce far niente*, so compelling we use the phrase in English too. It means indulgent lolling, 'to do sweet nothing.'

Billet's ancestor in Old French is *billette* (in French print by1389 CE) which was a letter of safe conduct through strange territory. Billette stems from a medieval Latin word *billia* attested by 1198 CE that meant 'important short document on parchment,' a possible relative of *bulletta*, diminutive of *bulla* Latin 'anything globular or spherical like a bubble, a ball, a knob, a stud. Papal bulls or edicts were so named because a round lead seal, *bulla*, was affixed to the bottom of the parchment page. In England *bulla* was a Latin translation of the phrase "The King's seal."

It appears that the name of the round seal at the bottom of the parchment came to stand for the whole parchment or paper itself, and that bulla underwent dialectical vowel gradation to billia and then was made diminutive as billette, here the diminutive form means not so much 'physically smaller' as 'less important,' in the sense that a short love note is less important than a papal pronouncement. Some atheists would disagree.

Synecdoche, Why Don't You Take All of Me?

This common verbal development in languages where part of something eventually names the whole thing (e.g. the bulla seal names the whole document as a papal bull) has a fancy name as a figure of speech in rhetoric, synecdoche (sin-NEC-do-kee). The classical Greek was means 'understanding (*doche*) something extra (*ek-*) at the same time (*syn-*).' *Syn*, of course, is a Greek preposition and a prefix that means literally 'with, together with, accompanied by.' In the catalogue of Latin rhetorical terms, synecdoche had two categories: *pars pro toto* where a small part names the whole thing and the less common *totum pro parte* where a whole thing name refers only to a part of the whole thing.

Bulletin Just Arrived like a Bullet!

Bulletin meaning 'a brief report of an event, often of official issue' is from French *bulletin* whose formal analysis finds it to be a double diminutive of *boule* 'ball.' As early as 1299 CE in French, *bulletin* signified the seal on a message, often a warm ball of wax pressed flat by a metal seal and used to conclude or to fasten shut an important short document.

A bullet was also a small ball, of lead, from Middle French *boulette* 'small missile' and *boulet* 'cannonball,' both diminutives of *boule* 'ball.'

What about Soldiers' Billet?

How does billeting soldiers in a village inn during a war relate to a love letter? Because the root meaning of *billet* in French is 'short note,' then 'ticket' as in *billet d'avion* 'airplane ticket' or *billet aller-retour* 'roundtrip or return ticket.' Originally *un billet de logement* 'lodging ticket' was the ticket or little note assigning quarters to soldiers looking for a night's rest and presented to the owner of the village house, stating that the owner **must** let soldiers eat and sleep in his house for whatever duration the army ordered.

Citations, both modern & ancient:

"A SECRET letter from a loyal servant telling of his employer's passion for marriage into Britain's Royal Family is revealed in The Times today. . . But the billet doux is not about Paul Burrell, the late Diana, Princess of Wales, and the Queen, but about a royal affair from half a millennium ago." — *The Sunday Times*, November 2002

"Young lovers in Victorian England, forbidden to express their affection in public and fearful that strict parents would intercept their billets-doux, sent coded messages through the personal columns in newspapers." — Susan Adams, "I've got a secret," *Forbes*, September 20, 1999

"His Officers and Soldiers; who were by those Billets dispersed into Quarters in several Parts of the Town." — *London Gazette* No. 6152/3, 1723 CE

"With tender billets-doux he lights the pyre,
And breathes three amorous sighs to raise the fire;
Then prostrate falls, and begs with ardent eyes
Soon to obtain, and possess, the prize:
The powers gave ear, and granted half his prayer;
The rest the winds dispersed in empty air."
— Alexander Pope, *The Rape of the Lock*, (II, 40-45), 1712 CE

The Concept of Love-Letter in Other Tongues

Comparison is odious. Among languages it is also somewhat silly. Nevertheless, in the verbal stakes for words meaning 'love letter,' as far as euphony and "sonic appropriateness" goes, French wins hands down with *billet doux*, especially compared with the creepy German *Liebesbrief*, the utilitarian Russian *lyoobovnoi pismuh* 'amorous written note,' and the merely serviceable Italian *lettera d'amore*. Spanish borrows the French word and gives us *il billete amoroso*. Swedish *kärleksbrev* sounds like it might slice open your fingers while you read it!

So, having perused the billet-doux, let us open the mahogany drawer of our Louis Quatorze escritoire, store the letter away, and tiptoe to a velvet-pillowed settee, thereupon to swoon.

Chapter 68

Juju: African Magic Word
Materializes in English

Juju is a West African magic charm or amulet or gri-gri (see below) used by a shaman, medicine man or witch doctor. Many objects may contain a magical juju spirit. Juju can be the fetish object itself, the magic power inside the object, or juju may be the tutelary spirits who superintend and wield juju, at the behest of the witch doctor, who can insert juju into certain objects like dolls or a familiar fetish object like blood-soaked chicken feathers tied in a bundle and fastened to a small animal or human bone by snakeskin ribbon.

World's Greatest Dictionary Still in Error?

The Oxford English Dictionary maintains, even in the face of modern comparative linguistic evidence from the study of African etymology, that the word *juju* was made up by Africans repeating a French nursery word for toy, namely *joujou*. This French word is an example of the reduplication of a root that occurs in many Western languages nursery words. *Jou* is the singular imperative of *jouer* 'to play.' So the word for toy means literally 'play, play', precisely what a parent offering an infant a new toy might have said long ago. Consider other infantile reduplication words like the English nursery toilet words: poopoo, kaka and doodoo.

Surprise! There is an African Origin of This African Word!

The problem? There exists a perfectly cogent African etymology for the word. Consider the Hausa word for fetish or bad spirit, *djudju*, with its root **not** in French. The word was around in Africa, centuries before French imperialists showed up to mess everything up!

Hausa, by the way, is one of the principal languages of Nigeria, spoken by nearly twenty million people there, one-fifth of the population. It is also the language of an additional three million people in Niger. Hausa is a Chadic language in the Afro-Asiatic language family. The word *juju* was noted in English as long ago as 1894 in a book about West Africa.

In the Yoruba language *jù* means 'to throw.' The general West African root is the Chadic etymon *ju* 'throw,' so that *juju* is 'throw-throw' because the amulet was tossed by the witch doctor or thrown from hand to hand as he induced the powerful spirit to enter the object. Then the fetish was thrown on the ground in front of the person seeking a magically charged object. The witch doctor also throws the juju power into a waiting object with his potent spell. If it were a fortune telling, the sorcerer foretold his fate from the way the juju landed in front of person. For other nefarious purposes, the seeker might also take the object away and use it to perform evil upon another person. If you need a quickie juju and can't wait for the witch doctor to get his act together, you can skip off to a fetish market, where pre-juju-ed objects await sale.

Good Juju & Bad Juju

A dead monkey's paw is a common juju object in West Africa. Good juju cures diseases of mind and body. Bad juju works to get revenge, to assuage jealous rage, or to bring bad fortune crashing down upon the fate and body of someone who has thwarted you in business, in love or cheated you at the marketplace. An individual can accrete good juju to his or her person by doing good deeds: saving a starving dog, giving a crippled beggar a bowl of soup. You can build up juju reserves; then you visit a witch doctor and he deftly transfers the units of juju goodness to a cow's horn and away you go! All juju-ed up.

Meaning Extended When Word Reached America

Black slaves brought the word and the practice of juju to America. From the 1960s onward, arising in American hippie slang, the word *juju* took on far broader meanings that juju magic. Juju came to mean the general spirit of a place, a situation, or a plan.

Citations & Usage Examples:

"No way was I going to step inside that dingy motel room. Bad juju."

"Horsetit, the dealer, said he was going to meet us under the bridge. No way! His shack smelled like dead toads, reeked of major-league, evil juju."

From the internet: "Juju of the more sinister sort was mentioned in 1997 by Reuben Abati, member of the editorial board of the Guardian Newspapers of Lagos, Nigeria. He told of a Nigerian in the United States who 'had built a strong network for credit card fraud. He repatriated funds regularly to Nigerian banks. After his arrest, his associates were afraid to testify against him. The fellow was said to have strong 'juju.' Even the presiding judge was advised to be careful lest the accused gave him an incurable ailment by 'remote control.'"

In Yoruba, juju names a style of local African music. King Sunny Ade was crowned King of Juju Music in a grand ceremony in 1967. Nowadays in American slang, juju can also mean marijuana or a frowsy woman.

Grigri: A Quasi-Synonym for Juju

A grigri is a charm, a fetish, an amulet, a spell or an incantation that can ward off evil or summon it to befall a victim. It's a word in the Balante language of Africa. A greegree man is an African magician or fetish priest, one who makes and sells charms and talismans: pieces of jewelry thought to be a protection against evil.

Juju and grigri are very primitive concepts. I, a cool modern type, don't need them. After all, I have my lucky rabbits' foot and my four-leaf clover.

Chapter 69

Hawaiian & Latin Breath Words

And the Lord God formed man of the dust of the ground, and breathed into his nostrils the breath of life; and man became a living soul. - KJV Genesis 2:7

Ha as Hawaiian verb means 'to breathe, to exhale the breath of life.' *Ha* is onomatopoeic. As a noun, *ha* is the breath of life. Polynesian *ha* imitates the sound of a human exhaling, and thus demonstrates the same linguistic ploy, imitation of the sound of the concept being defined by the word itself, used by the ancient Romans when they needed a Latin verb meaning to breathe and came up with *halo, halare* 'to breathe.' Both words imitate the sound of inhaling and exhaling.

Haole

The most interesting island term that contains *ha* is the Hawaiian word for foreigner or stranger or non-islander. The story, possibly apocryphal, concerns the traditional Hawaiian mode of greeting. Two people say hello by touching foreheads, then breathing in and breathing out alternatively. Thus one's breath of life is exhaled into the person you are greeting, and then she or he inhales your breath-spirit and reciprocates.

The tale is told that, in 1778, when Captain Cook became the first European to visit the islands, he was revolted when King Kalaniopuu puffed a greeting into his mouth. Cook turned away in revulsion at this very unBritish and to Cook unsanitary act. Thus were these strange white creatures dubbed in Polynesian *haole* 'humans with no breath of life in them.' Still today haole is the common word for foreigners. But it is an insult. There are more neutral words in Hawaiian for foreigner and the most common one is *malihini* 'stranger, newcomer, tourist, guest, one unfamiliar with a place or custom; new, unfamiliar, unusual, rare, introduced, of foreign origin.'

Aloha

This is the most famous Hawaiian word that does NOT have *ha* in the word.

True Root

The word *aloha* derives from the Proto-Polynesian root *qarofa, with cognates in other Polynesian languages such as Samoan *alofa* and Maori *aroha*, also meaning 'love.'

False Root

A spurious and false folk etymology — but a beautiful thought nonetheless— claims that aloha is a compound of the Hawaiian words *alō* meaning presence, front, face or share + *ha*, meaning breath of life. But alō is spelled with kahakoo (macron or long vowel mark) over the *a*, whereas the word *aloha* does not have a long *a*. O pshaw, you say. Does a mere macron make any sort of difference at all? In a language with far fewer vowel sounds and consonants than our Roman alphabet, it certainly does! Every little vowel lengthening has a meaning of its own. Aloha's prime meaning is 'love.'

Animus

Many words throughout all world languages use imitation when coming up with words about breathing and living.

Consider Latin *animus*. In Latin, *animus* named the sentient, thinking center of a human, the rational soul, the mind, and some mental powers like courage and passion. The Proto-Indo-European etymon was *ane 'to blow,' hence 'to breathe,' with reflexes in most later PIE languages, for example: Greek *anemos* 'wind,' Welsh *anadl* 'breath,' Old Iranian *animm* 'soul' and Old Norse *anda* 'to breathe,' and Sanskrit *aniti* 'he breathes.'

The *animus* root produced dozens of current English words like animal, animation, animated, equanimity, animadvert, magnanimous and pusillanimous.

Controversial Meaning of the Place Name *Hawaii*

Elsewhere in Polynesia, Hawaii or a cognate is the name of the underworld or of the ancestral home, but in Hawaii the name has no meaning.(!) So state innumerable tourist-as-chump brochures and pamphlets of travel blather. But, really, does that seem compelling to reason?

The hypothetical Proto-Polynesian ur-form of the word is perhaps *Sawaiki with a reconstructed meaning of 'homeland.' Cognates are found is other Polynesian languages such as the Maori word *Hawaiki*, the Rarotongan *'Avaiki* and Samoan *Savai'i*.

Everywhere else in Polynesia the word has a double semantic cast: in its negative sense, Hawaii means hell or underworld; in its positive sense it means homeland or ancestral home. But in the very islands of Hawaii, it doesn't mean that. It has no meaning? Shark shit! No word is void of reference or empty of meaning. Even nonsense word are nonsensical. What that denial of its root meaning represents is mealy-mouthed, suck-hole linguists who have been told by tribal chieftains or the viler sort of politician (native or not) not to sully the fair name of vacation paradise with a label that means 'hell.' What a trembling, cringing, crawling coterie of abject toadies and lickspittles!

The ancient Romans were asked where the name *Roma* came from. They had no clue. So they made up an ancestor named Romulus and derived their city's name from this unhistorical, quite mythical founder. Hawaiians did the same thing. They made up a traditional discoverer of the islands named Hawaii Loa, of whom there is not the scantiest evidence anywhere. No such plumed and plumeria-leied dude ever lived.

As in every other language, illiterates and fools can find any root they want in a word, never mind linguistic sense or historical proof. Sometimes, on cheap postcards that show comely maidens hula dancing, you'll see this nonsense about the origin of Hawaii.

'HA-'
Means the "breathe of life".
There is no literal English translation. (Hey, postcard-writer-fool, you just gave a translation!

'-WAI-'
In literal English means, "fresh water."
(No, it does not, dingbat.)

'-I'
This word is literally, the word or tone denoting or implying the concept of a supreme God. (As Hawaiian etymology, this is utter poppycock and twaddle!)

Correct Spelling of Hawai'i

The state's name should be spelled with an apostrophe or comma indicating that the penultimate letter of Hawaii is a glottal stop. The glottal stop is actually a letter of the short

Hawaiian alphabet. When you produce a glottal stop, you open and close your glottis at the back of your throat. When you say ee-ee, you have to open and close your glottis to produce the second ee sound. Ditto at the end of Hawai'i. The Hawaiian name of the glottal stop letter is 'okina.

Vog: New word from Hawaii

In common use in the Hawaiian islands, vog is volcanic smog or fog, a form of air pollution that results when sulfur dioxide and other gases and particles emitted by an erupting volcano react with oxygen and moisture in the presence of sunlight. Vog is a portmanteau word, a blended compound made up of *volcanic* and *smog.*

And so, to all my isle-minded readers, aloha oe!

Chapter 70

Fishmonger, Meet Wordmonger

The Oxford English Dictionary lists more than 306 compounds ending in the –monger suffix: duty-monger, god-monger, lie-monger, maxim-monger. In most current uses, -monger as a suffix makes the word an insult: whoremonger, warmonger, slander-monger, flesh-monger, monger of clichés, gossip-monger. The compounds reek of depreciative dismissal and sneering contempt. "Robbie Burns was a mere ballad-monger." But once, earlier in the history of English, monger had a neutral meaning of 'trader' or 'seller,' hence simple occupational descriptives, common at British markets, like fishmonger, hay-monger, ale-monger, cheese-monger and pear-monger.

The Fetid Joys of the Grievance-Monger

Some older –monger compounds are worth revival, for example, grievance-monger is a phrase worth recalling. It fits today's professional protesters and injustice-collectors, the self-pitying whiners who parade at public events, their young, angry, unlived-in faces smug with the disdain common to all of history's junior anarchists, the grievance-mongering losers who never vote, the protesters who have never tried to do anything but wail and bitch, put-upon-pie children whose sole innocent purpose is to destroy a world. As their rocks through windows and burning police cars shatter public order, so their moans pollute our civil air. The psychotic joy in their animal faces as they ignite buildings and burn down peaceful assemblies tells onlookers all we need to know about these ring-nosed, buttock-tattooed scum. Seeing their own reflections in the glass shards of the windows they have just smashed reveals the origin of their brainless anger. As that supreme American essayist Gore Vidal once wrote, "It is the rage of Caliban seeing his own face in the mirror."

Fellmonger

I happened upon the noun *fellmonger* recently as I began to reread the English novel *Lorna Doone* by the Victorian lawyer and classicist, R.D. Blackmore, whose style of English, a sturdy amalgam of Shakespeare, Milton and the King James Bible, presents guidance to the modern writer about how best to embed a spine of word iron into anemic, round-shouldered prose.

There is still a guild in England entitled The Fellmongers Company of Richmond in Yorkshire, an ancient craft and trading organization which had its origin in the middle ages and was an early trade union, originally made up of skinners and glovers. A fellmonger is a dealer in fells or sheepskins, who separates the wool from the pelts.

Among the oldest words in English, *fell* is a common Teutonic root whose prime meaning is 'the skin of an animal.' In the novel *Lorna Doone*, the fellmonger sells sheepskins. The Indo-European etymon was perhaps *pelno 'animal skin' making fell cognate with Latin *pellis* 'skin' and Greek *pella*. Our English word *pelt* also may be related, through the syncopation of an Anglo-Norman diminutive form like *pelette* or *pellette* 'little skin, foreskin.'

Syncopation or syncope in linguistics is the deletion of phonemes from a word or phrase. *Wanna* is a syncopated form of *want to*; *don't* is syncope for *do not*. Using *o'er* in poetic English instead of *over* is syncope. Although syncope usually describes the loss of unstressed vowels, it may also refer to dropped consonants.

Monger — Etymology & Semantics

By itself as a noun meaning 'salesman,' 'dealer,' 'trader' or 'seller of goods,' *mangere* existed in Old English and had acquired its /o/ by the time of Middle English as *mongere*.

Old English is the earliest form of our tongue spoken and written by the Anglo-Saxons between about 450 CE and 1050 CE. Middle English is a term coined by linguists to describe our language from the late eleventh century and to about 1470 CE, when Chancery Standard, a form of London legal English, began to become widespread through the introduction in England of William Caxton's printing press in the late 1470s.

Mongere had early cousins all over northern Europe, such as *mangari* in Old High German and *mangari* in Old Icelandic. They all derive from *mango, mangonis*, a Latin word borrowed very early into northern European languages. Compare the German verb *mangan* 'to trade goods' or the Spanish *mangon* and *mangonear*.

Small Class of Latin Agent Nouns

In Latin, *mango* belongs to a small group of agent nouns that end in /o/. *Caupo* is a Latin word for an innkeeper or tavern-owner. *Gero* is Latin for a porter or carrier of loads on his back. The standard agent noun suffix in Latin is –*or* or –*ator*, seen in agent nouns like emptor 'buyer,' known to us in the Latin phrase *caveat emptor* 'let the buyer beware.' The longer agent noun suffix is seen in the Roman word *gladiator*, literally 'one who carries and fights with a *gladius*.' A *gladius* was a small Roman sword. There is plant whose slender leaves reminded an early naming botanist of the blade of a small sword or *gladiolus*. The Latin agent noun suffix -*or* is, of course, cognate and equivalent to our English agent noun suffix *-er*, in words like speaker and fighter.

Watch That Specificity!

Latin abhors semantic specificity, in general. All that means is this: Latin has a small vocabulary; therefore single Latin words must bear many different shades of meaning. So, generally, Latin nouns have many meanings rather than one specific one. But *mango* is an example of an agent noun that did develop a quite specific meaning. There are several Latin words that mean trader, seller or agent. The more common word in Latin for salesman was *mercator*, related to current English words like *merchant* and *merchandise*. But *mango* came to mean a specific type of salesman, a slave trader, a dealer who bought up at bargain prices injured or malnourished slaves, fed them and brought them back to a reasonably robust health, so the *mango* could resell the poor wretches at a hefty profit.

A *mango* refurbished slaves and some buffed, repainted and repolished shoddy merchandise so it too could be resold. A *mango* might put a new glaze on old pottery and render the wares more easily saleable. Some etymologists use that fact to suggest the Romans may have borrowed their word *mango, mangonis* directly from classical Greek, where they posit an unattested noun like *mangano, manganonis from a real Greek noun *mánganon* 'deception, trickery, juggling, contrivance, means of enchantment.' Note that a vowel followed by a doubled gamma in Greek usually indicated a nasal syllable. The Greek term from which English gets its word angel was *aggelos* 'messenger,' pronounced *angelos*. Among their other winged duties angels are messengers of a god.

Mango is possibly cognate with the Late Latin military word *manganum* 'ballista' from Greek *manganon* 'philter, ballista,' from Greek *manganeuein* 'to deceive,' cognate with Middle Irish *meng* 'deception,' Tocharian A *mank* 'guilt', Sanskrit *mañju* beautiful; basic Indian meaning: to beautify with a derogatory sense, that is, to tart up, to dress up something dowdy to make it appear beautiful.

Some of these surnames may derive from *mango*: Mangone, Mangan, Mangano, Manges, Mangault and Mangold.

To show just how early in English the word *monger* appeared, we can quote from the Latin in a Royal Charter of King Aethelwulf: *unum merkatorem quem eam lingua nostra mangere nominamus* 'a seller whom we now call in our language a mangere [monger].' Aethelwulf was King of Wessex from 839 to 856 CE.

We'll conclude with a couple of mongers you may not know.

1. A costermonger is a term still used in London, England to name a person who sells fruits and vegetables from a street cart or barrow. Costermonger originally meant apple-seller and the word referred to one variety of large apple, a costard, an English apple with prominent costes or ribs (French *coste* 'rib'). London's famous and colorful Pearly Kings & Queens Guild evolved out of costermongers' associations.

2. "The clothes look straight off a tat-monger's street barrow." A nice British coinage by J. Gash in Lies of Fair Ladies (1993). Tat is used or shoddy goods.

3. A doom-monger peddles end-of-life-on-earth horror stories for the delectation of the terminally depressed and the professionally pessimistic.

That, friendly readers all, shall suffice for this essay, lest I dwindle into a mere monger-monger.

Chapter 71

Of Pygmies and Nuns and Amazing Nano-Scaffolds

Nanos is a classical Greek word for 'dwarf.' By using a nanoscaffold of ultra-fine polymer fibers, researchers have been able to regrow damaged or missing organs and limbs on small animals. A nanoscaffold forms a substructure for healing muscle, bone, and nerve tissue, this scaffold being composed of a grid or scaffold or *reticulum* (net) of fibers hundreds of times thinner than a human hair. Fluid containing the tiny fibers is injected between the severed nerve endings to build a nanoscaffold. The net-like grid of such fibers can be seeded with human growth cells and perhaps even with architectural chemical instructions on how and where to grow! With the help of this initial support grid, the nerves grow back together more quickly and more efficiently and more densely. The very title of the one of the earliest journal articles to use the term (2002) summarizes the tale: *Nano-Fibrous Scaffolding Architecture Enhances Protein Adsorption and Cell Attachment*, Kyung Mi Woo, Victor J. Chen, and Peter X. Ma, University of Michigan.

Extracellular Matrices

An early synonym for nanoscaffold is also explanatory: artificial extracellular matrices. The original idea was that these artificial nano-fibrous polymer strands and nets and lattices would mimic the structure of natural collagen fibers (fibroblasts). And they do! The fibrous reticulum is more porous, has more tiny holes for cell attachment and protein adsorption than natural fibroblasts provide. To quote the journal abstract, "results demonstrate that the biomimetic nano-fibrous architecture serves as superior scaffolding for tissue engineering."

Take a Gander at a Salamander

One piece of research that set scientists thinking of nanoscaffolding was analysis of a salamander's tail. No matter how many times a tale is lost or cut off, a salamander's tail grows back. But a human toe chopped off does not grow back. Why?

When first amputated, human and salamander limbs respond similarly. Yet shortly after such an excision, human and salamander healing processes differ. A human stump bleeds and the wound or amputated part develops a scar whose tough horny tissue inhibits the human body's ability to regenerate the body part and the healing process terminates with abundant scar tissue.

A salamander's tail stump does not scar over. Instead salamander blood vessels contract quickly and a layer of thin skin is rapidly produced to cover the wound. After a few days, this new skin layer signals cells called apical epithelial caps (AEC) that are essential for regrowth. Fibroblasts move in to form a structural framework for new tissue and eventually to form a blastema, thus forming a new limb.

In 2006, a team of neuroscientists recreated in mice a traumatic brain injury by severing the optic nerve causing the mice to experience blindness. The scientists injected nanoscaffold particles and watched as the nerves regrew and the mice's sight was restored.

Researchers from the University of Sheffield in England used nanoscaffolding in 2006 to repair skin damage in people with third degree burns. An American soldier's lost fingertip has been regrown including the bone, the nail and the digit's tissue.

Scientific Use of Nano- Prefix

Nano-, the chiefly scientific prefix is common in twentieth-century technical terms like nanotechnology, nanoplankton, nanolitre, nanobacterium, nanorobot and nanotube.

Precise Metric Use of Nano-

In the nomenclature of the metric system, the prefix nano- has a specific mathematical meaning, namely, 'one billionth part of', so that a nanosecond is one billionth of a second and a nanolitre is a teeny droplet indeed, being one billionth of a litre.

My New Etymology of *Nanos* and Derivatives

Greek *nanos* 'dwarf'

Some dictionaries claim *nanos* is akin to other ancient Greek words like *nanna, nenna* 'aunt.' Merriam-Webster claims a relationship with our English word *nun*!: "Etymology: Middle English, from Old English *nunne*, from Late Latin *nonna* nun, child's nurse; of baby-talk origin like Greek *nanna, nenna* female relative, aunt, Welsh *nain* grandmother, Albanian *nanë* mother, child's nurse, Russian *nyanya* child's attendant, Sanskrit *nan* mother, little mother."

All fine and dandy as a source route for aunt and granny terms, but I don't think *nanos* fits here. This is not the origin of a word for dwarf. I posit that the etymology of *nanos* is a primitive reduplication form, a simple doubling of a negative particle. The word did not arise from baby talk. In origin, *nanos* is a rejective, reductive, abusive compound. In other words, a dwarf to primitive speakers of Indo-European was a *no-no* of human form (in Proto-Indo-European **ne-ne* or **na-na*) hence an eventual Hellenic reflex like *nanos*.

Is there any proof for my supposition? None — except for the meagre cogency of semantic logic. Were our ancestral aunts and grannies all dwarves, living under toadstools and riding wee beetles like teeny fairy folk? Could the ancients not distinguish between the shrinkage of old age and dwarfism? I imagine they could. Were little people routinely vilified in unenlightened eras of human life as stubby no-nos? Of course they were!

I suggest that the Latin word for dwarf, *nanus* is not a cognate but a direct borrowing of the Greek etymon. The Latin word for dwarf is *nanus*. The Latin word spread through the Romance languages of Europe early, giving us forms like:

French *nain* 'dwarf'
Italian *nano* (thus "Snow White and the Seven Dwarves" in Italian is *Biancaneve e i sette nani*. Snow White in Italian is White (bianca) Snow (neve).
Portuguese *anão*
Maltese *nanu* (Was Robin Williams listening?)
Sardinian *nannu*
Spanish *enano*.

Dos enanos, two dwarfs, appear in Velazquez' most analyzed painting, Las Meninas (Spanish, 'the maids of honour') one of the earliest meditations (1656 CE) in paint on the blurred line between reality and illusion. Dwarves populated many a European court during the sixteenth and seventeenth centuries, not always, as in the Velazquez work, as playmates for royal children, but also as tokens of good luck and as deformed curiosities of nature. Due to courtly inbreedings, the incidence of achondroplasia, the most common form of dwarfism, was high, and often dwarves were the unwanted spawn of royal women, too misshapen ever to be allowed legal inheritance or public admission to the recognized family.

A Latin Proverb about Little People

Inter pygmaeos regnat nanus.
My translation: "Among pygmies, even a dwarf is king."

Its semantic match is found in a similar proverb: In the land of the blind, the one-eyed man is king. It is a nifty putdown of a bad leader.

Although the word *pygmy* today refers to short-statured tribal peoples who live in central Africa and also in southeast Asia, the word *pygmy* is first found in Greek mythology. The Greek word *pygme* was a measurement term, the length of the arm from elbow to wrist, hence a very short measure of length, around 13 inches. So the original sense of the noun *pygmy* was 'a human being only as tall as a man's arm.'

The mythological Greek Pygmies were especially famous for their battle with the cranes, as described in Homer. Depictions of their battle were very commonplace, particularly on pottery. No reason for the widespread popularity of this Greek story has been adduced by classicists.

Pugnacious Pygmies

The prime meaning of *pygme* in Greek was 'fist.' It is cognate with the Latin word for fist, *pugnus*, more familiar to English speakers because of the Latin word's many derivatives like pugnacious, pugnacity and related Latin derivatives like pugilist 'a boxer who uses his fists.' Both the Greek and Latin words stemmed from an Indo-European root like **pug* 'thick.' When you made your hand thick, you made a fist.

In 1601 Philemon Holland published a delightful translation of Pliny's *Natural History*. The *Historia naturalis* by Gaius Plinius Secundus, 23-79 CE, was the famous enclycopedist's attempt to "romanize" the extant scientific knowledge of the day, to take it from Greek and make it at home in Latin. In his *Natural History*, Pliny gives his version of the pygmies and the cranes:

"And these pretie people Homer also reporteth to be much troubled and annoied by cranes. The speech goeth, that in the Spring time they set out all of them in battell array, mounted upon the backe of rammes and goats, armed with bowes and arrowes, and so downe to the sea side they march, wheere they make foule worke among the egges and young cranelings newly hatched, which they destroy without all pitie. Thus for three moneths this their journey and expedition continueth, and then they make an end of their valiant service: for otherwise if they should continue any longer, they were never able to withstand the new flights of this foule, growne to some strength and bignesse. As for their houses and cottages, made they are of clay or mud, fouls feathers, and birds egge shels."

Although there is no cogent, extant explanation for the story of the pygmies' battle with the cranes, it may have been a mightily garbled and botched attempt at telling the story of European crane migration, a lively little tale that became mingled with the supposition that cranes were large enough to pluck pygmy babies from their reed cradles and gobble the wee babes up with unseemly delight.

Chapter 72

Deep-Sea Words like Abyss
& Benthos & Pelagic

Abyssal benthos is a phrase that names the animals and plants that live near the bottom of the sea, whereas littoral benthos is the flora and fauna living in water nearer shore (*littora* Latin 'shore')

Abyssal, of course, pertains to the abyss, primal name of scowling sunken chaos, chasmic grotto of Hell, undersea penetralia, unfathomable gulfs unplumbed. The word has had several spellings during its long underwater trip through English. Abyss is the current common form but I like two archaic ones too, abysm and abysmus. Both sound deeper and more infernal. In Latin *abyssus* was borrowed from Greek *abyssos* 'the deep' but literally *a* Greek 'not' + *byssos* Greek 'depth' or 'bottom,' itself akin to words treated below like benthos and bathos. Abyss may stem from even older tongues of the ancient Middle East. The Sumerian language had a word that named the waters beneath the earth and that word was *abzu*.

Tennyson and Shakespeare both liked the dark hollowness of the word *abyss*. Tennyson's short and stirring "The Kraken Wakes" presents an excellent poetic glimpse of an abyss.

The Kraken Wakes
Below the thunders of the upper deep,
Far far beneath in the abysmal sea,
His ancient, dreamless, uninvaded sleep
The Kraken sleepeth: faintest sunlights flee
About his shadowy sides: above him swell

Huge sponges of millennial growth and height;
And far away into the sickly light,
From many a wondrous grot and secret cell
Unnumbered and enormous polypi
Winnow with giant arms the slumbering green.
There hath he lain for ages and will lie
Battening upon huge seaworms in his sleep,
Until the latter fire shall heat the deep;
Then once by men and angels to be seen,
In roaring he shall rise and on the surface die.

There is now a commercial rum, black and spiced, whose brand name is The Kraken.

In *The Tempest,* Shakespeare has Prospero ask Miranda whether she can remember their life before they arrived on the island. Miranda remembers "Four or five women once that tended me." Prospero says:

"Thou hadst, and more, Miranda. But how is it
That this lives in thy mind? What seest thou else
In the dark backward and abysm of time?"

Prospero wonders if any more childhood memories are vivid for Miranda.

Benthos

The Greek noun *benthos* meant 'the deeps of bodies of water.' Benthic depths are the deepest parts of the sea. *Benthos* is related to the Greek adjective *bathys* 'deep,' which appears in dozens of English scientific words like bathymetric, bathysphere 'a deep-sea diving machine' and paleobathymetry 'scientific study of the depths of ancient seas.' Bathys' corresponding Greek noun *bathos* 'depth' could refer to depths other than those of water. For example, in the critical language of modern

English, in the study of literature, bathos is a sinking, a letting-down, a lapse, an anticlimax in which the mood or action of a story sometimes unintentionally falls from the sublime to the trivial. "The horrid giant broke the whole mountain apart, then stopped to pick his nose." That's bathos! Quite bathetic!

Marine organisms have excellent names based on how they move through water. Plankton comprise the flora and fauna that drift, from a Greek neuter singular adjective used as a collective noun *plangkton* 'drifting things.' Marine life forms capable of swimming by themselves are referred to collectively as nekton, from Greek *nekton* 'swimming things.'

Pelagic

Over the gunwales washes one more Greek word for the sea still in use in modern English when we speak or write of pelagic sea birds or pelagic fish and other organisms that thrive on the open surface of the ocean. Littoral regions describe waters near shore, benthic regions at the deepest parts of the ocean, and pelagic regions on the bounding waves of the water's surface. Classical Latin borrowed *pelagicus* 'of the sea' ultimately from ancient Greek *pelagos* 'the sea.'

We can't leave this root without dropping a word redolent of swaying coco palms and rippled dunes and tawny sand: archipelago. It began in Italian as *arcipelago* 'chief sea' referring to the Aegean Sea and made up from Greek roots, although it was never an ancient Greek word. Then, because the Aegean is absolutely spotty with islands, isles and islets, archipelago came to refer to any sea with many islands, and then a transfer of meaning to 'any group of islands' gave the word its most common modern English sense.

Assailing We Will Go

These sea words summon up to memory's harsh courtroom my first voyage on a great cruise ship. Here I ask you to permit me a longer-than-usual diversion from language, so that I may share a few of its sailing delights, particularly the onboard food.

I chose the sleek Bilgewater Queen sailing monthly in fair weather from Athen's port, the Piraeus. This star vessel was but one of a fleet from the world's only cruise line owned by a husband and wife team who had made their first millions in a chain of worldwide Greek restaurants. They were the billionaire Greek shipping couple Sam 'n' Ella Streptococcopoulos.

So dense are the happy memories of that cruise they seem to crowd one another aside in their hurry to be recalled. I cherish the thrill of playing obligatory shuffleboard with the sclerotic but mercifully mute gentleman from Idaho who operated two — count 'em, two! — all-night chicken stands. His wife Betuna shared with us her exquisite collection of bronzed toothpicks. Sadly the collection was portable.

But so many modern features on the seven-deck ship speak forth from that blissful odyssey. In the Bilgewater Queen's exciting new Kitchen-Theater, foodies could enjoy daily culinary lectures delivered by obscure Eurotrash royalty. Why, my first night aboard, I attended a talk by the last living remnant of Austro-Hungarian illustriousness, the Hapsburg Baroness Dita Puszta von Dipf-Shtick who spoke to us assembled peasants on the topic "Heritage Goulash."

Ship of Drools

What was so enticing were the many luxury restaurants on board the cruise liner. Three of these eateries were open to all the passengers, however humble and cheapskate (like me) they might be:

- The Okay Canal: Erie Food from Just South of Buffalo. Highlight: Love Canal Slushies. Head Chef? Sanborn Patterson. The galley crew's nickname for the head chef? Foodborne Pathogen.

- *El Gringo Muerto* presents the fiery spices of Central America in traditional fare that is to die for.
- For Proud Americans: The Donner Party Deli (Our Specialty: Mom's Leg of Dad)

Here are two examples of onboard, upscale restaurants (No riffraff, please).

(1) **The Milkmaid's Buttery** specializing in Old English Cuisine, its menu somewhat mangled by semiliterate Spanish chefs who are only peripherally acquainted with the English language and are deaf to boot. Thus every day The Milkmaid's Buttery offers entrees like Stake-in-Kidney Pie. Boeuf Wellington, a hearty meat dish with French fries, can be exchanged for the milder gay fare, Poof Wellington which features minced meat and merry ribbons of dyed potato purée encircling wee beeflets.

(2) *Le Pavillon Privé de Vichy* on the top deck features only six tables and is so exclusive that, at the entrance door, blood tests, gene scans and MRIs are obligatory, to prove that you are Aryan. Genealogy papers attesting to your family's arrival in America before 1800 must be carried on your person throughout the seventeen-course repast. In a sleek alcove tastefully partitioned from the vulgarity of the busy central corridor, where diaphanous curtains of Chantilly lace billow softly in the sea-borne breeze, a trained Bavarian nurse orders you recline into a special nasometric settee and there measures the length of your nose.

Waiters in jack boots are permitted to ask for your identity papers at any time during the festive meal. The *KellnerStaffel* (the K.S.) may approach any table and scream, "*Sie haben*

Verwandte die jetzt in Deutschland wohnen? (You have relatifs now livingk in Chermany?)

Digital photos of your family standing beside a Porsche Boxter or Mercedes Benz may be emailed weeks ahead of your on-board arrival to insure the elite seating you richly deserve. *Bon appetit!*

Forbidden Luau!

But none of the aforementioned *salles à manger* were as much fun as the welcome-aboard-the-ship feast which took the form and title of: Forbidden Luau. Each guest was handed an invitation: "Captain Cyril Krill requests the immeasurable pleasure of your personal company at the captain's table." Said passenger Wade Bunson of Minnesota proudly to his better half, Lil' Becky, "We've been invited to dine at the captain's table tonight. How's that fer ritzy?" Lil' Becky did not have the heart to inform Wade that the captain's table ran the length of the ship and sat 500.

So that all aspirants to the Higher Happiness, all attendees of the after-dinner party, would be on the same ecstatic page, each passenger received one crepe-paper grass skirt ("must be worn over long pants") and one antibacterial lei of fern fronds intermingled with plastic plumeria blossoms. Wearing of the ordained Polynesian apparel was obligatory. And that coconut bra! Haw! Haw! What a riot when a guy with a hairy chest put on a coconut bra! A note on the back of the invitation card read: "Please turn your coconut bra in at the end of the luau. They are made especially for us at great expense by one-legged blind women living in reduced circumstances on a small island near Malta."

Shall I ever sail the benthic seas again? Yes, when Charon, the grim boatman, comes to fetch me on the raft preparatory to crossing that well-known stream, The River of Death.

Chapter 73

Ocotillo: A Noise in the Desert
with a note about the joys of desert solitaire

Once upon a dune, inland due-east from the California city of San Diego, solitary I walked into the Anza-Borrego desert. On that late spring morning long ago, the scrub lay quiet, subdued as Eden after the fall. A sonic minimum hummed among humble cacti, over mesquite, tarbush and *paloverde*. Dry wind shushed across pebbled desert. Then I heard sharp, vivid clacks! The noise startled, as when the devil snaps a whip over his mule team. This rasping of dry ocotillo sticks clattered "thwick-thwock."

The ocotillo, also called the coach-whip plant, stands up in a spiky nest of long, dead-looking, slender branches often eight to fifteen feet tall, as if someone stuck ten tall brittle branches in the sand. The desert wind knocks ocotillo stems against one another and they clack, frequently providing the sole sonority on a desert walk.

If you happen upon spindly spines of ocotillo right after a spring or summer rain, you are rewarded by flashy red flowers exploding from the tips of the seemingly dead branches. Hummingbirds and carpenter bees pollinate the bright, arterial-red ocotillo flowers. Locally, in their native bajada landscape, ocotillo twigs are stuck in the ground to make a fence and the sprigs may sprout to make a living fence. Because they bristle with nasty spines, ocotillo fences exclude all manner of fauna from a southwestern garden.

Etymology of Ocotillo

The apt-sounding Mexican-Spanish word harks all the way back to the Aztecs. The conquistadores named the plant with a diminutive version of the Mexican word for a kind of pine tree, *acote* Mexican Spanish 'pine' but literally 'torch tree' < *ocotl* Nahuatl 'torch'+ *-illo* diminutive suffix inherited by the embryonic Spanish language as it grew out of and evolved from Roman soldiers' street Latin. Montezuma himself proceeded along Aztec palace corridors as slaves held high *ocotl* torches to light his way toward the treacherous Spanish soldiers awaiting him in the court of welcome.

Acote is a Mexican pine so rich in resin that its tree limbs were burned as torches by the Aztecs and other peoples of ancient Central America. Acote's botanical name recalls the Aztec king, having the scientific moniker of *Pinus montezumae*. Or it may have been dubbed 'the little torch tree' because of its red flowers.

Nahuatl is the name of the language spoken by the Aztecs and still used by their descendants. Through the medium of American Spanish, English has borrowed important words from Nahuatl, including *tomato, chili, cacao, chocolate, coyote, ocelot* and *avocado*.

Casselman of Arabia? I Don't Think So.

I am a lover of deserts and an appreciator of ocotillos. I did not touch toes to desert sand until my twenties, but have since made up for my late start. In one of a convoy of Land Rovers I have been driven across part of the Sahara, setting out from Marrakesh on the way over sandy *pistes* to Timbuktu. A *piste* is a so-called road in the desert, a scarcely visible sand track, often as faint as an albino's eyebrow, a road able to be deleted by the lightest cough of a sandstorm. I have taken safer guided hikes through the American deserts: the Sonoran, the Mojave, the Anza-Borrego, Joshua Tree National Monument and the Chihuahuan Desert.

Now, a sophisticated viator, however keen, ought not to adopt travel mottoes and life motives from film dialogue. Although it is beneath chic dignity, in two instances I have done so. I respond to these words put into the mouth of King Feisal speaking to Lawrence of Arabia in the 1962 movie script by scenarists Robert Bolt and Michael Wilson. Says the king played by Alec Guinness: "I think you are another of these desert-loving English: Doughty, Stanhope, Gordon of Khartoum. No Arab loves the desert. We love water and green trees; there is nothing in the desert. No man needs nothing."

Oh, Kingy, Kingy, Kingy, I beg your royal indulgence, Feisal, to disagree utterly. And, Feisal, may there be no reprisal. Sometimes, to accompany our being and to tame its pain, we require most ardently *momentitos* of nothingness. From the same movie, a character named Bentley, much like the real-life Lawrence-interviewing American newspaper reporter Lowell Thomas, asks this: "What is it, Major Lawrence, that attracts you personally to the desert? Lawrence (staring at Bentley as a dowager might observe a dung-beetle): "It's clean."

Lawrence meant clean of people, fervid hope of all hermits. Desert joy is the absence of scummy humans. The French existentialist Jean-Paul Sartre got it almost right when he wrote "*L'enfer, c'est les autres.*" I would amend Sartre's truth with one extra word: Hell is other stupid people. They make restorative solitude a necessity.

Indeed, solitude, rarest of companions in our Western world, may be found in the desert, where the dune mirage is not anything so vulgar as rippling water or date palms dancing the dance of the seven fronds. Instead, alone in the void, having sought yourself in the silence, sometimes with luck you see to the bottom of your heart. The tepid shallows of your squandered soul are rendered clear and oyster-lustrous, reflected back at you fiercely, so that, if fortunate, you may purge the dross of a shabby self and come back to the oasis of life or to approaching death rinsed, scrubbed free of the washable demons and renewed to an Edenic vigor.

As any mystic will tell you, the desert is not empty. It is full of God. For no other reason did Jesus decamp into the wilderness. The New Testament's Koine Greek uses the word *eremos* 'forsaken, desolate place.' Of Jesus' trial in the wilderness, the Latin Vulgate, thus eventually giving us our English word *desert,* uses *desertum*: *tunc Iesus ductus est in desertum ab Spiritu ut temptaretur a diabolo* 'Then Jesus was led into the barrenlands by the Holy Spirit in order that He might be tempted by the devil.'

Desertus, deserta, desertum is a Latin adjective, here in its three gender presentation forms. As an adjective it is a perfect passive participle of the verb *deserere* 'to abandon, to forsake,' literally *de* a negative prefix+ *serere* 'to join together,' hence 'not joined together, abandoned.'

Here's a note of intrigue from Wikipedia. I don't agree with it but still it lingers hauntingly: "The transliteration of the Ancient Egyptian term for the *Red land* (i.e. the deserts on either side of the fertile Black land irrigated by the Nile) is *dšrt* (conventionally pronounced *deshret*); it has been stated that 'it is not impossible that the very word *deserta* entered the Latin language by way of Egyptian'." This is ingenious but highly unlikely, given the clear Latin ancestry of *deserta.*

By the way, the word *dune* is a mere variant of the noun *down*, possibly influenced in its English spelling by French *dune.*

Here endeth my note, not too far, I trust, from the thorny ocotillo bush where we began.

Do visit a desert soon, even if in mere semi-solitary accompaniment. Such a sabulous foray may invigorate your soul.

Chapter 74

Samara, Pappus & Other Seed Words
plus memories of making boyhood whistles from maple keys

Pappus is the botanical name of the kind of air-borne, wind-blown seeds of plants like milkweed. Such aerial seeds in flotillas of tiny, silky parasols are dispersed by the winds of autumn. Filament-topped thistle-tufts and the velutinous and plumose pappi of dandelions belong also to this family of sky seeds.

The word *pappus* is a Latin form of an ancient Greek term for white down or fluff on certain seeds. Before that developed meaning in ancient Greek, *pappos* was a word for grandfather. Gramp's white hair probably suggested this second meaning of a white-haired seed.

In form, *pappos* is an affectionate diminutive in which the root *pa 'dad, father'* is duplicated, for example *pappas* was a Greek child's word for father, much like papa in English and some European languages. In Hellenistic Greek, *pappos* was the first down on a boy's cheeks. Note that reduplication of a word's root often indicates diminution and/or affection. And a form of the word is still kicking around in modern Greek as *poupoulo* 'fluff, down, bird's feather, soft stuffing.' In other botanical names this Greek root shows up. The botanical term for an American aster called Thrifty Goldenweed or Ring Grass is *Haplopappus* from Greek *haploos* 'simple' + *pappos* which means "down, fluff" referring to the plant's single pappus ring.

Samara or Maple Key

The little boy I left behind me on the September banks of the Grand River in southern Ontario used to make keen whistles from samaras, the dry winged fruit of riverside maple trees. Maple keys were also called "helicopters" or "whirlybirds." On certain fall days, sky-wide armadas of maple keys set sail across the heavens, their tendrilling parachutes corkscrewing down to earth. Still today, exuberant gyres of samaras can dervish, aloft on the gusts of autumn.

Each samara carries a single maple seed encased in a terminal nut to which nature appends a papery, feathery, veined winglet, evolved to insure a coiled path of flight. Elm trees, ashes and sycamores also produce samaras.

Maple keys helicate. Yes, dear patient readers, I must now coin a new verb to describe the spiral convolution of a samara's whirl down into the loamy bed of soil into which it needs to twist its potent seed. My coinage is "to helicate," from the same Latin word *helix* which the Romans borrowed from Greek *helix* 'anything spiral in form,' the noun from an older Greek verb used by Homer, *helissein* 'to spin, to roll.' The combining stem is seen when the genitive case of the Latin noun is given, namely *helix, helicis*. In English, the best scientific plural of helix is helices, whereas the clumsy-to-say, trashy American plural is helixes. What an odious, tongue-clicking clatter that sound is: helixes. Enunciating it aloud conveys an unpleasant sensation of trying to cover up cold sores on lips as one speaks or of swallowing some vile, supposedly restorative, gulpable unguent.

In any case, I judge *helicate* legit, since there is a recorded Latin form *helica* 'a spiral.' Thus we compose from the lonely noun, a verb, to helicate 'to spin like a falling maple key.'

Why does the maple samara come equipped with helicating possibilities? Most northern maple seeds require nature's stratification, that is, dormancy-breaking requires a seed to overwinter in soil, where cold and frost and weathering soften the seed coat, and then trigger the maple embryo to sprout and to break through the compromised seed coat in a quest for sun and food and leafy life.

The Seedy Origin of Samara

Pliny and Columella, writers on Roman agriculture and other topics, used the Latin word *samara* to mean 'elm-tree seed.' *Samara* is a classical Latin version, with a dialect-broadened first vowel, of an earlier form like *semera related directly to Latin seed words like *semen*.

Further back in time's verbosphere, samara derives from the Indo-European root *se and its extension *sem, roots that mean 'one and the same.' Thus the metaphor behind semen words and sowing seeds was basically: making more of the same living thing.

Russian Cognates

PIE cognates and relatives include our English adjective *same*, Russian *sam-* 'self' or 'same,' as in a borrowed word in English for self-publishing *sam-izdat*, a compound from Russian *sam-* 'self' + Russian *izdat* 'to give out, to publish.' Consider too the Russian word *samogon* 'moonshine' or illegal, home-distilled liquor similar to vodka. *Samogon* contains two Russian roots, *sam-* 'self' and *gnat'* 'to distill.' The pronunciation is sam-oh-GON. Samogon, wrote one food writer, "holds a special place in Russian drinking culture as a kind of Robin Hood of alcohol." But be careful for samogon is sometimes toxic. Drinkers have died after quaffing samogon.

Samoyed is a dog breed named after an insulting Russian name for a Slavic people: Samo-yed in Russian means 'self-eater,' that is, the Russians thought these people were so primitive that they were cannibals! Ha! And that bit of Slavic insight arises from a nation that spawned Stalin, Lenin and the fascist Gollum, Putin!

Other PIE cognates are Lithuanian *séju*, Gothic *saian*, Anglo-Saxon *sawan* 'to sow.' Semen in German is *der Samen*, Lithuanian *sémenys*, Old Church Slavonic *seme*, and of course our English verb *to sow*.

English derivatives of the Latin noun *semen, seminis* and its verb *sero, serere, sevi, satum* 'to plant seeds' 'to sow' include:

to disseminate — to spread like seed, for example, to disseminate knowledge of this new process to all the employees.

to inseminate —literally 'to put seed into something'

seminiferous tubules — in human anatomy, little tubes inside the testes that participate in the making of sperm and the carrying of semen; the suffix -ferous from Latin *ferre* 'to bear, to carry' appears in dozens of English words like aquifer, coniferous, difference, fertile, infer, Lucifer, pestiferous, refer, suffer and transfer.

seminivorous — seed-eating, said of some birds; the morpheme -vorous stems from the Latin verb *vorare* 'to swallow, to gulp, to eat greedily,' source of many scientific words like insectivorous, devour, voracious, carnivore (eats meat), herbivore (eats plants), and a creature that eats almost everything, an omnivore (Latin *omnis* 'all').

seminary began as Latin *seminarium*, a patch of ground where seeds were sown. Its next major developed meaning was a training college for English priests, on the thought that it was a seed-ground of religious knowledge.

seminar is a shortened form of seminary that came to mean a small number of students selected for advanced study and research by an individual professor.

season of the year is a hidden example of a derivative from a Latin 'seed' word. Its protean path to modern English from Latin looks something like this: Modern English *season* <Middle English *seson* < Old French *seson* (modern French *saison*) < Latin *satio, sationem* 'act of sowing, time of sowing, seed-time.'

sativus, sativa, sativum This botanical Latin adjective known to those who study crop science treating seed-grown domestic produce is perhaps the best hidden of derivatives from the Latin verb *serere* 'to sow.' The adjective, means 'cultivated,' that is, sown by seed by man as part of agriculture. *Avena sativa* is common oats. It may mean found once in the wild and then sown by man as a cultivated cereal crop. The expensive spice saffron is the dried and pulverized stigmas and styles from the flowers of *crocus sativus,* an ancient Mediterranean spring bulb widely planted in Spain and Morocco by saffron-harvesters. *Daucus carota* subspecies *sativus* is the species to which our common carrot belongs. Common domesticated rice is *Oryza sativa. Cannabis sativa* is the hemp plant.

Sativus' formal etymology identifies it as the perfect passive participial stem of the Latin verb *serere* 'to sow,' so that its literal sense is 'having been sown or planted.' It comprises the bare stem *sat-* added to a common adjective-forming suffix in Latin *–ivus. Sative* and *sativous* are obsolete English versions of botany's Latin adjective.

Boys Whistling in the Dark

A sound from my childhood echoes back to me now: the long, sharp whistle of a dry samara, produced by exhaling through a vibrating maple key, placed at just the right spot on a ten-year-old boy's lips. In the matted brown tangle of cat-tail beds, on the town side of the Grand River, we hid out on early fall nights, after supper, playing a twilight game of cowboys and we signaled our location to one another in the dense reed beds by whistling through maple keys.

I hear us now and that high, sweet sound of innocent adventure. But it is heard only in my mind's ear, for such stirring amateur flute notes ceased long ago, dissolved in night wind, diluted by the squall of boyhood's end, and drowned by mothers' voices calling from lighted back porches, "Time for bed, boys. Come home. Come home."

Chapter 75

Highbrow has a Low Origin

One of the adjectives most beloved of intellectual snobs, namely "highbrow," originated in the utterly discredited quackery of phrenology or reading the bumps on a person's head as a method of analyzing personality, talent and intelligence. The bigger the bump near the "talking surface of the skull" then the more adept one was at speech and words and writing. Try as I may, I keep feeling the bumps on my head but am only able to locate the evidence of the time I fell off the back porch during an unwise and immoderate imbibition of plum wine. Phrenology was a fallacious fad that reached the zenith of its popularity in the latter part of the nineteenth century.

Highbrow began as a simple descriptor of a human physical reality, a brow that was high. But in phrenology the incorrect belief was that a high forehead denoted extra brain material packed into that high forehead. We even know the ding-a-ling who made the word *highbrow* a part of our English language. It began in 1902 when a reporter for the *Baltimore Sun* newspaper, Will Irvin, began using the notion that high foreheads betokened deep thoughts. Not too bright, Will!

What balderdash, piffle and nincompoopery! Phrenology bears the same intellectual heft as palmistry or divination of the future by reading the cooked entrails of sacred hamsters. A high forehead could just as well be a symptom of a difficult birth during which the mother's narrow birth canal made Wee Jimmy emerge with a skull reminiscent of a cucumber, hardly a sign that Mensa would be telephoning any time soon.

Or Wee Jimmy might be merely the scion of a long line of coneheads.

From its deceptive stirrings in phrenology, highbrow came to be applied to describe classical music or the ethereal echelons of intellectual achievement, chiefly by middle-of-the-road snobs who were nervous about their own status on a scale of human intelligence. Of course, middlebrow and lowbrow have now joined their dubious sibling as easy putdown adjectives.

How lunatic were these early phrenologists? Some of them turned into grave-robbers in order to support the flimsy tenets of their charlatanism. In 1812, after the Spanish painter Goya died in French exile in Bordeaux, phrenologists opened his grave and cut the head off his corpse, in order to study its cranial terrain at leisure in a nearby, makeshift phrenology "lab."

The pseudoscience ("false" science, Greek *pseudos* 'fake, false') of phrenology stems from the common Greek word *phren* 'mind, heart, will, midriff' + a Latinized Greek noun suffix –logia 'the scientific study of…'

Schizophrenia, Frenetic & even Frantic!

Our most familiar English word containing this root word is schizophrenia from Greek *schizein* 'to split' + *phren* 'mind'+ ia common noun ending in science. Schizophrenia originally denoted a mental disorder in which the mind is split up into segments not easily reconciled. Here too, in the very word *schizophrenia*, a word like phrenology from *phren*, is a term whose usefulness in American psychology and psychiatric study has degenerated into meaninglessness because of its too general application. In one of the current psychiatric dictionaries reside impudently more than 100 definitions of schizophrenia!

Frenetic meaning first 'insane, mentally deranged' derives from a Latin form *phreneticus* from late Greek *phreneticos* 'delirious,' ultimately from Greek *phren* 'mind.' Frantic is a Middle English syncopated (shortened by letter-loss) form of frenetic which suffered a generalization of meaning also, until it eventually signified only the rapid, jittery movements of a delirious person but not necessarily their mental instability. "In order for the ship to meet its hour of departure, activity on the loading dock was frantic." So shall be my egress to the holiday of the next chapter!

Chapter 76

Take a Holiday Word

This sweet word, once festive, once abounding in the celebratory promise of work suspended, is nowadays rendered shoddy by commercial overuse and corporate corruption. A holiday once meant a day off for poor peasants to celebrate a saint's birthday, perhaps by a beaker of cheap wine, a brief dance in the village square, followed by dumping their last three turnips into the fat lap of their local priest.

The Old English form *haligdaeg* 'holy day' makes clear its religious origin. By the time of Middle English, between the late 12th and the late 15th century, the word was spelled as *halliday* or *halidae*. The same rounding of /a/ to Middle English /ô/ also occurred in English words like *halibut* and *hallow*.

The modern sense of holiday as a ceasing of work to enjoy a vacation began quite early. In a letter written in 1573 CE we read "in the hallidais he tooke a iurni into the cuntri" 'in the holidays he took a journey into the country.'

A Personal Holiday Tale

Perhaps at this arthritic juncture, I shall permit myself to retail a single holiday-of-horror story. All of us have several. When I was rather too old a lad (is it proper for a 38-year boy to leave home?) I served a term in a pet shop as an apprentice hamster shampooer. Exciting work, although I was not certain it would lead to law school.

However my sudsy dexterity won me the annual staff holiday generously provided by the owner of the pet shop, Mrs. Krendle. This prize-giving, her sole act of largesse, was utterly out-of-character, for Mrs. Krendle was a scoliotic crone bent double by natural venom, a penny-squeezing virago straight out of a Victorian melodrama. She was so tight one couldn't drive a flax seed up her ass with a mallet. I tried, but Mrs. Krendle confiscated the mallet, claiming it could be better used euthanizing the more recalcitrant hamsters.

In any case I won a free, resort holiday weekend in a small Northern Ontario town. My suspicions were aroused when I learned on the eve of the holiday departure from the pet shop that the resort was called "Vern's Live Bait."

Once I had arrived in Vern's stomping grounds, namely the pleasant Canadian hamlet of Moose Crotch, I found that in the shack out back of his bait shop, Vern had a fetching straw mattress beside the Coke machine where that night I was to rest what was left of my weary head. It was one of those older cold-drink machines where the glass soda-pop bottles were placed neck-high in cold water. The water-refrigerating motor caused the pop bottles to rattle gently all night. What a weekend! Vern was a natural storyteller, in spite of the fact that he had spent the majority of his life conversing with minnows. He convulsed us repeatedly with the tale of the day his cistern was full. Then, in a twist worthy of Edgar Allan Poe, Vern told the story of the day the cistern was empty.

Modern sociological studies show that many of us require a day or two after a holiday to rest and recuperate. When I returned to the shampoo stand at the pet shop, I began the furtive collection of a "good-riddance fund," raised among the staff so that we, her employees, might hire a hit-man to take Mrs. Krendle "for a ride." Alas, the only one taken for that holiday ride was yours truly.

Chapter 77

OASIS

green in the dune-strewn brown of desert

Thanks to spade work in the garden of word roots, chiefly by the late etymologist Eric Partridge, we know that oasis is a term of Nilotic provenance, to achieve which the Greeks dressed up an Egyptian word they heard on early forays into the dune-strewn Afric deserts.

Among the Hieroglyphs

The Greeks, as well they might, put a Greek noun-forming suffix *–asis* at the tail end of a basic Egyptian etymon *uah* or *wuh'*, a hieroglyphic root that signified 'bloom, be green, flourish, thrive, grow,' all meanings carried by the ancient Egyptian verb *uakh.* One of the earliest Greek writers to employ the word *oasis* was the historian Herodotus of Halicarnassus (484 BCE – 425 BCE) often called "the father of history" because he was among the first of history writers to check his sources and inquire of the reasons for human actions rather than merely recording their temporal progression.

The word is alive in ancient Egyptian's closest modern relative, the still-spoken language Coptic, where *ouahe* means 'place one can live or survive.' Even Arabic borrowed the Egyptian term. The Modern Literary Arabic word for oasis is *wah, waha,* as in the title of a Lebanese literary organization, *Wahat al Adab* 'Oasis of Literature.'

Apposition Anyone?

The English adjectives from oasis are ugly and quite unsuitable to pronounce. Who would use oasal or — yech! — oasitic? They both sound like skin diseases. When an oasitic reference is required, the writer careful about how words sound will employ nounal apposition, that is, will put a noun against another noun in an adjectival function but will maintain its noun form. For example, oasis greenery has usually evolved very tough outer tegumental tissue, to withstand the blistering of sandstorms and to conserve precious interior water.

"Wind, Sand and Stars"

One of the most evocative musings on *oasis* occurs in a memoir by Antoine de Saint-Exupéry, that pilot-philosopher-writer of clear, serene French prose. "Wind, Sand and Stars" is the beautiful English title, while the original French title is drab: *Terre des Hommes* 'Man Planet' but the book is full of wonders. In 1935 the author and his co-pilot crashed a small mail plane in the Libyan Sahara somewhere between Benghazi and Cairo. As the two men contemplate their possible deaths, seeking but lacking the discovery of an oasis, Saint-Exupéry unfurls a charming scroll lettered with the meanings of his life, one all of us may peruse to our existential betterment.

English Use

Are there visual memes, iconic images saved so deep in sight's memory-bank that they can spring to mind effortlessly? Then oasis is such a meme. Technically, oasis is a Libyan reference, for *Uakht* in ancient Egyptian referred only to The Great Oasis in what is now Libya, *Uakht* being a region of fertile green ringed by a vast waste of sand. Pondering the quondam Libyan beast, Colonel Gaddafi, leads one to remember what Shelley wrote in his poem "Ozymandias":

> "And on the pedestal these words appear:
> 'My name is Ozymandias, king of kings:
> Look on my works, ye Mighty, and despair!'
> Nothing beside remains. Round the decay
> Of that colossal wreck, boundless and bare
> The lone and level sands stretch far away."

Playing a lighter musical note, Maria Muldaur may sashay by, long-tressed songstress of the dance-inducing "Midnight at the Oasis." I think I'll join her dance.

Chapter 78

Eat These Words

Here on the taut quilt of a summer lawn, for picnic nibbling, are toothsome morsels of word lore, ambrosial as porcini freshly meadow-plucked and crisped in fermented Normandy butter, tidbits about the verb *to eat* and its Proto-Indo-European relatives, that is, the cognates (Latin 'born together') of the PIE root *ak-, *ako- 'eat.'

The close Latin relative of English to eat is *edere* 'to eat.' From that Latin verb there descends into English a borrowed feast of chewy terms. Most familiar is the adjective *edible* 'able to be eaten safely.' Then come the less-used literary and scientific terms. Edacious means greedy or voracious. The Latin adjectival root of edacious *edax, edacis* appears in the old Latin tag *tempus edax rerum* 'time consumes all things.'

Botany uses as one of its species adjectives *edulis*, another Latin adjective meaning eatable. Consider the botanical name of the edible porcino mushroom, *Boletus edulis*. Toronto, Ontario even boasts a fine restaurant named Edulis. *Canna edulis* 'edible cane' is the source of arrowroot in arrowroot cookies.

Esculent is a learned adjective that means 'suitable for food, eatable' from Latin *esculentus* from Latin *esca* 'animal food, food for beings lesser than human, hence bait for fish etc.' Consider too the common European frog whose meaty limblets the French love to devour as frog legs. The doomed amphibian's zoological tag is *Rana esculenta* 'edible frog.'

Esurient means greedy for food, peckish. It is built from *edere* 'to eat' with a verbal suffix called a desiderative, often in Latin -*urire* added to the verb stem so that *esurio* 'I desire intensely to eat, I am starving, greedy.' A desiderative ending adds an element of intense desire to the root meaning of a verb.

Comestible is both an adjective and a noun. It tacks to the front of the *ed-*, *-est-* root a Latin preposition *cum* that becomes con- or com- in front of certain letters. The Monty Python cheese-shop sketch has the customer ask for "cheesy comestibles" because he is "esurient." Comestible. What a pleasantly munchable vocable!

One of the hidden Latin *edere* verbs lurks in our common word, obese, from the past participle of *obedere*, *obesus* 'stuffed full, eaten to the brim.' The compound has the intensive prefix *ob-* added to the *–ed* stem.

Hellenic Gobbling

Greek has a similar series of 'eat' words from the same PIE root. There is *edmenai* 'to eat' and *edo* 'I eat' and *edode* 'food' and *edodos* 'greedy, ravenously hungry.' An intensive verb of eating exists too, *katedo* 'I devour, I eat up to the last piece of flesh.'

Interestingly a similar verb occurs in German where to eat is *essen* but to eat like an animal, ripping and chomping and glugging flesh down the throat in a wolf-like manner is *fressen*, from *essen* with the intensive German prefix *ver-* added, to give *veressen > fressen*. Yiddish has an agent noun, *fresser* which names a sloppy, vulgar eater with no table manners but plenty of appetite. Well, meals over, you may leave the chapter table.

Chapter 79

My Vocabulary has Lapsed

Today, class, I hold aloft my magnifying glass, the better to inspect a Proto-Indo-European root, a fascinator that leads to all these cognates: *lip, lapse, prelapsarian, prolapse, labia, lap, labor, collapse*, and — my favorite medical chart word — *labile*.

In medical chartese and in the more coherent realms of psychiatric mumbo jumbo, labile means liable to burst into tears at any moment, emotionally unstable. Once in the merciful long-ago, I knew a person who, viewing a pleasant sunset through a living-room window, was likely to begin gently weeping. "Why?" asked courtly *moi*. "Because another day is dying. Sob. Snurfle. Boo-hoo. Blub. Wahhhhh!'" Now that's labile! If such lachrymosity is allowed to fester and left unattended, then the future may hear the faint tinkle caused by the snapping open of an ampoule of Thorazine. Kleenex is cheaper.

Lip, lapse, prelapsarian, prolapse, labia, lap, labor, collapse — all these words are related to a PIE root given by Hofmann as *lab with its plosive variant *lap meaning 'to lick, to lap with the tongue.'

Labile

In everyday hospital use, labile means prone to mood changes or uncontrolled emotional upset. From Latin *labilis* whose literal sense is 'able or liable to slip' and made up of the Latin verb *labi* 'to slip, to fall' + a Latin suffix *–ilis, –ile* that gives English many adjectives like *agile, civil, docile, facile, fragile* (and its doublet *frail*), *juvenile, motile,* and *percentile.* But labile finds use in other sciences too. In physics and chemistry, labile means 'chemically unstable, liable to change its chemical composition.' In medical literature, one may read of labile hypertension (being subject to blood pressure fluctuations) or labile diabetes (fluctuations in glucose tolerance).

Of Lips & Labia

English *lip* and German *Lippe*, both name the two fleshy parts that form the upper and lower edges of the opening of the mouth, both lips having important functions in human speech.

The Latin word for lips is *labia.* The Latin plural noun *labia* 'lips' is cognate with an ancient Greek verb *laptein* 'to drink greedily like an animal,' whose basic meaning is to make a lot of noise with the lips while you are drinking, like a thirsty dog lapping up water.

Labia and its infrequent plural *labium* are cognate with English *lip* and German *Lippe*. That is, the words are not borrowed from one another' rather they stem from the same PIE root. The adjective *cognate* is shortened to *co-* from Latin *cum* 'together, with' + Latin *gnatus* 'born. Cognate words were born together, in the sense that they both stem from the same primitive root, rather than partake in borrowing and lending.

Today in English *labia* customarily refer to the inner and outer folds bordering the vulva, exterior and at either side of the vagina. There are two pairs of labia: the outer labia, or *labia majora* are larger and fatter, while the *labia minora* are folds of skin between the outer labia. The labia surround and protect the clitoris and the openings of the vagina and urethra.

Lap up This Lap

The lap as a body place descends from the same PIE etymon through a medieval English verb *lappen* 'to fold.' The human lap is where the sitting human body "folds." To lap up water is to fold the tongue, to lick up water with the lips.

Prelapsarian

Prelapsarian is an adjective confined nowadays for the most part to theological writings. Nevertheless it recently appeared in a newspaper's book review. "The allure of these kinds of stories is the idea of catching a glimpse of some prelapsarian civilization – humankind before the fall from grace brought about by technology and "civilization" and all the corruption and self-consciousness that comes with it." So wrote Nicholas Hune-Brown in *The Globe and Mail* (March 21, 2014). *Pre* from Latin *prae* means 'before' + lapsarian, referring to Latin *Lapsus*, the Fall of Man, the expulsion from the Garden of Eden, the end of perfect human innocence and unspoilt virtue. The theological Latin word for the fall of humankind is *lapsus* which means 'a stumble, an error, a slip, a falling down.' In non-theological use, lapsus survives chiefly in rather literary Latin phrases, two of which, though sooty with Victorian word dust, are still used: *lapsus linguae* 'a slip of the tongue' and *lapsus calami* n. a slip of the pen.

Prolapse

Prolapse is almost exclusively a medical term where it usually refers to prolapse of the uterus. The Mayo Clinic explanation is clear: "When pelvic floor muscles and ligaments stretch and weaken, providing inadequate support for the uterus, then the uterus slips down into or protrudes out of the vagina. Uterine prolapse can happen to women of any age, but it often affects postmenopausal women who've had one or more vaginal deliveries."

Prolapse as a word was invented around 1834, from *prolapses* "a falling down' in Late Latin, from *prolabi* 'to fall or slide forward' made up of a prefix *pro-* 'forward' + *labi* 'to slide.'

Other Quick Lapses

To collapse is to fall together *col<cum* 'with, together' + *labi* 'to fall, to slide'

To elapse is etymologically to glide out, from Latin *e, ex* 'out of' + *labi* 'to flow, to slip, to glide.'

To suffer a relapse then is to fall or slip back to a previous state from Latin *re* 'again' + *labi* 'to fall, to glide, to slip.'

Labor or labour appears to be a Latin noun from the PIE *lab root. The great etymologist Eric Partridge educes it as labor in a prime and sensuous meaning of 'weight' or 'work that is heavy and makes you slip or fall.' Partridge's learned guesses are constantly ingenious. If a worker bends under heavy work, he is engaged in *labor.*

In the classical Latin of that sententious old blatmouth Marcus Tullius Cicero we are reminded that 'work' to ancient Romans was always plural, *labores.* One of the gabby old shyster's maxims was: *acti labores jucundi sunt.* 'Work done abounds in joy." Cicero had a slave follow him throughout the day with a wax tablet and a stylus, to jot down any little gems of twaddle which Cicero might spew forth and thus save his pronouncements from the oblivion which daily utterance usually merits. What a pompous old fart! Perhaps, like a youthful me in long-ago Latin classes, you too had to peruse reams of Ciceronian balderdash wrapped in a lawyer's overweening self-congratulation?

Chapter 80

Halcyon: Kingfisher Days

This word of calming tenor, both adjective and noun, has largely disappeared from contemporary written English and is now confined to bad nautical poetry of the apostrophic ilk, e.g. "O helmsman brave, how stand the winds, as we do halcyon days approach?"

Halcyon days at sea meant breast-soft swells of plumping ocean. The often tempestuous brow of the sea was placid, all aqueous subsidence and liquid composure. Halcyon days in ancient times were two weeks of calm at sea supposedly occurring during the winter solstice. In the northern hemisphere, winter solstice (sometime between December 20 and 23) still marks the day of the year with the least hours of daylight. The days were named after a Greek word for a bird, the kingfisher.

Ancient Greek classical legends mistakenly claimed that the kingfisher nested floating at sea when brooding. Because of the bird being favoured by the deities of Olympus, the Greek gods made the sea calm so that the kingfisher could lay its eggs and brood in peace.

The watery balm of a glassy midwinter sea, fair weather and blissful waves of sweet tranquillity, unrippled, unruffled, unperturbed were called by Greek sailors *alkyonides hemerai* 'kingfisher days' borrowed directly into Latin as *alcyonei dies* and *alcedonia*.

Etymology

The Greek word for this kingfisher was *alkyon*. An incorrect derivation claimed it was a compound of Greek *hals* 'salt, the sea' + *kueo* 'I conceive,' because the kingfisher eggs were supposed to be laid at sea. The Romans borrowed the word which then made its calm way into the European languages and English. In fact *alkyon* is not a Greek root. The bird's name existed long before the Greeks ever arrived in the Hellenic homeland. *Alkyon* belongs to some now-lost, preHellenic language.

Our dear friends of the world-doping big pharmaceutical conglomerates once came up with a mind-blitzing hypnotic tranquilizer and they obscenely appropriated the name of this lovely adjective and called their knock-out drops Halcion (generic name: Triazolam). I am pleased to report that Halcion is now banned in Britain and several other countries.

I conclude by quoting Michael Drayton, Elizabethan poet and contemporary of Shakespeare, who wrote in his poem *Noahs Floud* (1630):

"There came the Halcyon, whom the Sea obeys,
When she her nest upon the water lays."

Chapter 81

Laundry & Latrine & Lavatory
Share the Same Word Root.
How, in the name of all that is sanitary, is such a derivation possible?

All the following words used in English stem from the same Latin verb: *lotion, deluge, latrine, avalanche, ablutions, lavish, dilute, laundry, lavatory, lather, lava, lavabo, alluvial* and two rarities, one from Christian ceremonial: *pedilavium,* and one from possibly obsolete medical jargon, *pediluvium.* All descend from the Latin verb *lavare* 'to wash.' We'll examine some of derivatives. *Lavare*'s traditional citation forms are: *lavo, lavare, lavi, lautum* (two alternative forms of the past participle *lotum* and *lavatum* also contributed greatly to the Latin verb's many descendant words in later languages, for example English *lotion* and *lavatory.*

The merest of these derivatives are dowdy toilet terms. But even the most fastidious word-lover ought to pay heed to the words' seed.

Cognates of Latin *lavare* in other Indo-European languages include ancient Greek *loutron* 'bathing room' and ancient Greek *lousthai* 'to wash the body.' Several "Know Greece" internet sites proclaim that Latin *lavare* and *louere* DERIVE from Greek *louein* and *lousthai.* No, the Latin does not stem from Greek. The words are cognate, literal meaning 'born together,' developed meaning in linguistics "belong to the same Indo-European language family.' Also related as cognates to *lavare* are some modern Greek words like *loutro* 'lavatory' and *lousimo* 'shampoo, bath.'

Lavatory

Lavatorium began in Medieval Latin as 'a place to wash,' just as *laboratorium* was originally 'a place to work' and then as laboratory became a place to do scientific work. The lavatorium first referred strictly to the basin, bowl or vessel that held the water used for ritual cleansing in the Roman Catholic Church during which the celebrant of the Eucharist washes his hands.

But euphemism raised a blushing face, as it always has throughout the history of English toilet terms. Whenever there existed a clear, simple mode of referring to a locus of excretion, one may safely bet that the English found a namby-pamby, pussyfooting courtly word of evasion to replace it. Because early toilets eventually had a shelf or stand with a washbasin, decorous and demure defecators had to hand an easy circumlocution. Instead of "going for a dump," they, as we still do, could whisper, "I have to wash my hands" or "Where is the washroom?" Or, one hundred and twenty years ago in a Mayfair mansion: "I say, Colonel Pizzlethwaite, where lies the lavatory?"

Victorian lavatory

By the way, I'm not an uncouth beast in matters of language. But euphemism is politically dangerous, leading the overuser into a verbal fen of niceness, into habitual dandification of language. Those 43 babies were not machine-gunned into a protoplasmic pulp. Oh no, they "suffered the consequences of revolution." Euphemism is addictive. By using it, unpleasantness that we human beings ought to face becomes quickly avoidable, first at the linguistic level, then at the level of needed political action comfortably left undone.

Bill Casselman

Lavabo

Another bit of Catholic Latin that named the bowl itself was *lavabo* (Latin, 'I shall wash'). Any ritual washing of a celebrant's hands can be termed the Lavabo in Catholic liturgical language. The word enjoyed a brief popularity in Edwardian English to name a washstand or washbowl, borrowed from modern French where *lavabo* still means a washbasin and, in the plural, is a polite euphemism. *"Où sont les lavabos?"* may be used to ask "Where are the restrooms?"

The word is borrowed from Holy Writ. It originates in the Latin of the Vulgate, Saint Jerome 's translation of the Bible into Latin, where Psalm 26, verse 6, begins *"Lavabo inter innocentes manus meas . . ."* The King James translation is "I will wash mine hands in innocency: so will I compass thine altar, O Lord."

Ewww, Don't say THAT!

When did lavatory become a euphemism for a place to urinate and defecate? Guess who gifted English with that evasive circumlocution? The fecally frightened Victorians, who else? The same imperialist world-conquerors who thought the word *leg* was obscene and so — truly — referred, in Victorian English, to the "limbs" of a piano! Of course, in the stately home where Lord Fuddley was shocked to hear a toilet called by underlings "the shitter" or "the pisser," that same Lord Fuddley had to be daily pried off raped milkmaids and sometimes forcibly dis-inserted from ewes out in the sheepfold of his stately estate.

One still current, wonderfully silly British toilet euphemism is W.C. for "water closet." Think of the grown Englishmen, dainty prisslets all, who might have fainted dead-away, waylaid by an attack of the vapours, if they had had to ask directions to the toilet.

"Prithee, Gentle Knight, Where be the Stool of Easement?"

Now, I don't want to give the dauntless reader an impression that I am obsessed with fecal periphrasis, with an unseemly quest for synonyms of excreta. Still, I must share my favourite roundabout phrase for toilet. It is now obsolete and belonged to English during the fifteenth and sixteenth centuries. It was "stool of easement" or "house of easement." To do one's easement was to evacuate one's bowels of excrement. The stool of easement, by the way, gave rise to the euphemism "stool" for fecal matter.

Latrine

This too began as a place to wash, because medieval Latin *latrina* 'toilet' is a contraction of *lavatrina* 'washbasin, washing room.' Starting as a French euphemism for military trench toilet, the English borrowed it during the seventeenth century to name a barracks privy, a camp toilet.

Laundry

Laundry has kept its three chief historical meanings: (1) washing, (2) the place where washing occurs and (3) the objects to be washed. Its newest meaning, money-laundering "making dirty money seem clean," does not arise in common English until the early 1960s, but gained widespread popularity as part of newspaper reporting on the United States Watergate scandal of 1973.

Laundry is a contraction of an earlier form perhaps introduced into England from Norman French as *lavandiere* 'washerwoman' itself contracted in England to *lavender* 'washer.' There are many reflexes in all the modern Romance languages: *lavendera* in Spanish, *lavanda* in Italian, all harking back to Latin neuter plural gerundial forms of the verb *lavare* like *lavanda* and *lavandaria* 'things that ought to be washed.' Gerunds are verb forms that can be construed as nouns.

But, gentle persons all, let us wash our hands of these lower matters and climb forward into the sunlit uplands of politer discourse which, in the next chapter, abound.

Chapter 82

GAZPACHO
cold Spanish soup & its hot etymology

A Spanish Soup Endures the Rigors of Sloppy Derivation

Poor, odd-looking word *gazpacho* suffers highly disputed, multiple-sourced etymologies, claiming that this lively word for a cold Spanish soup descends from every known language on earth and a few buzzing languages spoken only by the giant bumblebees who rule the planet Nargon.

Persons unacquainted with any deep knowledge of Latin have claimed Mozarabic origins, sources in Sanskrit dopewords, an origin in the Greek word *gazophulakion* literally 'treasure-guarder,' but in fact meaning a Greek Orthodox church collection box into which pious parishioners tossed old goat-hair coats etc. From that to a Spanish soup? Are you *caballeros* out of your minds? First, neither etymology nor printed evidence of transitional forms supports any of those unlikely metamorphoses. But they are only the silliest of the notions presented, all founded in a total ignorance of simple Latin.

True, Clear, Cogent Origin of Gazpacho

To me and many scholarly Spanish etymologists, gazpacho is most likely compounded of the late Latin street word *caspa* 'bit, piece, wine dregs, tatters, refuse, flakes, little pieces of bread'+ Spanish pejorative suffix *-acho* < Latin adjectival suffix *–aceus*, in other words gazpacho is a soup with all kinds of scraps and bits tossed into it.

This omnium-gatherum concept, this culinary meme, is not foreign to *la cocina española*. After all, it is Spanish cuisine that gives us the kitchen-scrap-saving tradition of *la olla podrida* 'the stinking pot,' the big kettle on the kitchen stove into which anything remnant but nutritious is tossed to make tomorrow's stew. *Caspa* may not be a Roman word, but, early on, it appears in Italian dialects as *caspu* 'the residue left when grapes have been stomped and squeezed.' In Spain, in Asturian Spanish, *caspia* is apple residue, left after cider-making. The chaff left after cereal grinding in France is *gaspaille*. So there is the root, possibly a Celtic morpheme, embedded in the daily speech of all southern Europe, wherever its ultimate source. There too is the prime meaning: leftovers, bits and pieces— perfectly apt for our soup word, gazpacho.

Suffixal Notes

Contrary to the know-no-Latin babblings of some internet "philologists," the suffix *-acho* is not of Andalusian Mozarabic origin. (!) It is a pejorative/augmentative suffix, from the common classical Latin suffix *–aceus*, productive of thousands of Latin and later English and French adjectives. Reflexes of it appear in all the Romance languages. For example, as a pejorative, it is still a richly productive suffix of nouns and adjectives in everyday modern Italian street speech, where, as *-accio* or *–accia*, it is an ending of newly made insult words. *Posto* in Italian means 'place,' *posto al sole* 'a place in the sun, a happy retreat' — but with the pejorative suffix, the Italian word takes on a negative import so that *postaccio* is a common Italian word for a bad place, for example: *Prigione è un postaccio* 'Jail is a bad place.'

Let's Focus on Kepler!

Or consider that humble proto-pizza, the lovingly ovened flat bread, *focaccia*. It harks back to ancient Roman kitchens where, as *panis focacius*, it was put down even in Latin as a lowly quick bread, for its name stems from the Latin word for kitchen fireplace *focus*, so that *panis focacius* means 'that low-class bread stuff that one bakes so quickly in the oven.' Since the kitchen-stove was the centre of slave activity in a Roman house, it is no wonder that the later astronomer Johannes Kepler (1571–1630 CE) took the hearth/fireplace word and used *focus* to name the spot where a lens makes a burning point. All our other English meanings of the word *focus* stem from Kepler's metaphorical borrowing.

Testaccio Detour

Let's discuss one more use of *–accio*. Testaccio is a once shabby but now solidly working-class part of central Rome. Testaccio has a wonderful market now and many inexpensive places to eat tasty Italian food. It makes a pleasant stroll in central Rome where you will meet amiable Romans who cheerfully talk to tourists, especially if you make an effort to speak Italian. *Testa* is ancient street Latin for 'pot' or 'jar.' Testaccio is Italian for shards (of broken pots). The Italian pejorative/diminutive ending *-accio* is a suffix that makes the noun smaller and negative. Testaccio is built on a hill that was an ancient garbage midden for broken pots and junk. Hence *testaccio* = 'place of shards and broken pots.'

Testa was also the common Latin word for the human head, much more frequent in everyday Latin speech than the formal and literary Latin word *caput*. Roman soldiers took the slangy term for head with them on their postings throughout the Roman Empire. Its use is very much as if a British soldier were to say "I took a hit on the old jar today." Consequently *testa* is the source of the modern French word for head, tête.

And so, having sipped like Spanish sybarites upon the broth spoon of gazpacho, we may go forward with our feast by ordering *paella de mariscos* (a sort of rice and sea-food pilaf) and hear the clack of crab-claw against chitonous pincer of lobster. *Buen apetito.*

Chapter 83

Legal Source of the Words *Farm* & *Farmer*

Farm and farmer are terms often reeking of disdainful contempt for those who have grown our food all through history. Embedded in their very syllables is the concept of land leased by a poor peasant, of money or crops paid to a rich lord so that the low-born, field-ploughing underling may perform his servile tillage of the soil and then at harvest give over most of what he has grown to the moneybags. In the very etymology of the word is planted the seed of every agrarian revolution that ever did sever a princely head from its lard-assed, paunch-bloated body.

Sources

Farmer first meant one who signs a lease for rented land. Like many of our words that appear steeped in an essential Englishness, it is pure Latin in origin. As *feorm*, it appeared in Old English around 600-800 CE, and was thus one of the very earliest of Latin words to enter Old English, where its plethora of meanings are yet within the same semantic barnyard: provision, food, supplies, provisions supplied by a tenant or vassal to his lord, rent, possessions, stores, feast, entertainment or haven.

After the Norman Invasion of 1066 CE, the word seems to have been reborrowed or at least newly influenced by a French agent reflex, Norman French *fermer* and later *fermier*, but possibly later and thus derivative Medieval Latin *firmarius* 'one who has signed any fiduciary pledge,' or its near synonym *firmator* 'lessee, one who has signed a lease for land,' both from classical Latin *firma* 'a person's signature.' Note here the derivation of the current Italian and Spanish words for signature on a document: Italian *firma*, Spanish *firma*. In Latin *firma* is a noun from the verb *firmare* 'to settle, to confirm, to fix payment by signature,' from the same morpheme as our English adjective *firm*.

The Word Cropped Well

Very quickly *fermer*, then *farmer*, drove out of our language all the various Old English words for farmer like *ierthling* 'ploughman' and *gebur* 'person who works the land or who keeps livestock,' with its relationship to other Germanic farmer words like Dutch *boer* and German *Bauer*. The French and English forms performed similar mop-up jobs in a few European languages. For example in Russian, native Slavic terms for farmer still have use but most common is the borrowed-from-French import *fermer*. Slavic farm names exist, but so too does *ferma*. The process or act of farming in Russian is *fermestvo*.

The Belligerent Ignorance of Those Who Do Not Know

As to the dismal, unproven nineteenth-century notion that *feorm* is not Latin but Germanic — a supposititious positing you will find on all sorts of semi-literate, spurious internet "word expert" sites where the resident no-nothings have copied all their word lore from very old dictionaries. *The Oxford English Dictionary*, Second edition, 1989, sums up the evidence succinctly: "Not found outside English, and no satisfactory Germanic etymology has been proposed. On the assumption that the primary sense was 'fixed portion of provisions, ration', it would be admissible to regard the word as < Late Latin *firma*."

Thinking to end this note with a snatch of farm poetry, I remembered the epitaph of the greatest Latin poet Virgil, author of the mighty national epic of ancient Rome, *The Aeneid*. Tradition claims Virgil himself wrote his own gravestone inscription. That is unlikely, but the last sentence does possess a characteristic Virgilian terseness.

Mantua me genuit, Calabri rapuere,
tenet nunc Parthenope. Cecini pascua, rura, duces.

'Mantua gave birth to me, Calabria snatched me away, now Naples holds me firm. I sang of pastures, farms and leaders of men.'

In its last sentence the epitaph refers to Virgil's three most renowned poetic works, the pastoral *Eclogues*, the farm-haunted *Georgics* (Greek, literally 'Farmers' Things') and the sweeping national epic of the leaders who founded Rome, *The Aeneid*.

Chapter 84

Were You Shriven before Lent?
origins of the Words 'Shrove Tuesday' & 'Lent'

Many Christians don't know a precise meaning of Shrove in the feast name Shrove Tuesday. One devout little disciple, wagging the finger of pious disapproval in my face, explained that a shrove is a pancake. No, Saint Martha, you are wrong, unleavened-bread-breath. In its simplest sense, 'to be shriven' implied that, before the renunciatory rigors of Lent, before the merrymaking and feasting that might come before Lent, one skedaddled off to church to loll encompassed by incense and swaddled in Holy Writ, there to take communion.

"Pastor Fred, for Lent, may I give up guilt?"

"No, my son, your Deity wants you on your knees!"

In earliest English, *to shrive* meant 'to hear the confession of, to administer priestly absolution to.' So one might say, "The priest shrove me Tuesday morning. I was shriven by the priest. The priest will shrive my wife this afternoon," that is, hear her confession.

The Teutonic root appears in modern German as *schreiben* 'to write,' itself borrowed from Latin *scribere* 'to write' hence our multiplicity of derivatives in modern English words like *scribe, circumscribe, conscription, describe, inscribe, manuscript, proscription* and even *scribble.*

All the ancient meanings of 'to shrive' begin with that original 'writing' sense. Among other senses, Old English *scrifan* could signify to assign, decree, impose as a sentence, impose penance, to regard and to take care of. In the antique spelling of John Ford's 1633 play *'Tis Pitty shee's Whore* a holy man pleads, "Give me leave to shrive her; lest she should die un-absolu'd."

Lent

What was the first Old English or Anglo-Saxon word for spring? Lent. That's why the season of religious personal deprivation is called Lent. Compare the Dutch word for spring, *de lente*. The northern *Hoch Deutsch* word for spring is *Frühling*, the early or *früh* part of the year; the southern German word is *Lenz*. Among the Germanic tongues, only English uses Lent with an ecclesiastical meaning. The ultimate root of *Lenz* appears to be an Old Teutonic form of 'long' (*lengs*) referring to lengthening spring days.

Chapter 85

Spindrift & *Unda* & Spinnaker
words nautical and nice

Spindrift

Beloved of poets, spindrift names sea-spray. stirred up by wind on thalassic and pelagic water. Spindrift is the conversion of tempest-chop, of ocean-wave crests, whipped tips and barmy tops roused into a driving salt spritz, then lifted and propelled across the surface of the briny main. Spindrift is the scud and spume of ocean's blown foam.

It began as a Scottish pronunciation of any earlier word *speendrift* from a verb *to speen* 'to drive a ship before a strong wind, itself a Scottish alteration of English *to spoondrift*, of that spoon's ultimate origin we have not the foggiest — or should I say — the windiest notion.

Unda

One of my pet nautical words is the throaty and volvent Latin word for wave, *unda*, pronounced not to rhyme with English *under* but rather with the /u/ of *soon* as in the hypothetical English SOON-da. *Unda* always seemed to me in early Latin class as a reptilian sneak of a word, waiting to coil a swimmer in its gagging, lethal folds. But then *unda* also gives rises to many calmer, less threatening words in modern English:

undulant 'in a wavy motion'
redundant 'washing back in meaning or purpose,'

surround ultimately from Late Latin *superundare* 'to overflow,' which was surround's first meaning in English
Undine or *Ondine* name of a wave-nymph, as in French playwright Jean Giraudoux's 1938 drama *Ondine*, all about a knight who falls in love with a water-sprite.
Inundate 'to flood with waves of water'

Comparative Etymology of *Unda*

Unda belongs to a wide Indo-European family of water words. Here are a few of *unda*'s close relatives:

Old English *wæter*
High German *wazzer;* Modern German *Wasser*
Swedish *vatten*
Russian *voda* (hence 'little water' or *vodka*)
English *wet, winter*
Greek *hydor* (genitive *hydatos)* and all the English words which begin with hydor's prefixal combining form *hydro-*, e.g. hydroelectric and hydrolysis
English *otter* 'water creature'
Sanskrit *udan*
Lithuanian *undu*

So — as the poet Coleridge wrote, "water, water everywhere" and not an aqueous droplet that cannot be etymologized. "Nyuck-nyuck," as Curly of the Three Stooges so wisely said.

Spinnaker, the Neatest Sailing Term

Sail words billow plumply on the pronouncing tongue and keep aloft the adventurous word-heart. Listen to sail words: moonraker, lateen, flying jib, spinnaker, topgallant and skysail. And should the ship run with the wind abaft the beam, wave-thrusting across fair weather, then light-canvas kite sails may fly to reap the breeze. Scudding over Neptune's fathoms we may reach port safely and never need to know what lurks in the benthic deeps of ocean or what gelatinous secrets beach waves may spread upon the sand for our morning discovery. So, let us spinnaker onward.

Spinnaker has No Valid Origin?

Racing yachts have spinnakers on right-angled booms at the yacht's side opposite to the mainsail. Fluffed taut to the snapping point while running before the wind (that is, when the wind is blowing from behind) spinnakers are powerful drawing sails that help win races. The origin of the stout name is lost. Folk etymology suggests that it is based on an illiterate pronunciation of Sphinx, the name of the first yacht said to have carried the sail. What? An illiterate sailor? One who says *spinx* instead of Sphinx. *Ompussible*!

One of the most metaphorically delirious and therefore memorable uses of the word *spinnaker* occurs in a well-known passage of critical analysis of the poetic diction of American poet Wallace Stevens as displayed in his 1937 collection of poems *Owl's Clover*. His fellow American poet Marianne Moore wrote in a review of Steven's glorious word use, "But best of all, the bravura. Upon the general marine volume of statement is set a parachute-spinnaker of verbiage which looms out like half a cantaloupe and gives the body of the theme the air of a fabled argosy advancing." However extravagant Miss Moore's clever but prickly praise may be, it is apt. Both Steven's language in the poems and a spinnaker sail filling with wind are beautiful and bountiful and may be overblown!

Chapter 86

Gehenna, Sheol, Tophet & Other Names for Hell

Hell

The root meaning of English *hell* is 'hidden place' or 'secret place.' Hell is directly related to an Old English Teutonic verb *helan* 'to conceal, to cover up.' Indo-European cognates include Latin *celare* 'to hide.' Think of cellar, ultimately from Latin *cellarium* 'storeroom.' I don't know about you but my pack-rat cellar is hell. The basic sense of the word *occult* as an adjective is 'hidden,' from a Latin verb *occulere* 'to hide' with the **cul* root smack dab in its middle. The ancient Greek reflex of the etymon is **kal*, showing up in the word *apocalypse*, literally 'uncovering' from Latin *apocalypsis* < Greek *apokalupsis = apo* Greek 'off' + *kaluptra* 'woman's veil, covering, lid of a pot' + *-sis* Greek suffix used to form nouns of action, abstract nouns and medical conditions. In Old Icelandic, Hel was a goddess who queened it icily on Hades' frozen throne. Through a series of vowel gradations like hel-, hal-, hæl, hul- (hol-), the root has reflexes and related terms in modern English, words like *hole, hollow,* and *hull.*

Sheol

The oldest word for hell in Tanakh, the canon of the Hebrew Bible, and in the Old Testament, is Sheol, Hebrew sheh-ol. Dead and in Sheol, you were shrouded in clammy darkness. Nobody, not even the rabbi's virtuous sister, returned from Sheol. You stayed subterranean and you stayed dead—which I always think makes for a nice, spacious, zombie-free, angel-empty world up here. This stern concept of Sheol probably predates formalized Judaism because Sheol boasts an attribute that is anathema to all organized religions. There was no moral judgment upon one's earthly deeds after one kicked the leather bucket and descended to Sheol, whose common meanings are 'grave, pit, abyss.' Do-gooders and do-badders, all alike, climb with doomed footsies down the one-way ladder of death.

Gehenna

Gehenna is one of the words for hell in the New Testament. No, it is not an afterworld where departed loved ones must use cheap hair dye forever. We human beings show skill at making ourselves feel guilty and pining for punishment. We therefore, throughout all known eons of cringing religiosity, with the eager connivance of holy men, have populated the underworld with myriad infernal abodes and manifold chasms of remorse. This New Testament *Gehenna* word for hell is taken from a real place name near ancient Jerusalem, namely *gei ben Hinnom*, 'the valley of the son of [a man named] Hinnom.'

Gehinnom was a midden in New Testament times, a garbage dump where butchers' waste was tossed to rot. However, in the Old Testament, that most fulminating of prophets, the ever-kvetching Jeremiah (Chapter 19, verses 2-6) tells us Gehenna was a frightful place of flesh-fed fires where living children were offered as burnt sacrifices to pagan gods like Baal and Moloch. This troubled time of untoward toddler-toasting, like so many hells, was always conveniently beyond precise human dating. You know, it was "back then." Islam borrowed the term Gehenna to give one of the classical Arabic words for hell, *jahannam.*

Hades

In Alexandria, circa 200 BCE, the Hebrew scriptures were translated into Hellenistic Greek and the Greek word *Hades* was used to translate Sheol. In *The Revelation of St. John the Divine* the dead abide in Hades. In Homer, *haides* was a synonym for Pluto, ruler of the underworld. Later Greeks named the whole dreary underworld after its ruler.

Facilis Descensus Averno

My own favorite inferno is Hellmouth as described by the Roman poet Vergil in his great epic *The Aeneid.* His hero Aeneas, for various reasons, must go down into hell. Aeneas finds out that the gate of hell is near *Avernus lacus,* a stinking lake in Campania whose sulphurous effluvia killed unwary birds that flew over it. Early Greek settlers in southern Italy (Magna Graecia) had first named the malodorous lake, naturally in Greek, *limne aornos* 'Lake Birdless' from Greek *a* 'not' + Greek *ornis, ornithos* 'bird.' Think of ornithology. Aeneas gets his hell-map and advice from a wrinkled seeress, the Sybil of Cumae, a crone who gives him good tips, in perhaps the most quoted passage from *The Aeneid*:

facilis descensus Averno;
noctes atque dies patet atri ianua Ditis;
sed revocare gradum superasque evadere ad auras,
hoc opus, hic labor est.

(my translation)

Easy is the climb down to Hell;
Night and day yawn wide black devil gates;
But to clamber back up

And smell again sweet airs of life
That's the trick, pal; that's the major task.

If you are planning to tiptoe through the tulips of fatality,
you could do worse than to read Book Six of *The Aeneid*.

Tophet & A Jewish Blood Libel

Another biblical garbage dump was Tophet. Its Hebrew shoresh or triliteral verbal root *t-f-th* means 'burn', thus tophet means 'place of burning or roasting.' It was a garbage dump for the bodies of animals and human cadavers which were burned to avoid contagion. The Jews who arrived with their genetic replicas, the Semitic Canaanites, claimed that the Canaanites had sacrificed living children at Tophet. Deeply unlikely. A small note of interest: the Jews and the Canaanites were ethnically exactly the same people, migrating farmers who settled what became Judea in the eighth millennium BCE.

The ancient Romans spread a widely believed bit of blood libel about their North African enemies, the Carthaginians. Romans claimed that citizens of Carthage burned living children as sacrifices to weird deities like their hideous moon goddess of death, Tanit. Two teams of modern forensic archaeologists have put the bones found in Carthaginian cemetery urns to scientific tests and discovered something startling. **All** the bones in the children's cemetery of ancient Carthage are fetal bones, from children **not born**. What does that tell us? It makes crystal clear that this Carthaginian children's cemetery was where still-borns were burnt and buried. There is no proof of living children being sacrificed at all. Nothing. *Nada. Zilch. Bupkes. Klum.*

Now the very same blood libel was levelled by ancient Jews against their "pagan" neighbors, the Canaanites. Jews claimed Canaanites sacrificed living children to those odious Canaanite gods Moloch and Ba'al. Notice that the Jews delayed this libel until AFTER the Jews had borrowed all kinds of Canaanite religious material and incorporated it into their Torah. For example, ask a rabbi who actually knows something about Hebrew etymology if the name Eve (*Chava* in biblical Hebrew) is even derived from Hebrew. It is not. The spurious etymology believed by thousands of modern Israelis is that Chava (Eve, of Adam and Eve) is related to *chai*, Hebrew for life. Think of the drinking toast in Hebrew *lo' Chaim* 'To Life!

Chava is not related to *chai* at all. Chava is a straight borrowing of the name Chavva, a prominent Canaanite snake goddess. What are some of the elements in Chavva's Canaanite mythology. How about these, Bible lovers? Chavva controlled snakes. Dedicated to Chavva was the fruit of a tree of the knowledge of good and evil. There was a prohibition on munching the fruit of this tree etc. Sound faintly familiar, O readers of Genesis?

All this Canaanite mythology predates the writing down of the Torah (the five books of Moses) by hundreds, perhaps thousands of years. Neat, eh? After Judaism borrows half of the creation myth in the Book of Genesis from their neighbors, the Canaanites, the Jews then condemn the very same Canaanites as godless infidels and baby-burning pagans. There is zero archaeological proof of moppets-on-the-menu. Talk about chutzpah!

In later Christian writings, Tophet became a synonym for Hell.

Chapter 87

Lemon & Lime Are the Same Word
both derived from Arabic limun *or Persian* limu

The earliest reflex of this root may be Indo-European, so that the words *lemon* and *lime* are not, as many dictionaries assert of "Middle Eastern" origin, but of South Asian provenance.

Sanskrit *nimbu* or *nimbuka* "lime"

In ancient India, there was a Sanskrit word for the Indian lime, *nimbu*, still used in Hindi. The Indian lime is a sort of cross between a lemon and a lime. *Nimbu pani* is a refreshing limeade drunk on a very hot Indian day. Nimbu may have been borrowed, as many Sanskrit terms were, into Persian as *limu*, and hence into Arabic as *limun*. Arabic has also *lima*, possible ancestor of lime, and a general collective plural form, *lim* 'citrus fruits.'

The path into English appears to have been: French *limon* < Spanish *limon* <Portuguese *limao* < Italian *limone* < Provençal *limo* < medieval Latin *limonem* < Arabic *limun* < Persian *limu*< Sanskrit *nimbu*.

Note about Utterance of Borrowed Words

In other Persian borrowings of Sanskrit words, initial Sanskrit /n/, not easily pronounced by Persian speakers, became an /l/ sound. And the Sanskrit /b/ is merely infixed and euphonic and dispensable (earlier Vedic Sanskrit form *nim'u*), since it was not needed in any Persian attempt at euphonious utterance. In Sanskrit and other Indo-European languages, a plosive like /b/ sometimes replaces a glottal stop, represented here in *nim'u* by the superscript apostrophe. Putting the /b/ sound into the word makes the word easier to say, quicker to enunciate.

Lemons & Limes of the Orient

When some languages borrowed the word *limun* or *lime*, the forms were altered. For example, the Japanese word for lemon is *remon*, because /l/ is difficult. Japanese *remon* is 'lemon' and compare Japanese *raimu* 'lime.' One Chinese word for lemon is an attempt at pronouncing a form of the word *lemon* borrowed from some language west of China. Chinese *ning-meng* 'lemon.' Mandarin Chinese gets a bit closer to lime with *lái méng*.

Persian Pun

The familiar English proverb is: One man's meat is another man's poison. Quite unrelated to this discussion but one of the best puns ever made in English is American humorist S. J. Perelman's proverb: "One man's Mede is another man's Persian."

Note that English borrowed from French *limon* (fourteenth century) and *lime* (sixteenth century) and they became the yellow lemon and the green lime. Then in seventeenth century French, another word that had been hanging around in French since the thirteenth century, originally borrowed from Latin, replaced both *limon* and *lime* first as the French scientific word and then as the popular French word too, and that word was *citron*. In modern French, lemon = *le citron* and lime = *le citron vert*.

Lemon and lime then are related. Lemon made its way to English through Old French as *lymon* in the fifteenth century.

Lime first entered English two hundred years later. Lime was borrowed from a Spanish form, *lima*.

Oranges & Lemons

Lemony references abound in English. But I'll conclude with my favourite from a British nursery rhyme and game: "Oranges and lemons / Say the bells of St Clements."

Chapter 88

Origin of the Phrase 'Christmas Carol'
plus a Shocking Personal Revelation by the Author!

Before filleting with deft scalpel the phrase *Christmas carol*, I must unfold, from the foxed parchment of my past, a childhood Christmas memory. "Oh please don't!" I hear you beg. But your qualms are of no avail, dear reader. Onward!

Each November in my Ontario public school, as Yule loomed, glutinous with psychological treacle and all sticky with false bonhomie, our junior school music teacher, whom I shall identify as Miss Treble Cleft Palate, would hold the dreaded Christmas choir try-outs on the creaky stage in the girls' gym. I, wee Billy, might begin in choir row A as "possible boy soprano phenomenon." Very soon however, after I had flatted out on the first lines of "O Little Town of Bethlehem," Miss Cleft Palate would move me back to choir row D, to stand glumly beside the "no longer possibles." My no-voice boy companions would be choral rejects, unsavoury local lads, spawn of moms and dads who were only seen in town when out on a day pass. But, of course, as we learned in Sunday School, "ALL God's chillun' got wings."

Row D included Grade Five boys like Mickey Wrongworm, a lad born with no discernible tongue, and Boris Pediculosivitch Impetigov, a New Canadian lad of Russian descent who was often absent from school because a medical research hospital located 300 miles away paid his mother handsome fees when she permitted doctors to perform incisional biopsies of her son's manifold skin diseases.

Other than the Christmas Carol Sing for the whole school, Miss Treble Cleft had many duties as junior school music teacher, so she could not take more than an hour to audition and cast the choir. Miss T.C. was a Maritimer and her proudest moment was her annual Nova Scotia-based ballet for the Grade Fours, "Afternoon of a Prawn."

Suffice to say, at the end of the choir audition, I was in the back row, my flat voice, like my small boy body, hidden by a row of hefty milkmaids, all of whom were from the Scottish side of town and could sing and had names like Fiona McSphincter, a scallop-shaped rotundity with all the allure of a shucked mollusc. All of which memory is placed before you to record that there are persons immune to the overdose of coziness within Christmas carols, stern hearts who do not wax all weepy upon hearing the opening notes of "Adeste, Fideles."

The Etymology of Carol

Carol has enjoyed dozens of spellings, and this orthographic bounty occurred in French as well as English. Consider: *karol, karolle, carole, carol, carrol, caroul, karalle, carowl, caryl, carrell, karrel* and *karil*. The French word may have come over to England during the Norman Conquest. It becomes frequent in English manuscripts at the onset of the fourteenth century.

The French carol was first a ring dance, then a dance accompanied by song, and finally the song itself. A carol was an ancient pagan round dance with singing by couples, a fertility ring dance first done on May-day celebrations throughout Western Europe. After spring use, the dancing and singing were shared by once pagan then Christian festivities celebrated at the midwinter solstice.

In the French dialect spoken in the Marne department, *carole* was a dance or a celebration. In the Swiss Romance dialect, *coraula* is a round dance. In Provençal and Italian *carola* is still a dance song or a round dance. The ultimate provenance is unknown. But two etymologists have proposed origins of this tricky word. Friedrich Christian Diez, a German philologist (1794–1876), proposed an origin in the Latin word *chorus*, from Greek *choros*, noting that most early forms took /o/ as first vowel, corol, coral etc. Karl Heinrich Wilhelm Wackernagel (1806-1869), a German-Swiss philologist of mellifluous surname, first suggested the /l/ of carol stemmed from *choraules*, the name of the flute-player who sometimes accompanied a Greek chorus as it danced and sang choral odes in early Greek drama.

Other guesses include *corolla* Latin 'garland, ring-shaped crown of flowers, coronet' especially if the original meaning was 'ring.' This not-now-popular suggestion conceives that the dancers wore flower garlands in their hair as they danced and sang, and that the name of the garland became the name of the dance and the song. Maybe.

Early Citations of the Word Carol

Here's a relevant English citation from CE 1387 "He saw a mayden . . . daunsynge in a carrole among other maydouns."

Long ago a British folk story told of circles of upright stones, like Stonehenge but smaller, that claimed they began as a blasphemous ring-dance, by a party of girls who were turned into stone for dancing carols on a Sunday.

In CE 1600, William Shakespeare in *A Midsummer Night's Dream* wrote this glum line: "No night is now with hymne or carroll blest."

How early did English speakers refer to Christmas carols? A famous early printer of London with the wonderful name of Wynkyn de Worde published a book in CE 1521 entitled *Christmasse Carolles*.

How Carol Turned into Carrel

The carrel in a library, an individual study desk or stall, is from the same word *carol*. Libraries borrowed the word from medieval monasteries, where the carrel was a small alcove or cubicle for individual monks and nuns to read Holy Writ or to meditate. That sense of small enclosure developed from carol's earliest meaning in French 'ring' or 'circle.' Carol also once meant precinct or small enclosed space, hence it became an apt word to name the little study carrels in a cloister.

More Citational Bounty

"I heard the bells on Christmas Day
Their old, familiar carols play,
And wild and sweet
The words repeat
Of peace on earth, good-will to men!" - Henry Wadsworth Longfellow

> "Christmas gift suggestions: To your enemy, forgiveness. To an opponent, tolerance. To a customer, service. To every child, a good example. To a friend, your heart. To yourself, respect."
>
>   - Oren Arnold

Chapter 89

Whales

"And God created great whales, and every living creature that moveth, which the waters brought forth abundantly."

So we read in Genesis 1:21 about the leviathan that later chugalugged Jonah. Of course, after disobedient Jonah had been in the belly of the whale for three days, he decided kissing a little Almighty posterior might be the wiser course, so, cringing lickspittle toady that he became, Jonah told the Big Guy he was really, really sorry. What happened next the the Book of Jonah, 2:10, KJV states clearly: "And the Lord spake unto the fish, and it vomited out Jonah upon the dry land."

Of course the biblical Hebrew does NOT say whales, because biblical Hebrew had no word for whale. They never saw one. The plural Hebrew noun *tanneen* means 'monsters, dragons, animal prodigies.' The deity is a much more inventive ha-Shem than He who is revealed in the prim prose of the dainty Elizabethan divines who gave us the (admittedly magnificent) English of The King James translation of Holy Writ. I mean, Wow! A deity who invents great lolloping sea monsters?

In stark ichthyological fact, many species of whales can't swallow human beings. Baleen whales, for example, have a hard-bone mouth filter called a baleen through which nothing as large as a man could pass. They dine on infinitesimal sea critters called krill or little clams.

But, class, please, come to order! Our educative purpose today is dispersal of morsels philological about the word *whale*, not spreading atheist doubt about Holy Writ's many factual errors.

"Got a Whale of Tale To Tell You, Lads!"

In Old English it was *hwæl* 'whale' related to German *Walfisch* and Old Norse *hvalr* and modern Swedish and Danish *hval*. It seems probable that our word *walrus* contains the etymon too, spirited into English by Dutch sailors (Dutch *walrus, walrus*) from a Viking or Old Norse form like *hvalross* or *hvalrusk*. With roots transposed *russhval* is also found. Thus walrus is literally 'reddish whale.' Sun-basking walrus do turn red.

My Faves = *Hwælweg & Hronrad*

Two whale words delighted me as a student reading Old English poems like *Beowulf* and *The Seafarer*. One was the word *hwælweg,* a poetic metaphor meaning 'sea' but literally 'the whale path.' Such a compound metaphor is called a kenning in Old English poetry studies. In the first part of the compound you can see one Old English spelling of whale and in the second part, what our modern word *way* looked like in OE, a Germanic etymon totally similar to the modern German word *Weg* meaning 'road, alley, lane, path or way.'

In Anglo-Saxon poetry, the sea was mentioned so often that the poet required many synonyms, needed to provide verbal variety. Among them were kennings for ocean or sea like 'sea-street,' 'the foaming fields' and 'the whale's bath.' Another kenning for the sea I thought apt was *hron-rad* or *hranrad* 'the whale road.' *Hran* was an Old English word for dolphin or whale. *Rad* is simply OE for road.

A ship could be a *baru fakr* 'a wave horse' or a *gjalfr-marr* 'steed of the sea.' These poems are filled with fearsome battles, so badly needed were poetic synonyms for blood; two good ones 'slaughter-dew' and 'battle-sweat.'

I'll stop this sidetrack with a kenning I really like, namely *foerg-bolt* literally 'life-house' but meaning 'the human body.' How's your life-house, dude?

Reading Tip: If you'd like to hear the sea-salty flavour, the thong-rich thrum and savour of Old English, but do not wish to take a few years to learn Anglo-Saxon, find and read Ezra Pound's rollicking translation of *The Seafarer.* An even more splendid achievement is *Beowulf* as translated into consonant-chomping English by Irish poet Seamus Heaney.

Narwhal the Zombie

The twisty-tusked narwhal's name may mean 'corpse whale.' Reflexes in the Scandinavian languages where the word originated include Danish *narhval*, Old Icelandic *nahvalr*, Norwegian *narkval* and Swedish *narval*, possibly all containing the initial element *nar*, Old Icelandic for corpse. Maybe the little whales were so named by early Vikings or sailors who noted the mottled coloration of the beast, a cadaverous murk of grey similar to skin on a long-drowned floating human body. The dowdy beast's scientific moniker is equally glum, *Monodon monoceros* from Greek roots that mean 'one-toothed one-horn.' Poor little narwhal! See, I'm a sympathetic atheist, not a big meanie.

Chapter 90

Rock Snot: Annals of Fresh-water Algae

Rock snot is a gomphonemoid diatom. And don't say I didn't warn you. More commonly, among hoi polloi, it is called didymo. By either name, you don't want 'em over at the house playing with the kids on Sunday afternoon. Rock snot is a kind of invasive algae that thrives in cold-water streams, messing up fish-food sources and befouling otherwise pleasant streams with dense, off-white mats of planktonic crud. Didymo attaches itself to the bottom stones and rocks and to underwater plants by means of a sticky stalk.

Its *raison de peste*, that is, why rock snot is such a plague of waters is neatly explained in this Wikipedia quote: "When the diatom cell divides, through vegetative reproduction, the stalk divides too, eventually forming a mass of branching stalks. The nuisance build-up is not the cell itself, but their massive production of extracellular stalks. Extracellular polymeric substances that form the stalks are made primarily of polysaccharides and protein, forming complex, multi-layered structures that are resistant to degradation." In other words, the crap sticks around and does not biodegrade in a timely fashion.

Rock Snot's politer nickname "didymo" is merely an abbreviation of its scientific binomial in botany, *Didymosphenia geminata*.

didymosphenia = Greek *didymos* 'twin, double' + Greek *sphen* 'wedge, wedge-shaped thing.' These algae were named because of their silica shell, called a frustule, which is cuneate, that is, it fits together in two halves like a pill box, seemingly composed of "twin wedges." *Cuneus* is the Latin word for 'wedge;' its translation in Greek is *sphen*. Think of cuneiform writing, wedge-shaped imprints in clay tablets.

geminata = Latin *geminatus* 'twin-born, doubled;' think of Gemini, the sign of the zodiac shown as twin boys.

gomphonemoid means 'like a gomphonema.' Really helpful! A gomphonema is a form of algae that makes undesirable slime in water, its presence an indicator of industrial waste and/or sewage in fresh water.

gomphonema = Greek *gomphos* 'bolt, spike, nail' + Greek *nema* nematos 'thread, filament, wire,' so that perhaps the naming scientist thought the alga (algae is plural) had nail-like filaments.

A diatom is a one-celled teeny-weeny alga, a plant with the ability to self-propel and that's why once it was thought to be an animal. Diatoms have silica in their cell walls, so that their fossil remains provide diatomaceous earth, widely used in modern products. Under the microscope their cells connect at odd, zig-zag angles so they seemed to be 'all cut up' which is what their Greek name describes. Diatom = New Scientific Latin *diatima* from Greek adjective *diatomos* 'cut through, cut in half,' from the Attic Greek verb *diatemnein* 'to cut through.'

Water-waders, consider yourselves warned. Stick not moist footsies into algous slime.

Chapter 91

Xanthic Means Yellow

If you wanted to insult a coward, you could yell, "Hey, chicken, you got a yellow streak down your back wide as the Jersey Turnpike!" Or, much more annoying to the semi-literate coward, you might hiss, "You dastardly poltroon, you have a mid-dorsal, xanthic striation of undue amplitude." Mind you, in Jersey, that prissy aspersion might earn you the five-finger sandwich, square in the teeth. However, there are other reasons to know the adjective *xanthic* means yellow.

This entry looks at scientific terms in English derived from *xanthos* 'yellow,' direct borrowings or coinages from that ancient Greek word whose initial letter is xi (k-sigh, rhymes with pi). In Greek, it is a double-consonant ks-sound; in English, usually a zee or zed sound. Xanthic 'yellow' is '*zanthic*' in English, but it is 'ksanthicos' in Greek.

Xanthophyll

Wanderers through the autumnal plume of any maple-leaved Eldorado have encountered xanthophyll, an accessory in photosynthesis and the chief pigment in autumn leaves that produces the glory of their golden-yellow hue, from *xanthos* Greek 'yellow" + *phyllon* Greek 'leaf.' Widespread through earthly nature, xanthophyll is a component not only of green leaves but also of carrots and egg yolks and human plasma.

Shakespeare had *Macbeth* (Act 5, Scene 3, lines 22-23) refer to the approaching autumn of his fate by saying, "My way of life has fallen into the sere, the yellow leaf. . ."

Generations of later poetasters and talentless versifiers took up the line, mangled it, and so poetry readers suffer still pamphlets of atrocious rhyme with titles like "Sincerely Sere and Yellow Fellow." These versicles of self-pitying tripe have couplets like this: "In Honda small, my Lydia hath left me deep in grief/and recommended that I *eat* a sere and yellow leaf."

Xanthochromia

This weightier word of doom from the pathology lab may arise from analysis of a patient's cerebrospinal fluid, where hemorrhage to the brain or spinal cord or nearby tissues is suspected. It means yellowish discoloration and may announce to microscopic view that diluted blood has escaped from its proper vessels. *Xanthos* Greek 'yellow' + *chroma* Greek 'color.'

Xanthippe

I'm stirring into this flavid cauldron one word that is not scientific but rather belongs to onomatology, the study of names. The Greek philosopher Socrates had a wife, Xanthippe. She was a nag and a scold and a shrew of toxic temperament. But here we care only about her single moniker. Her beautiful name meant 'chestnut mare (*xanthos* 'yellow, yellowish-red, auburn, golden yellow' + *hippos* Greek 'horse'). Only the well-to-do possessed horses in ancient Greece, so Xanthippe might have been the ugly daughter of a moderately wealthy man forced to marry an equally ugly philosopher, for history tells us that Socrates was no looker and would have turned an amphora of olive oil rancid in a trice. Being married to such a Socratic mug might have soured Xanthippe into the querulous quibbler she became.

Xanthophore

From zoology comes xanthophore, a cell, for example, in a cold-blooded animal's skin, containing a yellow pigment that contributes to its skin color. Other chromatophores may contribute other dermal tints and shadings. *Xanthos* Greek 'yellow' + *phoros* Greek 'bearing, carrying.'

Cryptoxanthin

This pigment is one of the deep yellow, orange-gold carotenoids, a precursor of vitamin A, found widely in nature, making fruits and plants yellowy orange and also tincturing egg-yolks to give them their yolky chromaticity. *Kryptos* Greek 'hidden' + *xanthos* Greek 'yellow' + *in* noun suffix used to name some organic chemical compounds.

Xanthopterin

There is poetry in chemistry. Knowing what scientific words mean is sometimes all that is necessary to find the poetry. Xanthopterin is a pigment that helps make new blood cells in anemic animals. It was first extracted from butterfly wings! Now a common source is the integumental tissue of wasps and hornets. *Xanthos* Greek 'yellow' + *pteron* Greek 'wing' + *in* noun suffix used to name some organic chemical compounds.

Fucoxanthin

No, adolescent boys, don't get your hopes up about this word root. *Fucus* here is a Latin word for rock-lichen or red dye, cognate with Greek *phukos* 'a seaweed from which a red dye was extracted.' But in present-day marine botany, *Fucus* is a genus of slimy brown algae, seaweeds with slippery leathery fronds. Fucoxanthin is the pigment that gives these watery slitherers their fuscous gloss.

Xanthodont is Worth Restoring to Daily Use

This is a now obsolescent zoological noun which once upon a time referred to rodents with yellow teeth. *Xanthos* Greek 'yellow' + *odous, odontis* Greek 'tooth.' I suggest its revival and application during denunciatory harangues against old, creepy, evil, witch-like music teachers who, when you first wrote the "Introduction to Harmony" exam at the conservatory on that grim Saturday morning, failed you and then mocked your low grade. Here's the very term to begin your screamed tirade against such injustice. You turn and address her: "You hideous old xanthodont! Obdurate virago! Leprous spawn of a thousand tuneless cicadas!"

In your fury, perched at the gunwales of your ship, U.S.S. Indignation, try not to go overboard in rage.

Chapter 92

Red

some 'red' words from Latin and Greek that appear frequently in English learned and scientific terms

Rubric

None of the derivatives of Latin ruber 'red' are common. The first two I learned were the medical adjective *rubifacient* 'making skin reddish' and the noun and adjective *rubric*. Rubrics were the letters or words painted red in ancient illuminated manuscripts. Rubrics were used to call attention to individual words and letters, and in later manuscripts to highlight titles, headlines and first words of a paragraph.

Rubella, a diminutive Latin form, refers to the 'little red' spots of German measles.

A rubicund countenance is a face healthy with the reddish glow of vim and vigour. A blush may be rubicund. *Rubicundus* as a Latin adjective means 'abounding in red coloration.' Think of other Latinate English adjectives like fecund 'abounding in fertility' and jocund 'abounding in joy'— not, as the *Oxford English Dictionary* claims, 'abounding in jest' but rather jocund derives from a common shout of joy in both Latin and Greek antiquity, "Io!" and "Iu!," both forms cognates of our English word *joy* and both attested in classical literature, so that jocund = *Iu!* + -*cundus* a Latin suffix of bounty; therefore jocund means 'abounding in joy.'

Ruby is a red corundum long treated as a precious gemstone. When the Norman Conquest of England in 1066 CE poured thousands of new French words into the English vocabulary, one of those precious stone words was Old French *rubi* < Late Latin *rubinus* 'reddish' < classical Latin *rubeus* or *ruber* 'red.'

Rubor – Soon or late, every medical and nursing student learns that the classic symptoms of inflammation are expressed as a mnemonic (memory aid) by three Latin nouns: rubor, tumor and dolor 'redness, swelling and pain.'

Incarnadine —This little pinkie began as an adjective, then a noun in English, meaning first 'pink' or 'carnation red' and later a noun colour name for carnation-pink, imported through French *incarnadin* from Italian *incarnadino* 'carnation' or 'flesh-colored < Latin *incarnatus* 'flesh-colored' < Latin *incarnare* 'to make flesh' (said of Jesus in fifth-century postclassical Latin) < Latin *caro, carnis* 'flesh.' Think of English derivatives like carnal and charnel house 'a house of dead flesh, a corpse room, a mortuary.' The same Latin word gives the French word for flesh, *chair.*

Flesh in Latin *'caro, carnis'* as opposed to *ruber* gives us the word *carnival*, a festivity traditionally held on the night before the start of Lent, Shrove Tuesday, during which revelers playfully bid adieu to bodily wants by crying in Latin *O Carne, vale* "O Flesh, Farewell!" That at least is the folk etymology. It is more likely that carnival stems ultimately from a Medieval Latin verb phrase like *carnem levare* 'to put away the eating of meat' (flesh) until after Lent.

Shakespeare used the verb *to incarnadine* with a new meaning in his play *Macbeth*, used it so memorably that afterward it acquired the meaning 'to turn blood-red' and Shakespeare's new meaning swamped all earlier senses. Macbeth is fretting about murder and all the blood he has spilled never to be washed off, when in Act 2, Scene 2, he says "This my Hand will rather The multitudinous Seas incarnadine, Making the Greene one Red."

Note: Some of the important Macbeth manuscripts have the word misspelled as incarnardine with that erroneous extra

r. I have chosen to correct it, as I am certain Shakespeare's actors did.

Contrary to many poorly-informed sites which assure us that Shakespeare invented the word *incarnadine*, he did not! The word existed before Shakespeare as a sixteenth-century learned adjective meaning "pink," ultimately from Latin *carnis* 'meat, flesh, the human body' with a midway form intervening like the Latin, then Italian verb *incarnare* 'to turn or to dye something flesh-colored.'

Does a "Red" Color Mean Something?

In the poppycock-laden annals of color-meanings, color charts and chromato-synchronicity babblings, red stands for anger, danger, sex, revenge, embarrassment, passion, positivity, war, determination and the hue of Tiffany's bustier. Quite a symbolic burden for one lonely basic colour to bear.

Blood is red. And the ferric spice of spilled blood corrugates the watcher's nostril and clutches a thumping heart. The sanguinous oozings of slaughter's gore and the clotted cruor of butchered corpses constricts his throat. *Sanguis* is the Latin word for blood and here I must add one of my favorite "blood-red" words, to wit, *sanguisugous*, literally 'bloodsucking' but figuratively 'cruel, miserly, cheapskate,' from Latin *sanguis* 'blood + *sūgĕre* 'to suck.' The sanguisugous old hag would not help her needy daughter with even one penny.

I have no wish to embarrass the pseuds, quacks and gurus of chromatic semantics (well, maybe just a smidgeon) for here we concern ourselves with the origins of a few exotic adjectives that belong in the red band of the spectrum, when naughty white light, prism-dispersed, shows forth its rainbow petticoat of refraction. There red has the longest wavelength of colours, violet the shortest.

Rarities & Obscurities

While ruber is the most familiar Latin red adjective, many other red words in Latin are used, especially in medicine, botany and zoological naming. Here are some:

atrosanguineus dark blood red
cardinalis cardinal red, a red bird
carminatus carmine red
cerasinus cherry red, French cerise 'cherry' is a color adjective,
cinnabarinus cinnabar red, vermilion
coccineous scarlet, deep red (rare to obsolete), but consider the zoological name of the lady-bug Coccinella and the name of a red dye famous in history and still used, namely, cochineal, made from the dried bodies of a Mexican insect Coccus cacti.
cruentus bloody, blood red
erubescens blushing, turning red
flammeus flame red
miniatus cinnabar red, vermilion
puniceus crimson
roseus rose-colored, red
rufescens light red, almost red
rufus red, reddish, red-haired, originally a boy given the name Rufus had red hair
russatus reddish, russet
rutilans red, becoming red
sanguineus bloody, blood red

Greek Morphemes

The standard ancient Greek adjective for red was *erythros*. Dozens and dozens of modern compound words in medicine, botany, zoology and mineralogy contain this morpheme (root).

erythrocyte = 'red' + -cyte 'blood cell' < ancient Greek *kutos* 'hollow receptacle, empty vessel,' hence in late

French –cyte 'cell' borrowed then into English; a cluster of red blood cells is shown above in macro-closeup.

Erythrocytopenia is a decreased number of red blood cells (erythrocytes) in the blood, symptomatic in some anemias. The suffixal part of the compound is from ancient Greek *penia* 'need, lack, deficiency.'

Erythrophobia is fear of red or fear of blushing from *erythros* 'red' + Hellenistic Greek suffix *–phobia* 'fear of' < classical Greek *phobos* 'fear.' But all fear of red is not irrational. A synonym is *hematophobia* 'fear of seeing red blood.' As wordman Anu Garg has written "Red screams danger or at the very least inconvenience and annoyance. It's no wonder we do our best to avoid it. Red ink is a sign of trouble in business. Red light stops us in our tracks. Who wants to be caught red-handed?" Red-handed means, of course, hands stained with fresh blood. He did it! Guilty of murder! Seize him!

Erythrophyll is the chemical that turns maple leaves red in the fall of the year after green chlorophyll production has ceased. The suffix is Greek *phyllon* 'leaf.'

Zooerythrin is a red pigment in bird feathers. Greek *zoon* is one Greek word for animal, literally 'something alive.' Consider zoology, the study of animals, sometimes seen at a zoo (short for zoological gardens) by a woman name Zoe (Greek 'life').

Not part of this discussion but worth perusing in further study are the many interesting English cognates of our word red, including ruddy, ruddle or reddle (a red ochre used in marking British sheep) and rust (red oxides of iron).

I'd like to conclude this red study with something profound and meaningful. But I can think of nothing weightier than this little ditty by the late pianist and comic Oscar Levant: "Roses are red, violets are blue, I'm schizophrenic, and so am I."

Chapter 93

English Words Derived from
Clavis, Latin for 'Key'

In a solemn Vatican conclave, within one of the most beautiful chambers ever created by human hands, the Sistine Chapel, cardinals of the Roman Catholic Church elect new popes. This chapter explores the Latin word for key, *clavis*, and its descendants in English, words like conclave, clavicle, autoclave, enclave, exclave, the surname Clavell, subclavian arteries, Bach's "The Well-Tempered Clavier," and even Moon Base Clavius in Stanley Kubrick's film "2001: A Space Odyssey." It's an awesome trip, dudes.

The word *conclave* is a Late Ecclesiastical Latin neuter noun *conclave*, Latin plural *conclavia*. Its prime meaning is 'any place or room that could be locked with a key.' Conclave < con = *cum*, Latin 'with' + *clavis* 'key.'

The Keys of the Kingdom

The armorial bearings of Vatican City show two crossed keys, a visual reference to the line in St. Matthew 16.18, *"et tibi dabo claves regni caelorum."* The Latin noun *clavis* 'key' (Latin plural *claves*) appears in familiar verses of the New Testament. In Matthew 16: 18,19 Christ bestows papal authority on his apostle Peter. In the Latin Bible authorized by the Roman Catholic Church and known as the Vulgate, these verses are:

18 *et ego dico tibi quia tu es Petrus et super hanc petram aedificabo ecclesiam meam et portae inferi non praevalebunt adversum eam.*

King James translation: And I say also unto thee that thou art Peter, and upon this rock I will build my church; and the gates of hell shall not prevail against it.

19 *et tibi dabo claves regni caelorum. . .*
KJ: And I will give unto thee the keys of the kingdom of heaven. . .

Matthew 18:16 also contains the great Latin Bible pun. *Petros* is the apostle name in Greek, *Petrus* in Latin, and *petra* is a Latin word meaning 'rock.' So Petrus is the *petra* (rock) on which the church will be built.

Clavicle

The clavicle is the long, slender, *f*-shaped collarbone that connects the breastbone with the shoulder blade. The clavicle or collarbone is the most frequently broken bone in the human body. The collarbone is near the skin, and it can be seen and felt easily in most people. The clavicle is designed to support the shoulder, acting like a strut that helps to align the shoulder with the rest of the chest. Some texts say the bone is S-shaped. No, it is *f*-shaped, like an italic f.

Etymology of clavicle

Clavicle English < *clavicula* Latin 'twig, little stick, hoopstick, human collarbone' < *clavis* 'key, bolt, stick' + *-cula* Latin diminutive ending, 'small'

What the *Oxford English Dictionary* & *Merriam-Webster* Do Not Tell You about the Origin of This Word

Yes, clavicula meant literally 'little stick' or 'little branch' but in Latin it also denoted a hoopstick, the water-bent wooden branch that Roman children used to trundle a hoop. This hoopstick was *f*-shaped like a human collarbone. The wooden stick with a slight hook permitted children to roll the hoop more quickly. That is why early anatomists gave this name to the human collarbone, not because it was a key or key-shaped or S-shaped but because it is *f*-shaped like a Roman child's clavicula. Do these sticks survive in museum collections? Yes! All the book-wormish, ivory-towered dictionary writers have to do is: be aware of them; go and look at them; then alter their oh-so-learned, lexicographical overlookings.

Autoclave

Several medical words derive from Latin *clavis* 'key.' Every doctor's office used to have a shiny metallic autoclave, although not as large as modern laboratory-size sterilizers. An autoclave is a self-locking device used to sterilize instruments by means of steam pressure. Autoclaving, also called steam sterilization, is the use of pressurized steam to kill agents of infection and denature proteins. This kind of "wet heat" is today considered the most dependable method of sterilizing laboratory equipment and decontaminating biohazardous waste. Autoclaves do not remove chemical contamination. The roots of autoclave look like this: autoclave < Greek *autos* 'self' + *clavis* Latin 'key.'

In Arthur C. Clarke's novel *2001: A Space Odyssey*, and in the Stanley Kubrick film of the same name, a mysterious black pillar is found at a lunar site named Moon Base Clavius. The base is named after an adjacent moon crater, itself commemorating a well-known 16th century mathematician,

Christopher Clavius, proposer of the leap-year rule. About 300 mathematicians have features on the earth's moon, mostly craters, named after them. One can easily find net photographs of the vast Clavius crater.

More English Words Derived from Latin *Clavis*

Johann Sebastian Bach finished the first part of "The Well-Tempered Clavier" at Cöthen in 1722, and the second part at Leipzig around 1740. This most famous of Bach's clavier works is a set of preludes and fugues. Each part consists of twenty-four preludes and fugues, one prelude and one fugue in each of the twelve major and minor keys. The German title is *Das wohltemperierte Clavier.* The tempering referred to is an altering of musical intervals to make their performance more practical on fixed-pitch instruments like pianos and modern organs.

Clavier first meant keyboard. After being borrowed into German from French, it is today the general German word for piano, *Klavier.* The names of some historical keyboard instruments also contain this root: clavichord, clavecin, and clavicembalo.

Clavier French keyboard instrument < *claviarius* Medieval Latin 'one who or that which bears keys' < Latin *clavis* 'key.'

Clef

Another familiar musical term from Latin clavis is *clef,* the symbol used in musical notation to indicate the pitch of the notes on a stave. There are three clefs: treble, bass, and tenor or alto. The term was first used in French musical notation and borrowed into English. French *clef* < Latin *clavis* 'key.'

Clavel – the lintel over a fireplace < *clavellus* Medieval Latin 'little key,' so named because of the lintel's shape. This word borrowed into English from medieval French gives rise to several French and now English surnames. The most renowned bearer of the last name Clavell is perhaps the late

Australian novelist, screenwriter and film director, James Clavell.

Enclave – French, literally 'locked in,' said of a territory surrounded by foreign land, then the meaning was generalized to refer to any minority within a larger grouping. The Italian town of Campione d'Italia is located on the shore of Lake Lugano in southern Switzerland and is an Italian enclave in Switzerland.

Exclave is a territory that belongs to a political entity but is not connected to it by land (islands are not counted) and is surrounded by other political entities. Alaska is an exclave of the United States of America. Hawaii is not, because it is made up of islands. Another good example is the region around the Russian city of Kaliningrad. It belongs to the Russian Federation, but is separated from the rest of that country by territory belonging to Lithuania and Poland.

Although both meanings are close, an exclave may not necessarily be an enclave. Kaliningrad is surrounded not by one state only, but by two: Lithuania and Poland and it also borders the Baltic Sea. On the other hand, the Spanish exclave of Llivia is an enclave in France. After World War I, East Prussia became an exclave of Germany.

Enclave < French *enclaver* 'to enclose, to make a dovetail joint in woodworking' < Latin *in* 'in' + *clavis* Latin 'key.'

Exclave < Latin *ex* 'outside of' + *clavis* Latin 'key.'

Subclavian arteries are two vessels that bring blood from the heart to the neck and the arms and that extend partially under the clavicles (Latin *sub* 'under').

I am now sticking my head back inside an autoclave, to see if I can really tell the difference between enclave and exclave. Even professional diplomats do get the terms mixed up!

Chapter 94

Magic Words, Appear! Magic Author, Disappear!

Magic was originally sorcery and conjuring tricks performed by an ancient Persian astrologer called a magus. The three Wise Men who brought gifts to the infant Jesus were magi. Magi began as Median priests in charge of cult rituals. Magus is the classical Latin form of ancient Greek *magos* from Old Persian *magush* 'cult priest.' In the history of Christianity most magical practices have been considered sacrilege and abomination. A 1565 engraving by Pieter Bruegel bears the caption "the magician is torn to pieces by demons." This is one of the archetypal tropes or plot turns in the Faust legend, the classic medieval "human dares to make a deal with the devil" story. The Faust figure, or whoever the duped magus may be, makes an obscene bargain with Satan, then, not too much later, Faust is knocked upside-down in his cart by Satanic imps and by misproportioned fiends from the brimstone womb of Hell. At the conclusion of his story, Faust is ripped to pieces by such demons and his corporeal scraps and bits of soul are dragged off to the ever-conflagrant inferno.

Was it Magic?

The name of the practices entered English from French *magique*, a word derived from classical Latin *magica* 'occult doings,' itself from the Hellenistic Greek phrase *magike techne* 'the magic arts.'

Sorcery

Sorcery goes back to an ancient Roman fortune-teller and the casting of lots. It shares an etymon (word root) with our common verb, *to sort*.

In European history, the casting of lots, deciding a winner by means of a lottery, goes back at least to Homeric Greece, where, in a multi-person dispute, pieces of wood (lots), each with an individual contestant's mark on it, were tossed into a war helmet. The helmet was shaken violently. The first wooden lot to fly out of the helmet and be cast on the ground was the winner.

In Latin, the word for a lot or fate or response from an oracle was *sors, sortis*. One of the derived Latin verbs was *sortiri* 'to divide or obtain by winning a lottery.' From its French reflex *sortir*, English has the verb *to sort*, original meaning 'to assign by category,' and eventually to sort out 'to arrange in order items first presented in disarray.' Assorted colours first meant colours picked out for a specific application. Assorted did not originally mean randomly mixed but rather selected. Latin *sors* appears in all the Romance languages, most felicitously perhaps in the Spanish wish for good luck, *Buena Suerte.*

The only common use in modern English is in the phrase 'the casting of lots.' This harks back to Old English *hlot weorthan* 'to throw lots,' similar to German *das Loos werfen*, Latin *sortes conicere*, Greek *kleron ballein* 'to throw lots.' From French, English still has *to draw lots* (French *tirer au sort*). While sorcery was first the mere casting of lots, eventual sorcerers dabbled in a variety of hocus-pocus, mumbo jumbo and pseudo-mystical flim-flam.

Thaumaturgy & Necromancy

These two Greek-derived words always lend a spurious sound of legitimacy to magical claptrap. Thaumaturgy is simply wonder-making < Greek *thaumatourgos* 'magician, conjuror, wonder-worker' < *thauma, thaumatos* 'wonder, miracle, marvel' + Greek *ergon* 'work.' The 'work' etymon lurks in many English words like surgery, allergy, synergy and ergonomics.

To skeptics of Christianity's bag of miracles and tricks, Jesus walking on water may be deemed a thaumaturgical performance.

Necromancy

Necromancy's prime meaning is predicting the future by communication with dead people. Just why the recently defunct members of our wayward species would know the future is never explained. While it is supposedly true that Jehovah can make anything happen, think about it briefly. I do realize that thinking is anathema to the true believer — but humour me: If our defunct ones' brains have already been nibbled to mush by worms or crematory fires, surely the deads' prognosticatory prowess would have diminished at least marginally?

Necromancy means literally in Greek 'dead magic.' It first appeared in the writings of one of the brighter fathers of the early church, a third-century Christian scribe named Origen where the Hellenistic Greek form *necromanteia* pops up signifying 'predicting the future by communication with the dead.' The word is made up of ancient Greek *nekros* 'dead body, dead person' + *manteia* 'divination, telling the future.'

The necro- combining form is widely used in English scientific vocabulary. Think of medicine's necrotic tissue, when organized masses of cells die. *Polis* is the Greek word for city. A necropolis is a city of the dead, a cemetery. A necrology is a list of people recently dead or an obituary. Necrophilia is having sex with dead bodies. To observe this, just visit Washington.

Two Rarities

Every now and then in this impish parchment I try to include a term or two of surpassing uncommonness, to assuage the true word nut's avidity. Here they are.

Stoicheiotical

The rarest, silliest word in this column is the obsolete adjective *stoicheiotical* 'pertaining to magic' which enjoyed the briefest span of popularity among a few seventeenth-century English writers. It was a literal borrowing from medieval Greek *stoicheiotikos* 'possessing an elemental, primitive, basic enchantment,' its ultimate etymon *stoicheion* 'foundation post or first stake, hence a beginning, rudiment, first element.'

The cognates of this Greek word are of interest, for it shares a Proto-Indo-European morpheme with Old English *staca*, Dutch *staak*, German *Stake*, Spanish *estaca*, Italian *stacca*. That PIE morpheme is *stak, a variant of PIE *stek, so that English verbs like *to stick* are cognate too. One of the morpheme's interesting Spanish lemmata (a lemma is a fully independent word form) is a grisly term borrowed into English descriptions of bullfights, namely the *estocada* or estocade, the final thrust by a matador (Spanish 'killer') with the sword, a plunge meant to kill the bull.

Dwimmercraft

Tolkien uses it in *The Two Towers* as dwimmercraft but gives it a darker than usual meaning. In Old English it was *dweomercraeft* 'skill [craft] in the arts of illusion and magic' from earlier Old English words like *gedwimere* 'juggler, sorcerer.' Dwimmercrafty is the even rarer adjective.

Odder words than that I cannot summon. Therefore, with the most rudimentary of incantations: Abracadabra, I vanish!

About the Author

"Bill Casselman is one of Canada's leading etymologists." So says Professor Jennifer MacLennan in *Readings for Technical Communication*, Oxford University Press, 2008. Bill Casselman has published 12 books about Canadian words and one medical dictionary. He was a columnist for *Maclean's* magazine and *Canadian Geographic*, and a producer at CBC Radio and CBC TV for many years. Bill was one of the founding producers of "This Country in the Morning," a seminal program that introduced Peter Gzowski to Canadian radio audiences. Casselman's work has taken him to every province and territory of Canada, where he has always found time to pursue his chief delight and hobby, the study of words, particularly words and sayings that Canadians have added to the mighty hoard of English. He is a proud Canadian. His word studies continue on his website: wordingdesk.com.(?) Readers may contact Bill with questions and comments at wordingmail.com (?)His word studies continue on his website: https://www.wordingroom.com. Readers may contact Bill with questions and comments at wordingmail@wordingroom.com

Printed in the United States
By Bookmasters